# Bill Sholin's

# "THE SACRIFICIAL LAMB
## (Who fought like Lions)

## The Kamikaze massacre of -- 157 -- US DESTROYERS.
*Okinawa, where 4,907 sailors gave their lives and 4,832 were wounded*
*--- in the greatest Air-Sea Battle of all time.---*

## DESTROYERMEN GO TO WAR, A DIFFERENT KIND OF WAR.
### EVERYTHING THE JAPANESE THREW AT THEM -- WAS SUICIDAL!
## HOW DO YOU FIGHT AN ENEMY LIKE THAT?
### HOW THEY LIVED, LOVED, FOUGHT, AND DIED.

# USS WREN, DD568, *a Fletcher class* DESTROYER

# THE SACRIFICIAL LAMBS
## (Who fought like Lions)
The entire story of Japanese Kamikaze
attacks against the U.S. Fleet, in WWII.
By William (Bill) Sholin
360-897-8040

Published by:
Mountain View Publishing
PO Box 7438
Bonney Lake, Washington 98390
360-897-8711

Writers Guild of America West Inc #516219
Library of Congress Catalog Card Number: 94-77042
ISBN: 0-9641754-1-X

Photographs by: The Naval Historical Center
National Archives Photographic service
Shipmates and crewmen of many destroyers.

Primary Research Material -- Dictionary Of American Naval Fighting Ships (All eight Volumes,) by the U.S. Naval Institute

Quotations from: U.S. Destroyer Operations in WWII By Thodore Roscoe, published by the U.S. Naval Institute, and The Battle Reports by Walter Carig, published by Holt Reinhart and Winstor.

*BUT MOST OF ALL THIS BOOK IS ABOUT -- THEIR TERROR.* ONE MINUTE THEY WERE ALL ALIVE, AN INSTANT LATER SURVIVORS WERE SURROUNDED BY MANGLED BODIES OF FRIENDS, TANGLED IN TWISTED WRECKAGE!

The untold story about the Japanese Kamikaze attacks against the US Fleet, from beginning to end. This book tells all! Told from the decks of USS *WREN*, DD568.

# USS WILLIAM D. PORTER, DD579

*Her men scramble to escape their sinking ship! The USS Smalley, stands by in the distance, to porotect survivors. Porter had relieved Smalley on RP15, a short time before -- but now it's Smalley's turn again!*

# Acknowledgments

## SPECIAL THANKS TO THE NAVAL HISTORICAL CENTER AND NATIONAL ARCHIVES FOR THEIR SPLENDID COOPERATION, PROVIDING PHOTOGRAPHS

Past assistant director of the Naval Historical Center and former XO of the USS *Wren*, Captain David Long made a special trip to the center on our behalf. Charles R. Haberlein Jr., Head Photographic Section, searched the extensive files of his section, as well as the National Archives, acting on Captain Long's request. To both of these gentlemen -- we will always be grateful.

## TO THOSE WHO PROVIDED SPECIAL HELP, SPECIAL THANKS

(TIN CAN SAILOR, Edward Ward)---BILL FERGUSON JR---COMMANDER JOHN POWELL---LT LOWELL CLARK---LT COMMANDER ROBERT PAULI XO---LT HOWARD COOK OD---LT DACRE DUNN---LT JACK CLEMENS---LT COMMANDER DAVID LONG---MRS. R. J. MILLER

## THANKS, TO WREN'S CREW WHO PROVIDED STORIES

LTjg LOWELL CLARK---COMMANDER JOHN POWELL---LT. JACK CLEMENS---LT HOWARD COOK---ENS L. D. CRISSWELL---M2/C JIM HUTZEL---CM1/C JOE MARTINO---PM2/C RENO PELLEGRINI---S1/C AL COPSON S1/C DANNY WANN---S1/C JIM PRIDMORE---QM3/C KEN KUTCHIN---S1/C L. J. ADAMS---S1/C BARNEY PULLEN---WT1/C HAP ROGERS---S1/C ROGER JONES---ET1/C BOB PIERCE---S1/C JACK JARC---BM1/C BILL FERGUSON---BM1/C DICK EASTER---GM1/C JOE REINDERS---MM1/C CLAY HARRIS---MM2/C WALLACE RUPE---MRS E. A. MACDONALD---MRS FRANK OLSON---MRS R. J. MILLER---MRS LOWELL CLARK---MRS ANNIE DUNN

## THANKS, TO CREWMEN OF OTHER SHIPS FOR THEIR STORIES

USS ABNER READ, DD526,---CHIEF ELECTRICIANS MATE LLOYD MEGEE
USS DREXLER, DD741, ----CAPTAIN COMMANDER RONALD LEE WILSON---GM2/C BUFORD MILLS---FC3/C ROBERT L. ANTEAU---TM3/C GEORGE REAM---WT2/C MORRIS E. CARLTON S1/C WILLARD L. JONES---S1/C GEORGE (DUKE) PAYNE---GM3/C GENE BRICK
USS HARDING, DD625,---MM2/C ROBERT HISKEY, (HISTORIAN)---CAPTAIN RAMAGE-WALTER VOLRATH JR---MIKE NEVORAH---LTjg WILLIAM CARTER---CE-LT FRANK STRATMAN---and JACK SINGER
USS HUTCHINS, DD476,---RM1/C JOHN TUCKER
USS LITTLE, DD803,---CAPTAIN MADISON HALL JR.--GM1/C FRANK WHALL
USS LUCE, DD522,---F2/C DWAINE ERSTAD
USS SCHUBRICK, DD639,---BOB JOHNS
USS WILLIAM D. PORTER, DD579,---JAMES J. GILLAN, NAVY CORRESPONDENT--S1/C H. E. FARNHAM---S. R. YURCHEY---MM2/C D.L. ANDERSON---MM2/C N.J. VERTERAMO---S1/C C.A. WILLIAMS--S2/C A.E. HINGLE--S1/C RICHARD J. STEVENS--RM3/C W.S. CLOVER (HISTORIAN) and---CYM JAMES GILLAN
USS WILLIAMSON, DD244,---MM1/C FRANK BOHN,

## REFERENCE MATERIALS

DICTIONARY OF AMERICAN NAVAL FIGHTING SHIPS--U.S. NAVAL INSTITUTE PRESS (ALL EIGHT VOLUMES)---TAPES, LETTERS, AND PERSONAL INTERVIEWS

# TABLE OF CONTENTS

# DEDICATION

Words cannot describe my gratitude to those who have made it possible to tell our story, by telling theirs. This is their story and I shall try to tell it factually.

This book is dedicated to all Americans who have ever seen a Kamikaze. I especially dedicate "The Sacrificial Lambs" to destroyer men who lived and died defending our country against the nightmare called, the "Okinawa Picket Line." American heroes of the highest order!

What is a hero? U.S. gun crews, people in magazines, handling rooms, engineering spaces and the bridge, had no place to hide. Americans -- "Looked them in the eye -- to stand and die!" Thousands of brave men faced unwanted but certain death. Undauntedly -- we all stood our ground. I ask again -- What is a hero?

A special thanks to all of my old friends and shipmates, who have given so freely of their time to tell their personal stories. But most of all, a special thanks to my dear wife, Marilyn, without whose help and patience "The Sacrificial Lambs" would not exist.

# PREFACE

**<u>TO ALL LOYAL AMERICAN READERS -- READ THIS ENTIRE DOCUMENT!</u>**

Never in my wildest dreams, in the United States of America, did I think we who fought the war in the Pacific would ever have to defend our actions. But liberal revisionists are forcing us to take a stand. Anti Pacific war feelings seem to be wide spread. During the 50th anniversary of the Kamikaze event, many veterans have taken "The Sacrificial Lambs" along with their personnel stories, to the local newspaper. They knew the story should be told. Most have been rejected. I have been told repeatedly by the U.S. press, television media and Hollywood, "We are not interested in the subject." It seems taboo -- not politically correct. With so much publicity about the European war, how could this be? Now they want to abolish the name, VJ-Day, consider the U.S. Military mass murderers, and sweep the truth under the carpet for another 50-years!

Japan raped, burned, plundered and conquered much of China. Then, without provocation or declaration of war -- she attacked the United States of America! While talking peace in Washington the Japanese Navy, in a sneak attack, destroyed most of the U.S. Navy at Pearl Harbor -- and killed thousands of Americans! Japan then quickly conquered the rest of Southeast Asia, the Philippines and most other sovereign islands of the South Pacific. Like in China, the Japanese brutalized the people.

Without question or reservation our youth answered the challenge. Young Americans, mostly teenagers, left home and spent valuable years fighting for places they had never heard of. Many of us were gone so long we forgot what our mothers, fathers, wives and sweethearts looked like -- then they died by the thousands to keep America free. We fought and won the war, without dissent or protest. Those of us who are still alive, continue to enjoy the freedom we saved for all Americans.

I challenge those who would say: 'Japan only defended her unique heritage and life style from United States "Imperialistic" aggression. After we had already won the war, the U.S. used excessive force against Japan; that we had over-estimated our casualties if we invaded Japan; that the U.S. should not have dropped the bomb.' Read the following Japanese operative and read about the Kamikazes -- then reconsider your position. The United States of America should never let Japan or any liberal revisionists, influence U.S. history of the Pacific war. Our history is great! All who fought the Japanese stand tall.

The most popular Japanese pulp fiction, at present time, is about how Japan won the war with the United States. Japanese books depict the battleship *Yamato* in Puget Sound shelling U.S. Naval installations. If this were true -- what would our life style be like now? Americans would be bowing and eating raw fish and rice. Our women would carry the groceries and walk behind their men. Thanks to our Navy -- *Yamato* is on the bottom of the Pacific! Our heroism is non fiction and we won. If we had not fought and won that war, what would those same revisionists be saying?

The following Japanese operative, from the USS *Wren's* secret papers, was given to me by LTjg Lowell Clark. Lowell, the officer in charge of *Wren's* record keeping logs etc. during the war, kept all papers after decommissioning.

Commander John Powell recalls: "We were the first ship to moor dockside at the Yokosuka Navy Yard. LTjg Ray Hudson, a *Wren* officer, took over the Japanese Admiral's house at Yokosuka for two months, to set up the first small boat pool. I believe he had a lot to do with obtaining that Japanese Operative, for the *Wren.*"

This order had been released to the Imperial Fleet November 1, 1941, thirty-seven days before Japan carried out her cowardly surprise attack against Pearl Harbor! Note the Japanese refer to that terrible rape, burning and plunder of their neighbor -- as **'The China--Incident.'** This translated, actual Japanese operative, outlines Japan's plan for the United States!

## IMPERIAL JAPAN'S PLAN AND ORDER -- TO "ATTACK PEARL HARBOR"
### (Every American should read and never forget this document!)

---

TOP SECRET:                                        Flagship Nagato, Saeki Wan
                                                   1 November 1941

### COMBINED FLEET SECRET OPORD #1

The Japanese Empire will declare war on the UNITED STATES, GREAT BRITAIN, and the NETHERLANDS.

War will be declared on X-day.

This order will become effective on Y-Day.

### GENERAL SITUATION
(A) Policy toward the UNITED STATES.

In spite of the fact that the Empire has always maintained a friendly attitude towards the UNITED STATES, the UNITED STATES has interfered in all the measures which we have taken in self protection for the preservation of our interests in East ASIA. Recently, she has blocked our speedy settlement of the CHINA Incident by aiding the government of CHIANG KAISHEK and has even resorted to the final outrage of breaking off relations. While senselessly prolonging JAPANESE-AMERICAN negotiations, she has continued to strengthen her military preparations. She offers a threat to us in the form of a concentration of her fleet in the PACIFIC OCEAN, thus attempting to exert on us both economic and military pressure.

(B) Policy towards GREAT BRITAIN.

Britain is aiding the government of CHAING Kaishek and, acting in concert with her Allies and the UNITED STATES, in interfering with our program of construction in East ASIA. Recently she has been steadily building up the defenses of her bases in East ASIA in an attempt to threaten us..

(C) Policy toward the NETHERLANDS INDIES.

Although economic negotiations of a peaceful nature have been underway with us for a number of months, the NETHERLANDS INDIES has been led by BRITAIN and the UNITED STATES to reject flatly the continuance of mutually beneficial economic relations. Recently she has threatened the fortunes of Japanese which have been built up as a result of persevering work through long years.

(D) The ports and the vast fertile regions of the coast of CHINA have been occupied by us and most of her great cities captured. CHINA, however, supported by BRITAIN and the UNITED STATES, has not yet awakened from the deluding dream of "Fight the War and Save the Country" and is attempting total resistance to JAPAN in the form of a "scorched earth" policy for all CHINA.

(E) Policy toward the SOVIET UNION.
The strength of Soviet forces on the SOVIET-MANCHUKUOAN border is formidable.

The USSR is maintaining a vigilant alert, awaiting developments. However, if the Empire does not attack the SOVIET UNION, it is believed that the SOVIET UNION will not commence hostilities

## SITUATION

The Fourth Fleet has largely completed preparation in the Mandated Islands as has the Eleventh Air Fleet (Naval shore-based air) at essential bases in CHINA, FRENCH INDO-CHINA and THAILAND. The state of repair of our ships and planes is generally excellent and the efficiency of their personnel has markedly improved.

## STRATEGIC OBJECTIVES

To drive BRITAIN and AMERICA from Greater East Asia, and to hasten the settlement of the CHINA incident. In addition, it is expected that when BRITAIN and AMERICA have been driven from the NETHERLANDS INDIES and the PHILIPPINES, an independent self-supporting economic entity may be firmly established. The vast and far-reaching fundamental principle, the spiritual guide of our nation, (the "Eight Corners of the World Under One Roof--KAKKO ICHIU), may be demonstrated to the world. To this end we will use all the military strength necessary.

## STRATEGY

The strategy to be adopted against BRITAIN, the UNITED STATES and the NETHERLANDS will be as directed in the Annexed Volume. X-Day and Y-Day will be announced later.

If before Y-Day the enemy is believed to have been able to ascertain our plans the execution of X-Day will be made the subject of a special order.

If before X-Day we should be attacked by the enemy, his attack will be crushed with all available strength. All commanding officers will act in conformance with "Strategy to be Adopted in the Case of an Enemy Attack".

In the case of the SOVIET UNION, every effort will be made to avoid provoking hostilities. At the same time, every effort will be made to insure the secrecy of our plans. If the enemy should ascertain our plans, military operations will immediately be begun in accordance with "Measure to be Taken in the Case of an Attack by the SOVIET UNION".

Circulation of this order is limited to Fleet and Force Commanders. These Commanders will take every possible measure to prevent leakage of these plans prior to their being carried out.

Precaution: Disposal of this order:
This order must be burned when no longer of use. If there is any danger to its falling into enemy hands as the result of a ship sinking or some other untoward occurrence, the responsible Commander shall personally make immediate disposal of it.

### Combined Fleet Secret OPORD #1

1. Joint Army-Navy operations will be carried out in accordance with the "Army-Navy Central Headquarters Agreement".

2. A striking Force (Carrier Task Force), having the 1st Air Fleet (Carriers and Escorts) as its main element, will depart its naval bases or operating areas about X-16 Day, and will set course, by way of TANKAN BAY (HITOKAPPU BAY, ESTOROFU ISLAND, KURILES) for PEARL HARBOR, the base of the American PACIFIC Fleet, where it will deliver a surprise attack.

X-Day is expected to be during the early or middle part of December.

3. Targets for attack are airfields; aircraft carriers; battleships, cruisers and other warships; merchant shipping; port facilities; and land installations in that order.

4. From the time set by the Force Commander for the Striking Force to leave port in JAPAN strict radio silence will be observed. Communications will be via ordinary broadcast system. The code book to be used will be "(not Certain)". The following communications abbreviations will be in effect.
"Many warships in PEARL HARBOR" -- "The fate of the Empire".
"No warships in PEARL HARBOR". -- "The cherry-blossoms are in all their glory".
"Weather clear and visibility good in the region. Suitable for attack." -- "Climb MT FUJI."
"The time to commence the attack is 0520". -- "The depth of the moat of HONNOJI TEMPLE is 0520".

"All forces attack" -- "Climb MT NIITAKA!"

5. The course and disposition of the attacking units will be determined by the Striking Force Commander

The Commander of the Striking Force will inform the proper authorities as soon as he determines on the course and disposition of the attacking units. Care must be taken to avoid ordinary merchant shipping routs and to keep the plans from disclosure under any circumstances whatever.

6. Procedure to be followed in case of discovery before the attack either by a ship of the nation against which war is to be declared, or by a ship of a neutral nation (including the SOVIET UNION).

(a) In case of discovery within 600 miles of the objective by a ship of a nation against war is to be declared, make immediate preparation to attack and sink it.

(b) In case of discovery within 600 miles of the objective by a ship of a neutral nation, the ship should immediately be detained until it can do us no actual harm; strict surveillance should be kept at its radio transmission. In case it should make any transmissions which might prove harmful to us or give us reason to fear that our plans might be revealed, the ship will be seized by a destroyer which will make immediate attack preparations.

(c) In case of discovery by a foreign ship more than 600 miles from the objective, the ship will be detained and radio transmission forbidden. However, if it seems highly probable that our general intentions have been guessed, attack should be made immediately, if between X-5 Day and X-Day. If before X-5 Day, the Striking Force Commander will decide the disposition of the ship, depending on the circumstances. In the case of detention of an enemy ship, "B" method will be followed.

7. The Commander of the Surprise Attack Force (Submarine Force), having the 6th Fleet (Submarine Fleet) as its main element, will have most of the submarines leave the western part of the INLAND SEA on X-20 Day to attack PEARL HARBOR. Its entire strength will be disposed so as to command the harbor mouth. It will attack any enemy warship which may have escaped from the harbor. It will also carry out reconnaissance before the attack, and if the opportunity presents itself will carry out surprise attacks on enemy warships with midget submarines. The time for such attacks will be after the flights of planes have attacked OAHU. Every possible means for recovery of midget submarines should be considered.

8. Joint Army-Navy preparations should be carried out in accordance with the provisions of the Central Headquarters Agreement. The disposition of forces will be determined by the Commander of the Advance Force (principally Second Fleet cruisers and destroyers). The Commander of the Advance Force will inform the proper authorities as soon as he decides on the course and disposition of the attacking units.

The point of departure for the ships of the MALAY and FRENCH INDO-CHINA Forces will be BAKO and the point of departure for the PHILIPPINES Occupation Force will probably be PALAU.

9. The Capture of English and American troops and ships in CHINA will be arranged by the Commander-in Chief of the CHINA Area Fleet. The occupation of HONG KONG will conform to the provisions of the Army-Navy Central Headquarters Agreement and is the responsibility of the Commander, 2nd CHINA Expeditionary Fleet.

10. English and American merchant ships which are in ports under Japanese sovereignty at the time of the outbreak of the war or which are in ports which may be taken are to be captured if possible.

SOVIET shipping is to be kept under surveillance after undergoing a ridged inspection.

It should be so planned that none of our shipping will be in foreign ports when the war breaks out.

11. Beginning on Y-Day the Commander of the 1st Combined Communication Unit will send false messages to give the impression that the main strength of the Fleet is in the western part of the INLAND SEA.

After Y-Day has been determined, the Commandant of the YOKOSUKA Naval District will allow as many men of his command as possible to go ashore so that the number of men on liberty in TOKYO AND YOKOHAMA will give a false impression.

(Another POW confirms this.)

(AUTHOR'S NOTE: (POW) -- Japanese Prisoners Of War -- possibly being held for "War Trials." They must have translated the captured documents for the U.S.)

After Y-Day has been determined, the NYK passenger vessel TATSUTA MARU, which is scheduled to proceed to the west coast of AMERICA, will sail; arrangements will be made to have her return while en route. (This was done, and Allied passengers were interned; the same procedure would have been followed with any trans-Pacific liner scheduled to sail in this period.)

12. The Commander-in Chief of the 4th Fleet (Mandates Fleet) will expedite the attack and occupation of British, American and Dutch bases in the North and South PACIFIC, acting in close cooperation with forces of the 11th Air Fleet in the South PACIFIC. Enemy air power within our sphere of operations will be checked and communication between AUSTRALIA and the mainland of the UNITED STATES will finally be cut.

(The dates for execution of assault and occupation of various British, U. S., Netherlands bases were then listed in this paragraph -- a few of which follow.

(1) GUAM      about X plus 2
(2) WAKE      about X plus 7

> (3) (The dates for the invasion of RABAUL and the Islands from the SOLOMONS to the FIJIS, SAMOA, and SANTA CRUZ groups were all entered)

13. The date for the seizure of MIDWAY is set as late Spring of 1942. The date for the occupation of the HAWAIIAN ISLANDS is scheduled for October 1942

---

Herewith are two of the above referenced documents.

### THE ARMY-NAVY CENTRAL HEADQUARTERS AGREEMENT

The objectives of Imperial Headquarters, Army Department and Imperial Headquarters, Navy Department in setting forth clearly the division of duties and command in joint operations was to promote a maximum display of efficiency. (According to POW it was issued at the end of October 1941. A resume of the contents follows;)

1. The highest ranking Army officer for SUMATRA, BORNEO, the MALAY Peninsula, CELEBES, and the PHILIPPINES (including FRENCH INDO-CHINA and THAILAND) will be Field Marshal TERAUCHI, HISAICHI. His Command will be called the Southern Army and its headquarters will be in SAIGON.

2. Plans for escorting large Army convoys and the place, time and date for landings.

3. Agreements on Aerial Warfare Agreements on the places to be attacked by both Army and Navy planes and on the places, dates and times of attacks by Army or Navy planes acting independently. Agreements on the airfields to be used, such as "XX Airfields will be used primarily by the Army and secondarily by the Navy."

4. Supply Plans

Plans for the supply of Army landing forces to be effected by Army shipping and for the Navy's support of same.

5. Communications Plans

6. Agreement on occupied territories, cities, and resources such as, "The BANDJERMASIN Oil Refinery will be controlled by the Navy."

---

## MEASURES TO BE TAKEN IN CASE OF A SOVIET ATTACK

(POW does not remember the date exactly, but it was the end of October -- and stated in effect.)

"It is believed likely that we shall not be attacked by the SOVIET UNION unless we attack first, but in case JAPAN is attacked first, the 5th Fleet (Northern Force) will counterattack with all its strength and maintain local supremacy."

YAMAMOTO, Isoroku
Commanding, Combined Fleet

---

Flagship AKAGI, SAEKI WAN
10 November 1941

## STRIKING FORCE OPORD #1

1. All ships will complete battle preparations by 20 November.

2. The fleet will rendezvous at TANKAN WAN. (HITOKAPPU BAY, ETOROFU IS. KURILES).

3. Inasmuch as the plans for the coming operation must be kept absolutely secret, strict security will be maintained in regard to them, up to the time they are explained to the crew after port of departure in JAPAN has been cleared.

4. Break-down of attack plane units.
     The AKAGI 1st Attack Plane Unit.
          Unit Commander: Lt. Comdr.XX
               1st Carrier Attack Unit
                    Etc.(details not recalled by POW).

5. Fleet cruising information  (Including retiring formations).

6. All transmissions of messages is strictly forbidden.

Transmissions and reception will both use the TOKYO #1 broadcast communications system.

NAGUMO Chucihi
Commanding Striking Force

---

Verbal explanation by the Chief of Staff, Combined Fleet of ambiguities in Combined Fleet

SECRET OpOrd #1/
(Printed version of an explanation of details not covered in the order delivered to the High Commanders in an information talk.)

1. That the coming declaration of war against ENGLAND and the UNITED STATES will usher in a great war of survival with the two leading naval powers of the world.

2. That this war is really one in which our existence is in question, and in which we have no choice but to strike with our military power. That our Navy, in engaging a worthy enemy, is about to realize an ambition which dates back to the foundation of the Imperial Navy many years ago.

3. That the alliance with GERMANY was not desired by the Navy, but was a project favored by the Army which thought it would hold the SOVIET UNION in check.

4. That the campaigns in the NETHERLANDS INDIES and in the PHILIPPINES will be preceded by the securing of advanced bases in THAILAND and FRENCH INDO-CHINA. It is believed that these operations will come off in extremely smooth order.

The Navy will be able to secure sources of oil supply swiftly by means of these campaigns.

5. In connection with the attack on PEARL HARBOR, reports indicated that a gigantic fleet, which includes the ATLANTIC Fleet, has massed in PEARL HARBOR.

This Fleet will be utterly crushed with one blow at the very beginning of hostilities. It is planned to shift the balance of power and thereby confuse the enemy at the outset and deprive him of his fighting spirit.

Our objective, however lies more than three thousand miles away. In attacking this large fleet concentration it is to be expected that countless difficulties will be encountered in preserving the absolute security of the plans. If these plans should fail at any stage, our Navy will suffer the wretched fate of never being able to rise again. The success of our surprise attack on PEARL HARBOR will prove to the "WATERLOO" of the war to follow. For this reason the Imperial Navy is massing the cream of its strength in ships and planes to assure success.

All of the planes of CarDiv 1, CarDiv 2, and CarDiv 5 will be concentrated in the attack on OAHU. If there are any ships which escape, almost the entire submarine strength of the 6th Fleet will be in command of the harbor mouth and will concentrate torpedo attacks on them. In addition to these, the destroyer strength of (DesRon 1) will be deployed in a screen (mainly for night attacks) and the fast battleships of BatDiv 3 deployed in a fourth echelon. If the main force of the enemy fleet should escape from PEARL HARBOR and make for the open sea, it will be waylaid by the Main Body of our Fleet.

6. The midget submarine unit has been studying and training at the KURE Navy Yard with the CHIYODA for a year and a half, but it is still too much to hope that it has reached a stage of perfection. In any case, the crew members are supremely confident. The 6th Fleet will attempt to use them in attacks within the harbor.

7. It is clear that even if AMERICA'S enormous heavy industry productive power is immediately converted to the manufacture of ships, planes and other war materials, it will take at least several months for her manpower to be mobilized against us. If we insure our

strategic supremacy at the very outset of the conflict by attacking and seizing all key points at one blow while AMERICA is still unprepared, we can swing the scales of later operations in our favor.

8 Heaven will bear witness to the righteousness of our struggle. It is hoped that every man will exert his full efforts toward the realization of the objectives of this holy war by determinedly carrying out our original purpose, in the full realization of the unparalleled opportunity which this war offers.

---

Communication Plans
    (POW does not know about these; no details)

---

Supply Plans. (outline)
The Naval bases of YOKOSUKA, KURE and SASEBO will be rear supply bases. BAKO, PALAU, TRUK and OMINATO will be forward supply bases. In addition to these, supply ships will be attached to each fleet.

---

                                       5 November

Combined Fleet SECRET OpOrd #2
    Y-Day will be 23 November

---

                                       10 November

Combined Fleet SECRET OpOrd #3
    X-Day will be 8 December

---

**(AUTHORS NOTE** -- All copy in parenthesis in the above document, not otherwise identified are the transcriber's notes. The entire layout is just as it was transcribed. Solid lines across the paper separate the individual documents. This author has changed nothing.)

    We are now in our third printing of "The Sacrificial Lambs" and our computer bank is full of input from thousands of sailors, soldiers, pilots and marines -- who were out there. To the man, we feel sickened by our countries refusal to even recognize what actually happened! This is not the America we fought and died for!

*Bill Sholin*
Author

# THE SAGA OF

# "OKINAWA PICKET DESTROYERS"

OKINAWA—"THE GREATEST AIR-SEA BATTLE OF ALL TIME"—TOOK PLACE 40-TO-70-MILES NORTHWEST OF OKINAWA—BETWEEN JAPANESE KAMIKAZES AND U.S. DESTROYERS. 148-DESTROYERS—OF ALL TYPES—TOOK PART ON "THE OKINAWA PICKET LINE." —122-80% FELL VICTIM TO JAPANESE KAMIKAZES—AND 43 WERE EITHER SUNK—SCUTTLED—OR SCRAPPED.

EACH DAY FROM MARCH 26 TO JUNE 30-1945—AN AVERAGE OF 55-AMERICAN SAILORS WERE KILLED AND 55-WOUNDED. (MOSTLY DESTROYER-MEN) TERRIBLE YES—HOWEVER— KAMIKAZES DID NOT COME OVER AT AN EVEN RATE. THEY OFTEN CAME IN SWARMS. APRIL 6-1945—13-DESTROYERS WERE HIT (7 SUNK OR SCRAPPED) APRIL 11&12—16-HAD THEIR DECKS CRASHED INTO. MAY 26&27—4; APRIL 14 TO 16—8; APRIL 27 TO 29—7; MAY 3 TO 5—9; MAY 25 TO 28—11; DESTROYERS FELL VICTIM TO JAPANESE SUICIDE AIRCRAFT OF ALL TYPES.

BLOOD AND GASOLINE MIXED FREELY OVER OUR DECKS. THE HARBORS QUICKLY FILLED WITH DESTROYERS—BATTERED BEYOND RECOGNITION. YOUNG AMERICANS-ON SMALL DESTROYERS—STOOD FACE-TO-FACE WITH KAMIKAZE PILOTS. EACH KAMIKAZE PILOT FACED HIS DEATH ONLY ONCE—BUT AMERICANS FACED THEIRS OVER AND OVER—LIKE A RECURRING NIGHTMARE. "WE LOOKED THEM IN THE EYE TO STAND AND DIE"! "I KNOW—I WAS THERE!"

IN JAPAN—KAMIKAZE PILOTS ARE IMMORTALIZED IN A MAJOR MUSEUM—ENSHRINED IN THE YASUKUNI SHRINE AS "THUNDER GODS"—AND REVERED AS RIGHTFUL HEROES OF THE HIGHEST ORDER. THEY EVEN ENJOYED A HERO STATUS IN AMERICAN DOCUMENTARIES. ON THE OTHER HAND-THE UNITED STATES HAVE MINIMIZED—TRIVIALIZED—AND STILL DENY THE TRUTH. AMERICAN KAMIKAZE SURVIVORS STILL RELIVE THEIR NIGHTMARES IN SILENCE AND SOLITUDE—55-YEARS LATER! WHY—AMERICA?

This event in U.S. history needs to be told--remembered. At Okinawa the U.S. suffered 49,159 casualties including 9,760 Navy men from Kamikazes. In the first 30-days at Normandy, Americans suffered 42,000 casualties, terrible; however, American documentaries seem to ignore Okinawa, and they never tell the entire truth about the Kamikazes. Why! This was, by far, Americas finest hour! Now England is working on a Kamikaze documentary (Asking for US Destroyer survivors)--will we have to go to England to see it?

(To see the "Joint Chiefs Of Staff's" statistics see page 114 "Truman's Decision")

THIS IS OUR PROUD U.S. HERITAGE—STAND UP AND BE COUNTED!

## WE ASK—WHY NOT TELL IT LIKE IT HAPPENED?

# ONE
# WHY "SACRIFICIAL LAMBS?"

This story is not about one sailor or just one ship; rather, it's about an event in U.S. history that needs to be told. Okinawa, bloody Okinawa, where 4,907 sailors lost their lives and 4,832 were wounded in the greatest air-sea battle of all time.

Okinawa, the scene of the last major battle of World War II, is a Japanese home island located about three hundred fifty miles off the southern tip of Kyushu, the most southern Japanese main island. The East China Sea is west and the Pacific Ocean east.

All out Kamikaze air-sea attacks threatened to destroy the U.S. Navy at Okinawa. Like swarms of bees, they swept across the East China Sea from mainland Japan, then crashed directly into troop laden transports, tankers, supply ships, aircraft carriers, destroyers, cruisers, and battleships. Never in the history of mankind had a warring nation imposed such a threat! How could we save our fleet? The U.S. Military was in deep trouble!

**FLEET CARRIERS HIT**

A total of 19 successful suicide attacks were carried out against major U.S. fleet carriers including: the USS *Franklin*, CV13; *Intrepid*, CV11; *Hancock*, CV19; *Belleau Wood*, CV24; *Lexington*, CV16; *Cabot*, CVL28; *Intrepid*, CV11; *Essex*, CV9; *Saratoga*, CV3; *Ticonderoga*, CV14; *Langley*, CVL27; *Enterprise*, CV6, and the English carriers HMS *Illustrious*, *Indefatigable* and *Indomitable*. Among the 28 escort carriers hit, the USS *St Lo*, CVE63, was sunk.

USS *Bunker Hill, CV17, May 11, 1945,*
*on fire after being hit by two Kamikazes*
*off Okinawa, 389 were killed and 264 wounded*

# EVEN MIGHTY BATTLESHIPS AND CRUISERS WERE HIT BY KAMIKAZES

*USS Missouri, BB63, deck gunners look them in the eye, stand and die.*

This picture taken April 28, 1945, at Okinawa, epitomizes the sheer guts and dedication required by gunners, for ships to survive. What these gunners did during the split seconds after this picture snapped would determine life or death -- theirs! Note: despite the conviction they are about to die, no one is running, hiding, or even ducking. Miraculously, they lived! Their efforts either killed the pilot, or shot the right wing off the "Zeke" (Zero). Believe it or not; this Kamikaze crashed in the sea. At the time of this picture, *Missouri* was spared. *"Mighty Moe"* remained in action despite damage from another Kamikaze that crashed into her on April 11, 1945.

## BATTLESHIPS AND CRUISERS HIT BY KAMIKAZES INCLUDED:

The USS *Nevada*, BB36; *West Virginia*, BB48; *Maryland*, BB46; *Idaho*, BB42; *Tennessee*, BB43; *New York*, BB34; *New Mexico*, BB40; *Mississippi*, BB41; *Colorado*, BB45; and *California*, BB44. The cruisers included USS *Columbia*, CL56; *Louisville*, CA28; *Reno*, CL96; *ST Louis*, CL45; *Nashville*, CL43; *Biloxi*, CL80; *Vincennes*, CL64; *Indianapolis*, CA35; *Birmingham*, CL62; *Salt Lake City*, CA24 and the two Australian cruisers HMAS *Australia*, and *Westralia*.

## SIXTY-NINE AUXILIARY SHIPS, INCLUDING TROOP TRANSPORTS, TANKERS, MERCHANT SHIPS, AND EVEN THE HOSPITAL SHIPS USS COMFORT AND PINKNEY, FELL VICTIM TO THE JAPANESE KAMIKAZE DEVASTATION AMONG THE 69, 23 WERE SUNK.

When suicide as a weapon was first encountered, reaction of the U.S. high command was disbelief. With the unmistakable truth thrust upon them, they reacted by minimizing its importance and censored the press. However, our research has now uncovered the reality regarding the extent of devastation.

In the Philippines and again at Iwo Jima, the Japanese had confirmed the effectiveness of flying an aircraft directly into a target ship. Several hundred suicide planes were committed to those battles. At Okinawa several thousand could be expected. The Japanese would launch everything they had in one fanatical, last ditch effort to stop the Americans and save their Empire.

*May 11, 1945, another Kamikaze strikes home. An unknown freighter explodes.*

Small, one man high speed, wooden suicide boats, nearly impossible to detect on US radar, were also used by the Japanese in defense of their home Empire. They had free access to US destroyers from the many small islands that make up the Ryukyus. *Wren* engaged fifteen of those elusive ghostly craft, in one high speed gun battle in the darkness off Okinawa.

Okinawa was the first Japanese home island the U.S. invaded. For the first time aircraft could fly directly from mainland Japan. The U.S. Navy had to stop them! But how?

U.S. destroyers were given the job and Admiral Moosbrugger was put in charge of this awesome task.

*USS LST447, April 6, 1945, exploded and sank. Many ships of this class felt the ultimate sting. Note the landing craft in the foreground loaded with troops*

## THUS ENTERED THE SACRIFICIAL LAMBS

American destroyers were singled out to stand between the Japanese mainland and the U.S. invading fleet. They alone were given the task of intercepting the onslaught of massive Japanese suicidal air-sea attacks, designed to annihilate the American invaders. Okinawa, the place remembered in nightmares, by all who fought there.

Men on small ships had never been called upon to face such odds. With no place to hide -- they had to look them in the eye, stand and die. Blood and aircraft gasoline mixed freely on decks of U.S. destroyers and many were swallowed up by the sea.

## BATTERED HULKS OF DESTROYERS STARTED TO FILL THE HARBORS IMMEDIATELY!

*USS William D. Porter, DD579,*
*June 10, 1945 -- sunk*

*USS Laffey DD724, April 15, 1945,*
*32 killed 71 wounded.*

*USS Morris, DD417, April 6, 1945, scrapped. They only had 255 survivors.*

4

## 157 DESTROYERS HIT BY KAMIKAZES
## 35 IN THE PHILIPPINES, AND 122 AT OKINAWA

Of the 35 destroyers hit in the Philippines; seven were sunk. USS *Abner Read* the first, followed by the USS *Ward, Mahn, Reid, Long, Palmer*, and *Hovey*, Captain Mac's last command before the Wren.

At Okinawa, 122 destroyers fell victim! Forty-one were either sunk outright or considered total losses by the U.S. Navy and scrapped. Some were ultimately sunk by U.S. gunfire, while they beached others to prevent their sinking. Among the other 81 repaired and returned to service were ships that should have been on the bottom. All 157 destroyers each have exciting stories that could fill a book by themselves.

*USS Aaron Ward, DM34, May 3, 1945, scrapped.*　　　*USS Hazelwood, DD531, April 29, 1945.*

*USS Sigsbee, DD502, April 14, 1945.*

## 148 DESTROYERS OF ALL CLASSES TOOK PART IN THE OKINAWA CAMPAIGN, OF THOSE 122, OVER 80%, WERE HIT BY KAMIKAZES.

*USS Lindsey, DMS32, April 12, 1945*

DMs, DMSs, and APDs, are all destroyer types that have been given equal treatment in this book. Many stood picket duty, and all had a very rough time with Kamikazes.

*USS Haraden, DD585, December 13, 1944*

Stories on most ships hit by Kamikazes are featured in our book.

*USS Ward, APD16, December 7, 1944*

We have given up five years of our retirement to research and write this account of those hectic, historically significant times. Both my wife and I hope you will enjoy reading about "The Sacrificial Lambs."

Two articles appeared in the New York Times in 1945. The true extent of the holocaust had not been divulged at that time and remains untold. This book will set the record straight!

**Those articles follow:**

*Ryukyus Glory Won by Little Warships*
*Picket Line Guarding Fleet off Okinawa*
*Balked Enemy Air Force in Blazing War*

*June 29, 1945*                                                *by W. H. Lawrence*

*By Wireless to The New York Times Aboard a Flagship, in the East China Sea off Okinawa, June 26 (delayed), the Navy threw a "Picket Line" across "Bogey Highway" to keep Japanese ship breakers out of the Okinawa transport area. These picket ships -- none larger than destroyers--fought and won the longest and hardest battle in the history of Naval warfare. They suffered the greatest losses in men and ships ever sustained by the United States Navy, but they fulfilled their mission of keeping the bulk of the enemy aircraft out of the transport area, where vital supplies for the soldiers and marines were being unloaded. It is no exaggeration to say that these little ships, which seldom have the chances for glory given to the aircraft carriers and battleships, performed a major role in our victory on Okinawa.*

*This thrilling story, which can be told for the first time now that the Okinawan Campaign is won, constitutes an epic that will live forever in the annals of the Navy. It is a story of tough little ships and brave men whose extraordinary gunnery took care of the best the Japanese Air Force could throw at our Okinawan operation.*

*They were at "general quarters" more than 150 times during the eighty-two days of the land fighting in Okinawa. These air alerts lasted from a few minutes to several hours, and came at all hours of the night and day, as the Japanese sent over one to 200 aircraft in a single attack. Only comparatively few of the enemy got through to the transport area.*

*Commanded by Commodore Frederick Moosbrugger, forty-four, of Philadelphia, himself a hero of the Naval fighting off Vella La Vella in 1943, these pickets stood guard as much as sixty miles away from the Hagushi Anchorage. They were the sentinels to fight approaching Japanese planes, surface craft or submarines.*

*The shattered Japanese fleet never got near our main anchorage, but the pickets did have to cope with small suicide boats carrying powerful explosive charges, which Naval men called "skunks." A few submarines were encountered and depth charges dropped. Whether any submarines were sunk or damaged has not been announced.*

*But it was the enemy aircraft, which fighting men call "Bogeys", that made this the toughest duty Naval men have had to face in this war. Here, less than 400 statute miles from Kyushu, southernmost of the Japanese home islands, and about equidistant from the enemy held China coast, the pickets had to engage the best of the Japanese air force. It was in this battle that the enemy employed Kamikaze fliers of the "Special Attack Corps" on the greatest scale, sending literally thousands of planes and their pilots in an attempt to drive the bomb laden air craft squarely into a ship.*

## *OKINAWA PICKET LINE*

*Out over the horizon, hull down from the highest peak on Okinawa, was fought during the eighty-two days of the land campaign the most bitter, relentless sea-air battle of the Pacific war, the Navy now has revealed. It was the battle of the destroyer squadrons against the "Kamikaze Corps", both sea and air. It is a battle that still is going on.*

*Day after day, sometimes hour after hour, the Japanese send down from Kyushu and northern Ryukyu bases their suicide planes and suicide boats. Their prime targets are the fat transports, oilers and supply vessels lying off the Okinawa beaches unloading men and supplies. To get to them they have to pass the two picket lines of destroyers, destroyer escorts and other fast escort craft deployed to meet them in two great arcs out in the East China Sea, twenty-five miles and fifty miles respectively from the unloading area. Some of the enemy get through, of course. Many of them do not. Part of the story of the picket lines was told in the single ship releases on the U.S.S. Laffey, worthy successor of the destroyer, lost in the Solomons on Nov. 13, 1942, and Commander Al Parker's U.S.S. Mannert L. Abele, which was sunk by a combination suicide plane and baka bomb attack off Okinawa. The Laffey withstood the crash of six suicide planes on her decks and got back.*

*Nine destroyers were sunk, twenty-one were damaged: one of every three. Almost a quarter of the naval losses of 4,907 men off Okinawa were suffered by these little warships. Their antiaircraft battles took toll of 490 Japanese planes, and uncounted number of suicide boats which attacked at night, and perhaps several suicide submarines, small enemy undersea boats, were detected and attacked. The work of the destroyer squadrons has been told before, but it cannot be told too often. A list of Navy vessels lost from Dec. 7, 1941 to May 31, 1945 shows 60 destroyers, 8 destroyer escorts and 7 destroyer transports (which often did destroyer escort and patrol duty) -- the largest single class losses among the total of 302. The only comparable loss by classes is that by submarines, of which forty-three have failed to return, forty-two from combat assignments. By the accident of name, the destroyer Aaron Ward leads the alphabetical list .*

# TWO
# WHAT IS A DESTROYER?

Our book features one destroyer, but it's not about just one. Not a super destroyer, perhaps not even outstanding, but proud, well-skippered and well manned -- that was the USS *Wren.*

*USS Wren, looking down at her stern*

Crewmen of any destroyer would probably resent being called ordinary -- but extraordinary was the norm for all Okinawa picket destroyers.

Destroyers, "Tin Cans, Greyhounds of the Fleet," by any name these sleek and graceful ships are the smallest, but faster among the U.S. Navy's ships of the line. They are maneuverable, gutsy and expendable. Standing Naval orders mandate that all destroyers must move between inbound aircraft, gunfire and torpedoes directed at larger ships.

*Wren,* is a Fletcher class destroyer, 376 feet

long and 39 1/2 feet wide, with a top speed of 40.9 knots or about 47 mph, recorded during class speed trials off San Diego. *Wren,* unofficially the fastest destroyer in the United States Navy, had twin screws that utilized her 60,000 shaft horsepower to the maximum. Turns could be accelerated by varying the speed of those propellers; thus moving *Wren* quickly in and out of harms way. Her bow taper started about midships, flowing down to a long point with rounded edges. This allowed her to dip easily under swells and shed water rapidly on the rise.

*Looking down at Wren's bow*

# WREN BRISTLED WITH GUNS, TORPEDOES, AND DEPTH CHARGES.

Her five, 5- inch guns could reach air surface targets up to 18,000 yards with extreme accuracy. The five twin 40mm mounts could be fired by radar, or visually, and delivered 160 explosive projectiles per minute.

Seven 20mm antiaircraft guns were her last line of defense. Fired locally, their rapid fired explosive rounds could devastate incoming aircraft. With a total of twenty-two guns, *Wren* was a fast, maneuverable, radar controlled gun emplacement.

When the guns all fired at once, her small deck space offered no refuge. Crewmen on exposed decks caught hell from flash burn and concussion. Empty shell casings came flying out of each gun and bounced around on the decks. They slammed back and forth with each radical maneuver. Destroyers created their own hell! They were exciting! The duty was tough, but any man who served on a destroyer will never forget it.

*Mount-1 in the foreground, mount-2 trained*
*to starboard, 40mm above mount 2 barrel,*
*and 5-inch director on top*

*Five-inch gun director*

*Wren's stern dropping depth charges and making smoke.*

Her offensive armament included two 21-inch torpedo launchers, each capable of firing five torpedoes. Wren also had four "Y" and two "K" guns. Those fired depth charges to each side of the ship and two tracks dropped them from the fantail for a devastating pattern against enemy submarines.

*Wren* was capable of dealing with any ship, aircraft, or shore installation she faced. While traveling at speeds of forty-seven miles an hour, the rooster-tail, a twenty-foot-high geyser created by her two powerful propellers, erupted at her stern. One of the most exciting places in this world to be is on the decks of a destroyer maneuvering at flank speed.

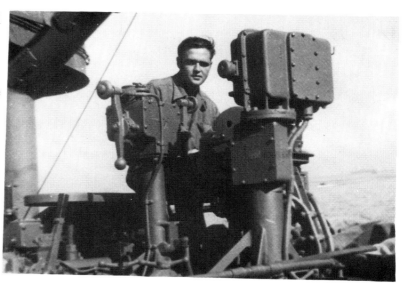

*Torpedoman First Class Bud Brennan sitting high upon his torpedo director*

*An ash-can -- looking for a home*

At such speeds *Wren* was often forced to execute emergency right angle turns to avoid being rammed by suicide boats, or hit by suicide planes. Those turns were necessary to keep enemy aircraft at right angles to the ship, which allowed simultaneous firing of all guns.

Her decks became alive with surging, vibrating power. As she heeled over, as much as twenty to forty degrees, the outside decks were suddenly under raging water. Gunners and loaders on the 20mm main deck guns and repair parties, had to move quickly amidships at the first sign of water on deck. Once water appeared, it cleared the stern in the blink of an eye. Fixed, welded items could be torn from *Wren's* decks. Anyone in its path could be ejected overboard.

In those desperate live-or-die situations all of *Wren's* guns fired at one deafening time, often at night. Gun flashes were all around and our crew felt as though they had been pelted by thousands of sand bags. Take ships like *Wren*, put them alone, exposed to massive suicidal air-sea attacks and you had **"THE SACRIFICIAL LAMBS"** -- who fought like Lions. This was the blood-bath called the **"OKINAWA PICKET LINE."** To tell this story at all, you had to be there.

# THREE
# COMMISSIONING AND SHAKEDOWN

Life began for *Wren* on April 24th, 1943, at Seattle-Tacoma Shipbuilding Corporation, when her keel was laid. Launched January 29, 1944, she was commissioned May 20.

*Captain Edwin A MacDonald*

Commander Edwin MacDonald, Captain, soon became affectionately known by his officers and crewmen, as Captain Mac. But not always to his face. At thirty-eight years of age, our Captain a rather handsome, slightly built, mild-mannered gentleman, took command.

After graduating from the Naval Academy in 1931, he served aboard the battleship USS *Maryland,* the destroyers USS *Long,* DD206-DMS12, and *Noa,* DD343-APD24. But, Captain Mac wanted to be a pilot and was elated when his transfer came through to the Naval Air Station at Pensacola, Florida. He graduated as a flying officer and served in squadrons aboard the carriers USS *Langley* and *Saratoga,* until an aircraft accident left him injured and grounded.

In 1941 Captain Mac returned to sea duty as executive officer of the minesweeper USS *Hovey*, DMS11; he soon became her commanding officer. He participated in the Solomon Islands campaign, then they gave him command of *Wren.* Captain MacDonald's experience in ship handling, plus his knowledge as a pilot, made him uniquely qualified to guide his crew through the hard months ahead. His reputation as a cool-headed, decisive leader, would soon be confirmed and spread throughout *Wren's* crew.

A major class-distinction and lifestyle separation caused division between officers and crewmen, aboard Navy ships. With 350 men, many of them boys, on such a small ship the potential for discord or even downright rebellion was great. Captain Mac, together with the skill and knowledge of our officers, helped pull the crew together.

A warship is like a city. Many different professions and skills are required to make her function effectively. The crew of a newly built destroyer had been selected weeks before the Navy accepted it. Some would be going to sea for the first time, while a few had previous sea duty. Many had been involved in various training programs.

Some seamen and deck rated men came to *Wren* from gunnery school at Point Montara, California and Norman, Oklahoma. Skilled personnel, including CIC men, fire controlmen, radarmen, gunner's mates and electricians also required special training. The ability of the captain to blend and mold these skills into a harmonious, smooth running team, was imperative.

LT Howard Cook, respected by officers and crewmen alike and considered a highly competent seaman, was always congenial and fair. He gives us his background:

"In December, 1941, I enlisted in the Navy as an apprentice Seaman, and went to officers candidate school, where I received my Ensign's commission in October, 1942. They assigned me to the USS *Edwards* DD619, a new 1650 ton destroyer. After shakedown, *Edwards* was assigned to convoy duty in the north Atlantic, heavy weather, but not many submarines.

*LT Howard Cook*

"In December 1942, *Edwards* transited the Panama Canal en route to the western Pacific. We became part of the first relief carrier task group to be sent to the area. Our group took part in the Solomon Islands campaign, the battle of Rennel Island, the Gilberts, Marshalls, Tarawa, and Attu.

"In the latter, *Edwards* was credited with a 'probable' in the sinking of a Japanese submarine that had launched a torpedo at the battleship *Pennsylvania*, the flag ship for U.S. forces in the Aleutian campaign. DD619, and another destroyer carried out a sustained attack, which lasted for about four hours. The sub surfaced, then plunged back into the sea, leaving men, debris, and a three day oil slick at the site. I learned later that the sub survived.

"My career developed somewhat unusually. While still an ensign, I had the rare opportunity of being appointed a destroyer department head and qualified officer of the deck.

"All of the foregoing experiences were good preparation for my orders to *Wren*, which came in early 1944, when I became part of the pre-commissioning team."

LT Dacre Dunn, gunnery officer: "I came to *Wren* after surviving the sinking of USS *Brownson*, DD518. We were in Cape Glochester, New Britain, when an attacking Japanese aircraft scored a bomb hit right down our after stack. *Brownson* sank in about fifteen minutes.

*LT Dacre Dunn*

"I joined the Navy in February, 1943, as a '90 day wonder,' with boot camp at the Notre Dame University, and Midshipman school aboard the USS *Prairie State* in New York City. Then I went to bomb disposal and gunnery school in Washington DC.

"After graduation, they transferred me to Orange, Texas for duty on the USS *John D. Rodgers*, DD564; in a short time I was reassigned to the *Brownson*, as gunnery assistant.

"After shakedown at Guantanamo Bay, Cuba, we were on submarine patrol in the north Atlantic; then went to Casablanca, North Africa, during the invasion. After that we went through the Panama Canal and up to the Aleutians for about eight months. During that time we were on sub patrol, but also bombarded the Kurile Islands. We then went south to New Guinea and were landing marines at Cape Glouchester, on Christmas day 1943, when we were sunk.

"We lost 108 crewmen! I found myself in the water, swimming among body parts, trying to avoid fires that were consuming the sea. Explosions were still erupting when the USS *Daly* finally took me aboard.

"After survivors leave, I joined the crew of USS *Wren* as navigator. When they transferred Hank Turner I became gunnery officer, and John Powell was my assistant, roommate, and friend."

Ensign Lowell Clark rose rapidly on the *Wren*, becoming Howard Cook's right-hand man during GQ. He recalls his early Navy life and introduction to the *Wren*: "While attending Midshipman's school, my wife to be, Pat, joined me. Graduation was a big day for us because we got married following the ceremony. I was assigned to the USS *Hill*, DE141, operating on submarine patrol in the Caribbean and went aboard at Bermuda.

"We left the area on orders for Charleston, South Carolina, and I'll never forget the storm we were in off Cape Hatteras. It was just a prelude of things to come, but at least I didn't get sea sick.

"*Hill* was assigned to Provincetown, Massachusetts, where we towed targets for the Naval Air Station's flight training program at Hyannisport. During that time we also tested new types of torpedoes. We had the soft touch of going to sea in the morning and back in at night, but I wanted to get off that old DE and aboard a full fledged destroyer.

"I was later sent to sonar school at Miami, then on to Key West for sonar training aboard a submarine. They eventually sent me to Treasure Island, for navigational training, before going to Bremerton for assignment to *Wren*.

"As sonar officer and assistant navigator, at 23 years old, I felt somewhat intimidated because of lack of sea duty. I knew I wouldn't get sick but what if I screwed up? How would I stand up to this rugged duty? What kind of an officer would I be? Those thoughts and consid-

*ENS Lowell Clark*

erable apprehension lingered while standing on *Wren's* bridge for the first time."

However, destroyer duty either brings out the best or worst in everyone and Lowell learned fast while advancing rapidly. LT Dacre Dunn, navigator, became gunnery officer and Lowell elevated to navigator.

Lowell must have excelled in ship handling, as they assigned him to the bridge during GQ, as JO-OD, and raised him in rank to LTjg. He remained at that job during most of *Wren's* exciting action. Assigned the additional task of keeping records for our ship's logs, allowed little time to dwell on his lack of experience.

LTjg Jack Clemens was second and later became *Wren's* chief engineer. Jack recalls the harrowing

*LTjg Jack Clemens*

15

experience on his last ship. "After graduating from midshipman school and attending fire fighting school in Boston, I helped commission the USS *Turner*, DD648, at Brooklyn Navy Yard, April 15, 1943.

"After three trips across the north Atlantic in convoy duty against German submarines --*Turner* blew up. It happened at 0600 on January 3, 1944, off Sandy Hook Light Ship. The undetermined explosion in number two handling room destroyed that mount, blowing the bridge and main battery director, aft. The mast lay on the deck house and the signal flag bags were against number one stack. Both sides of the hull below number 2-gun were blown open, as leaking fuel oil ignited on the water. Ammunition exploded and the ship sank 90 minutes later.

"Tragically, 138 men lost their lives and about 100 were hospitalized. I was extremely fortunate to be the senior survivor, an ensign with very limited experience. After visiting with all of the next of kin and hospitalized survivors; testifying at the Board of Inquiry; enjoying survivors leave; and attending Damage Control School in San Francisco, I joined the USS *Wren* in preparation for its commissioning at Seattle-Tacoma Shipyard."

Ensign John Powell, assigned to the *Wren* several months before she was commissioned, attended special schooling in Norfolk and Philadelphia in preparation for destroyer duty.

*ENS John Powell*

John advanced in the Navy the hard way. He joined after high school in 1937 and completed boot camp as an apprentice seaman. Assigned to the heavy cruiser USS *Astoria*, CA34, where he remained for over five years, John became a first class fire-controlman.

During the battle of Savo Island, John thought his career would abruptly end, he describes the action.

"The *Astoria, Quincy*, and *Vincennes*, all the same class of heavy cruisers, were assigned to block the entrance to Guadalcanal from the north, maintaining a station east of Savo Island. The Japanese, with a force of six heavy and three light cruisers, approached from the north, passing Savo Island to the west, and turned northeast heading into the area.

"They fired torpedoes at the USS *Chicago*, disabling it. The HMS *Camberra* was sunk. Those two ships were guarding approaches from the southwest. The Japanese ships then engaged *Astoria, Quincy* and *Vincennes*. *Quincy* and *Vincennes* were both sunk by torpedoes and gunfire. All three ships engaged the battle with the Japanese. *Astoria* was able to score 8-inch and 5-inch hits on the Japanese ship, and killed or wounded nearly all of the Japanese Admiral's staff.

"There seemed to be some confusion with the Japanese ships as well, when their formation split into two parts. Half the ships passed *Astoria* to port and the others to starboard while shooting at us. *Astoria* received well over 100 8-inch and 5-inch hits. She was set ablaze from bridge to hangar, half the length of the ship and sank about 10 hours after the battle of Savo Island. We took a lot of flack over the battle that we didn't really deserve.

"Our senior command was at fault for committing the unpardonable sin of splitting forces. We were split into four groups, but in my opinion it simply wasn't necessary. The normal tactic is to keep your fleet together, so you can present the largest possible force against an attacker. If we had stayed together, the outcome would have been one hell of a lot different. We would have been more evenly matched, and we had an early form of radar.

"One of our groups gathered at Florida Island, another at Guadalcanal, one on the south and we were on the north end of Savo Island. The attacking Japanese Fleet consisted of six heavy and three light cruisers, outnumbering each group nearly three or four to one. After being hit, the Japanese Admiral broke off the engagement. When the war ended he stated his fear of being caught by our carrier planes, the next morning.

"U.S. forces invaded Guadalcanal August 7, on my 23rd birthday and at times I didn't expect to live to see 24. *Astoria* sank August 9,1942, in spite of all our efforts to save her.

"We got 30 days survivor's leave, the longest I had since joining the Navy. When I returned to duty they assigned me to the destroyer tender *Cascade*. She was a new ship, with a rusty hull, being outfitted by the Matson Steamship Company for duty as a destroyer tender. We all thought we would have an extended time in the U.S., but they were ready to go in March, 1943."

John Powell's battle station on *Cascade* placed him in charge of the ship's offensive armament. He evidently did a good job as the captain recommended him for warrant gunnery officer; however, the Bureau of Naval Personnel decided he should be an ensign, as experienced gunnery personnel in the officer ranks were greatly needed. "Much to my surprise I became an ensign," John recalls. It might have been a surprise to John, but it was one of the best things that could have happened for the *Wren*.

After finishing his schooling on the east coast, John went to Treasure Island where *Wren's* crew was gathering. He recalls: "Shortly after arriving in California, the XO sent me on down to the Point Montara Gunnery School. Our gun crews spent days shooting hundreds of 5-inch and thousands of 40 and 20mm ammunition, for practice. When we went on board our ship, all gun crews had a hell of a lot of shooting experience. They had moved well beyond the initial fear of noise and concussion."

*Wren* was fortunate to have many experienced and skilled people like Robert Pauli, Howard Cook, John Powell, Jack Clemens, Dacre Dunn, Lowell Clark, Wally Rupe, Clay Harris, Dick Easter, Joe Martino, Bill Ferguson, and many others, among her officers and crewmen.

Prior to commissioning, May 20, 1944, the crew arrived early to get everything shipshape before the ceremony. Bill Ferguson stepped up to the PA system in the central passageway, blew his pipe and said: "Now hear this, all hands turn to, turn to. Sweepers man your brooms, clean sweepdown fore and aft, sweepdown all decks and ladders, empty all spit kits and trash cans -- turn to, turn to...." *Wren's* deck hummed with activity.

At 1100, May 20,1944 the commissioning ceremony started with a speech given by Captain MacDonald, he said: "This ship is going into Tokyo Bay, anyone who does not want to go with us, step forward." (No one did.)

*USS Wren, DD568, -- Captain MacDonald received our ship's colors from the sponsor.*

Later the same day officers gathered on the bridge prior to getting underway. Captain Mac said: "Set special sea detail." Howard Cook, OD, relayed all orders, saying: 'Aye aye Sir, all hands set special sea detail.' Ferguson blew his pipe into the PA system and repeated: 'Now hear this, all hands set special sea detail, all hands set special sea detail.' The men rushed to their individual stations with enthusiasm. Finally they were getting underway.

On the bridge, Captain Mac walked out on the starboard wing. (the conn) Looking down he could see Frank Olson and his deck crew, on location, waiting for orders. He walked to the port conn, looked down as tugs attached lines to *Wren* and shouted angrily: "You tugs cast off those lines -- we don't need you."

Our captain then walked back to the starboard wing looked down and shouted: "Single up."

Cook repeated, "Aye aye Sir, single up."

Olson's crew jumped into action, coiling the extra lines, and stowed them away, leaving only a single line fore and aft.

Captain Mac then gave the orders, "Cast off stern line, twenty degree left rudder, starboard engine back slow." Cook repeated his orders.

As the stern started to move from the dock, the Captain said, "Cast off bow line." The order was repeated and *Wren* slowly left the dock.

As the bow moved from the dock the captain ordered, "All engines back one third." As the bow cleared the dock Captain Mac said, "Port engine ahead one third." *Wren* turned slowly in her own length, until she lined up seaward in the narrow channel. The Captain then gave the order, "All ahead one third." Underway for her first time, *Wren* headed towards Elliott Bay.

Howard Cook recalls, "Our captain was like a kid with a new toy, roaring up and down Puget Sound, near shore, inadvertently knocking over floating outhouses with the wake."

May 27, *Wren* hit a partially submerged log, known locally as "dead heads," damaging her port screw, and returned to Bremerton for repairs. Next day they were back on Puget Sound, conducting gunnery practice. May 29th and 30th the magnetic compasses and radio direction finders were calibrated.

Fire Control Officer John Powell, a stern but likable officer, gained the respect of everyone. John took charge immediately. May 31st he decided to align the 5-inch-38 batteries. John asked Gunnery Officer LT Hank Turner, "How do you want to align the batteries? Do you want them lined up accurately, or by the book?"

Hank responded, "If you know a way to line them up so they are accurate, go ahead and do it your way. Don't bother me with details." John replied affirmatively, contacting Fire Controlman First Class Bill Harris.

John recalls, "Bill Harris was a real professional fire controlman. He served many years on new pre-war destroyers, and knew the Mark One computer like a book. I had complete faith in him; because he had much more experience than I did with our installed equipment at that time, but we really saw eye-to-eye when it came time to align the batteries. I told Hank we needed several targets around the compass about eight thousand yards from our ship, to check our work.

"Captain Mac obliged by anchoring the ship in a strategic place where this could be accomplished. When we completed our test firing, we had a real fine close 'Fall of shot pattern,' with all guns."

*Wren* continued her sea trials in Puget Sound, operating consistent with orders from the Thirteenth Naval District. DD568, conducted various maneuvers and speed runs, checked all guns, and removed bugs from her numerous complicated systems. June 8, she entered Todd Shipyard for minor repairs, returning to pier 91 the same day.

Captain R. C. Bartman, fleet operational training commander, inspected our ship and pronounced her in very good condition. He declared her ready for shake-down at San Diego and *Wren,* joined by the USS *Killen,* DD593, were dispatched.

On June 12, *Wren* arrived at San Diego and moored to buoy 8. At 1430 Captain Moosbrugger, of Fleet Operational Training Command, inspected her again and assigned *Wren* to Task Force 14, under Rear Admiral F.D. Denebrink, for training. The crew kept busy with the serious task of testing, learning to use all of her weapons, checking and working with the sound equipment, and fueling at sea.

Friendships established among the crew would last for a lifetime. There is something about men going to war together that creates a unique bond. Men of all backgrounds and fields of expertise must learn to get along together, on a small ship like a destroyer. This bond of mutual admiration, respect, and pride starts with the captain and his officers, and must develop throughout the entire crew. The urgency required this type of bond between the men and their ship. Our survival depended upon how well we accomplished the necessary coordination required to convert our ship into a fighting machine.

Many opinions have been expressed on this subject by *Wren's* officers and crew. LT Howard Cook remembers: "At San Diego we continued our ship's weapons tests and so on, while all the time, Captain Mac was performing that magic necessary to transform an inanimate metal structure, into a fighting ship."

In a tape to Captain Mac, LT Jim Rorabaugh recalled: "You managed so well to make the *Wren* a good fighting ship and still a "happy" one. I served on two destroyers, after *Wren*, and neither came close to being the fine fighting ship --*Wren* was."

Commander John Powell reminisced at a ship's reunion: "I served as skipper of three destroyers after the *Wren* and she was the finest combination of crew and ship I served on."

Reno Pellegrini, a tall, slender built, young, pharmacist's mate, aboard *Wren* from the beginning, had a pompadour of black wavy hair, a broad smile and everyone liked him. However, beneath that smile lived a wild, fun-loving, hell-raising kid. If any trouble could be gotten into, you could always depend on Reno to be in the middle of it.

*Joseph Precopio, and Reno Pellegrini*

The best way to describe Al Trombie, fireman second class, is simply to say he was one tough character. He would prove this to my personal satisfaction during a liberty together at Dutch Harbor.

*First Class Watertender Hap Rogers*

First Class Watertender "Hap" Rogers, another member of our crew like Reno, was friendly, well liked and his nick name suited him. For such a young man he had a lot of responsibility on the *Wren*. As "Oil King" he was in charge of oil, pumping it aboard and maintaining safe reserves. Liquids had the secondary function of adding ballast to our ship. Oil and water pumped from side to side kept her level, or created a list, allowing for such maintenance activities as painting the waterline.

Bill Ferguson, a slightly built, serious-minded, boatswain's mate first class, also put *Wren* in commission. Bill had the dubious duty, among many other important chores, of maintaining some degree of order onboard the *Wren*. Those who underestimated Bill's small stature were in for a rude awakening if they stepped too far out of line.

*Seaman First Class Al Copson*

Seaman First Class Al Copson had trouble figuring out what he wanted to do in the Navy. He started out in the deck crew, transferred to a fireman's rating where he worked and stood watches in the after engine room, then back to the deck crew, all aboard the *Wren*. He was tattooed and salty, well-liked, high-spirited, and enjoyed going on liberties with his shipmates. He found a real home on the *Wren*. Though small in stature, he also would defend the honor of our ship against anyone who attempted to bad-mouth her.

Al recalls: "Before coming aboard *Wren*, I served eighteen months on the Amphibious Flagship USS *Rocky Mount*, ADC 3. We participated in the Marshall Islands campaign. During this duty I gained experience on LCTs and LCVPs, helping me become a small-boat handler for the *Wren*."

*Seaman First Class LJ Adams*

Today, when asked about his duty aboard *Rocky Mount*, Al is very outspoken: "I hated every minute of my time there. We housed high-ranking officers from all branches of the service and we permanently wore our right hand in a saluting position. They literally had hundreds of steward's mates catering to their every need."

Seaman First Class "LJ" Adams came to *Wren* directly from Point Montara, Mark 20, 40mm director school. He also "skippered" the captain's gig. As such, he provided personal shuttle service for Captain Mac and other officers, to and from our ship.

One day while anchored out in San Diego Harbor, Captain Mac had his wife aboard to visit the ship. LJ was not available to deliver the happy couple back to the dock at the end of her visit, so Al Copson took his place skippering the captain's gig. Al had been running the whaleboat cradled on the starboard side. They were similar except for the passenger canopy on the gig. Al recalls his experience on that trip: "It was a typical clear, smooth, San Diego day, when the call came down for me to run the captain's gig. I was honored, but nervous about falling under the captain's scrutiny.

"Captain and Mrs. MacDonald came aboard pleasant and smiling. I welcomed them to the gig. During our short trip to the dock, I became distracted by porpoise crisscrossing our bow. They were having a great time swimming alongside the boat, diving then coming up ahead of the bow. They followed us all the way back to our dock. (Those boats were steered with a tiller, and the coxswain stood high up on the stern.)

"While distracted by my fascinating finned escort, I rammed full speed right into the dock pilings! The impact dumped me the length of the boat at my passenger's feet. As I looked up, embarrassed, Captain and Mrs. MacDonald were in a heap in the bow. I quickly got back on my perch and docked the boat. As they left the gig Mrs. MacDonald said, 'Thank you' and gave me an embarrassed smile. Our Captain remained silent! But that was the one and only time I ever ran the gig."

June 23rd to 28th *Wren* moored to pier 3 at the San Diego Destroyer Base, to have alterations to her main-battery computer. Our crew had liberty during that time.

Hap Rogers, Bill Ferguson, Al Trombie, Reno Pellegrini and Al Copson along with several other shipmates, decided to venture down to Mexico. After making several pit-stops in Tijuana, some of our boys wound up at the California Bar.

On their way in, Al Trombie accidentally bumped into the post supporting the swinging doors and the entire building front shook. Hap tells us: "We went in and had a few more drinks when all of a sudden there's Trombie up in front shaking the building. 'Hey, Hap,' he yelled, 'look at this fine construction!' The glass rolled like vertical ocean waves. Subsequently, a second shipmate decided to help Al check out the merits of that fine building. Going to the other side of the second window, together, they gave this building front its supreme test. The entire plate glass window wound up on the sidewalk -- in pieces." Hap concluded, "We had better get out of this place." But no way! Mexicans gathered around in front of the building preventing their exit. That's right, our boys all wound up in the infamous "Tijuana jail." Bill Ferguson still says: "I was roped in!"

*Boatswain's Mate First Class Bill Ferguson*

Reno and Al Copson avoided going to jail on that incident, but soon got into trouble on their own. Al recalls: "We were in this bar where they were selling large knives for about a dollar fifty, so Reno and I, along with several other crewmen, purchased one.

A friendly game of mumble peg ensued. We used the bar top to sharpen our skills. I don't know why the owners objected. Most of their Mexican customers seemed to like the idea. But, sure enough, the Mexican police returned with a paddy wagon and started rounding us all up. The police van had two doors, so we promptly opened the second door and exited as fast as they put us in. We disappeared back into the many bars. For some strange reason the Mexican police found us conspicuous. Once again, in about an hour, they gathered us all up.

"We were driven to the American border and handed over to the shore patrol, along with the official complaint, then promptly returned to our ship and released to the OD."

Captain Mac had been notified of his crew still in the Tijuana jail; so he sent his shore patrol to Mexico with funds from the ship's store, to make restitution and post bail. The Navy had enough clout to secure their release, fortunately,

Returning to their ship, they faced the wrath of Captain Mac. He said: "I do not read Spanish so I don't know what some of you guys did down there, but I doubt we will be available for any more Mexican liberties. As for you guys who were in jail, I expect to see every dollar reimbursed to our ship store fund." Captain Mac was like a mother hen with his crew, compassionate and forgiving. But, do not push it.

*Wren* remained at pier 3 until June 29th, then got underway for battle practice. Entering San Diego Harbor only long enough to replace fuel and supplies, they stayed at sea for a week at a time. *Wren's* crew practiced every conceivable battle tactic.

*USS Wren fueling at sea.*

It's always an emergency, if it becomes necessary for one destroyer to tow another. This potentially dangerous procedure must be practiced.

Underway, while traveling with the fast fleets, destroyers must fuel daily. To accomplish this difficult but necessary procedure, they must position themselves close alongside tankers, carriers, or other larger ships. Before the fueling hose can be sent over the two ships must be joined together, about thirty feet apart, first with a "heaving" or messenger line followed by large lines to secure the ships.

During fueling operations the sea between moving ships becomes very turbulent. If not held steady, all lines and hoses could easily part. During this operation both ships were vulnerable to attack. All lookouts and radar monitoring personnel must be extra vigilant.

John Powell says: "Captain Mac was very good at allowing all of his bridge officers to participate, hands on, taking the helm during fueling operations. Many captains prefer handling those close maneuvering procedures themselves. This gave all of our officers a chance to learn to handle the ship. Captain Mac just sat there and let them make their own mistakes. When they finished he would say something like, 'It might have been better if you had handled it this, or that, way.'"

Before our first Paramushiro bombardment, LT Commander Robert H. Pauli replaced Dan Henry, as Executive Officer. Robert recalls a fueling incident shortly after coming aboard: "While in the wardroom with Captain Mac, *Wren* was preparing to fuel. He said: 'Go ahead and take her alongside.' I approached the tanker at twenty knots, about five knots faster than he was traveling, and slowed to his speed as our bridge came alongside. Captain Mac looked out of a porthole and noticed the tanker going by pretty fast, so he rushed to the bridge about the time I slowed down. After looking around he

*USS Wren fueling at sea from a fleet carrier -- David and Goliath.*

went back to his cabin, saying nothing. But that was our Captain's way, so calm under fire, mild mannered, and effective. I believe he was the best Captain I have ever seen. I admired him greatly."

All delicate maneuvers had to be practiced extensively until they became smooth and routine. Gunnery practice was a daily routine. *Wren's* crew fired at towed sleeves, unmanned remote controlled drones, shore targets and each others wake. Simulated surprise attacks were conducted. This gave the skeleton crew's, "ready watch," an opportunity to retaliate before the full gun crew could man their stations.

Torpedo attacks were carried out and dummy torpedoes fired at ships. This required a coordinated effort between the torpedomen, radarmen and those maneuvering *Wren*.

They tested under water sound equipment and put it into play against submarines. Depth charges were released over the stern and fired by "Y" and "K" guns. Diversionary and emergency tactics were practiced for every conceivable situation.

The purpose of a shakedown for a new ship, is to expose defects by applying maximum stress to her structure, equipment, and systems. At maximum speed, with her 60,000 shaft-horsepower, *Wren* had been thrown in reverse with full throttle applied, until her stern submerged under the sea. Her guns had all been fired at once, while traveling headlong into heavy seas, at flank speed. The stress and vibration of those activities on a new ship caused all sorts of mechanical failures. Her electrical wiring systems were attached to the steel overhead and bulkheads by small drilled and tapped buttons, welded onto the surface. Those would pop off, leaving dozens of electrical cables hanging like tangled spaghetti. It is better to know those defects before a ship is in combat. Problems will continue to occur, under similar situations, but hopefully to a lesser degree.

On July 20, *Wren* moored to buoy 8 in San Diego Harbor. The 21st our ship received an inspection party, headed by Captain C. C. Adell, who pronounced her and the crew shipshape. At 1028 they got underway hosting Captain R. W. Sampson and his staff, the shakedown training officers. A potential tactical problem was presented to Captain Mac and his officers, which they solved and *Wren* returned to port. At 0650, July 23, *Wren* got underway for Seattle.

Hap Rogers, "Oil King," recalls an incident while pumping fuel on this trip: "We pulled fuel oil feeding the boilers from two service tanks in the forward fire room. They were located amidships so the ships balance would not be affected, as they drained down. When one tank became empty it was refilled from storage tanks, and after emptying the storage tanks they were pumped full of sea water for ballast. As a safety precaution we had Don Riggi on the empty tank, visually watching and taking soundings, during pumping. We were connected with JV phones. I opened the valve feeding oil into the empty feeder tank and started pumping. No chance for mishap? Wrong! I opened the wrong valve. We pumped oil into the full feeder tank.

"Each tank had a safety valve and one was in Chief Engineer LT John Maynard's stateroom. As we pumped I asked Don if it was filling. He said, 'No, I don't see anything.' I kept pumping and waited for verification, when Mr Maynard poked me on the back and said, 'Shut the pump off and come with me.' I obeyed his order, but wondered what was going on. When we reached his room I soon found out. The threshold of each compartment on our ship had a wall about 12 inches high. Maynard's room was filled to the point of overflowing with thick, smelly oil. His shoes floated like small boats in a bath tub. He was pissed! Now, Mr Maynard took himself and his job very seriously, yelling, 'You guys are restricted until further notice.' He screamed and threatened, 'You're going to be court martialed. I'll break you for this!' I think he thought we did it on purpose. When we got back to Bremerton they extended the pipe over the side of the ship."

DD568 arrived at berth A-5 Bremerton Navy Yard at 1750 on the 26th, and remained there until August 8th, while skilled tradesmen crawled throughout her. *Wren* emerged an awesome state-of-the-art weapon of war. She wore her crew like a snug fitting glove. While *Wren's* repairs were being completed her crew enjoyed their much deserved leave.

After getting underway to re-calibrate the Mark 22 radar they returned to anchor off Bremerton Navy Yard where a full load of ammunition was taken aboard. The following day they left to compensate the magnetic compasses, then moored at pier 91 until August 12.

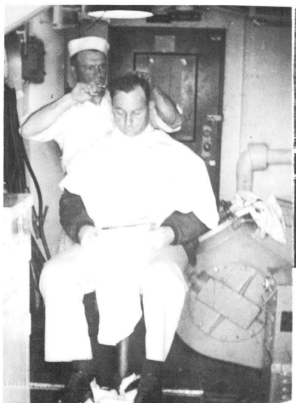

*Top -- Wren's deck crew mooring to buoy.*

*Left--Captain Mac gets a haircut.*

# FOUR
# WREN HEADS INTO WAR

Lowell Clark, sonar officer and navigator: "On August 12, I sensed the urgency to complete our last minute details, prior to becoming available for assignment to a combat zone. On that day I had said 'good-bye' to Pat and we got underway to adjust the radio direction finder. Much to my surprise and pleasure we returned to Indian Island to exchange 66 of our depth charges for Mark Mode 3, then tied up at pier 90 for the night. After making it very clear that we had to be aboard by 0600 on the 13th, Captain MacDonald, in his usual gracious manner, allowed those of us with families in Seattle to go home, one more time."

Lowell's wife, Pat, remembers: "I had taken Lowell to the ship the day before to say 'good-bye.' Watching him climb that gangplank and waving one last time, before saluting the colors, still brings tears to my eyes. We tried to remain upbeat and positive, but looking at all of those men, equipment and weapons and knowing they were going to war, tore our insides apart. When Lowell came back through that door, I felt overwhelmed with joy! No matter how temporary it would be we just wanted to hang-on as long as we could. Our time together was so precious! And we were always saying 'good-bye.'

*Dacre-Annie Dunn and Pat-Lowell Clark*

"We had been staying in a beautiful home just north of Seattle, high on a bluff, overlooking Puget Sound. It belonged to a Naval officer and his wife, who enjoyed sharing it with other officers. They were relatives of Dacre and Annie Dunn, who shared the home with us, and we appreciated their gracious hospitality, so much.

"Next morning we got up early for another emotional good-bye. Knowing we've had our last reprieve, Annie and I went out on the bluff to watch for *Wren*," Pat recalled.

Annie Dunn recalls: "The house we stayed in was located high upon Magnolia Bluff. Pat and I spent hours on the bluff, watching for *Wren*. Each time a destroyer went by we waved a sheet. If Dacre saw it they flashed *Wren's* lights, then Pat and I called the other officers wives, so we could all be on the dock when *Wren* returned."

"Our final trip to pier 90 was silent as Dacre and I treasured our private thoughts. No sooner were we aboard when we set 'special sea detail,' to move to pier 91. Four hours later *Wren* left, alone, for the Aleutians."

"After Dacre and Lowell left, Annie and I scanned the vast Puget Sound for one last glimpse of *Wren*. My thoughts returned to our first meeting in 1941 at Modesto Jr College, where Lowell had been an announcer for football games and I worked on the school paper. We were both heavily involved in school activities, had separate friends, and it wasn't love at first sight. Our paths continued to cross when he became student-body president and I was class representative and secretary. Even then we each had separate love interests, but no sparks for one another. Several months later Lowell was elected King and I became Queen of the 'Spring Frolic' (a week long celebration), but that still didn't stimulate our interests.

"In the spring of 1942, we had our first date, when Lowell offered me a ride home while attending a club meeting. We continued to date and fell in love that summer, becoming secretly engaged. But, now, I felt as though my entire life would slip away. We sat and stared, in our melancholy solitude, for one last glimpse of the *Wren*. We didn't see her!"

Lowell continues: "As we left Elliott Bay and turned north, I picked up a pair of binoculars and stepped out on the starboard bridge wing. Looking back, at our 16 knot wake, Seattle started to fade in the distance. The atmosphere on the bridge had been quiet and somber and I knew my gut-wrenching feelings were shared by everyone.

"Traveling north, I searched with my binoculars for the cliff home Pat and I had shared, with Dacre and Annie, for so many pleasant months. My thoughts, as though being pulled by a magnet, returned to late fall of 1942, when we were both enrolled at the University of California at Berkeley. Pat lived in San Francisco and I lived in east Oakland, so we dated seldom, but our love continued to grow and we were officially engaged on Thanksgiving Day. We both knew we had to wait fifteen months to get married, as I was in the Navy's V7 program and couldn't marry until I became an officer.

"I remember pounding my old beater up the many hills between my home and Pat's, trying to squeeze a few dates into our busy schedules. I had been working swing shift at the Richmond Shipyard, so dating was limited to an occasional week-end visit. It seems like something had always prevented us from being together. Now, I was leaving again! How long would we be gone? Would we all get back?

"I searched the hills one last time looking for Pat, but unable to locate the house among so many others, I returned to the bridge. We soon turned the corner at Point-No-Point, heading due west in the Straits, and I knew my life would be on hold. This was definitely one of the low spots in my life; however, idle minds breed ill thoughts, so I got busy and stayed that way."

They left the cities, night blackouts, cars with slits for headlights, humming defense industries shielded with barrage balloons, USO clubs, gas rationing -- and girls. They headed for the treeless, snow covered, wind-swept Aleutian Islands; occupied by soldiers, sailors, and marines, but -- no girls, just war!

The crew stowed their dress blues and broke out their dungarees, to the music of the Andrew Sisters singing -- Don't Sit Under the Apple Tree; The Bogey Wogey Bugle Boy from Company B; Praise The Lord and Pass the Ammunition; and Rosie the Riveter. Sayings like "loose lips sink ships," were common.

Steaming through Puget Sound and into the Straits of Juan De Fuca, our crew also experienced the dismal feelings of depression. Those feelings are known only by those leaving their homeland, heading into the uncertainty of war. As *Wren's* lonely crewmen looked back at Vancouver Island and Cape Flattery slipping away in the distance, they wondered if they would ever get back home. Thoughts of loved ones they were leaving behind, their fear and anxiety of going to war on such a small, aggressive ship, were overwhelming.

*Desolate Attu, land of the midnight sun.*

Attu, Adak, where are those places? Since no maps were available to the crew, they seldom knew exactly where they were going. The Aleutian Islands project westward from Cooks Inlet, Alaska and extend to within eight hundred miles of the Japanese northern home islands. Siberia is due west of Attu, the western island in the Aleutian chain. The Aleutians divide the Bering Sea, to the north, from the Pacific Ocean. Little doubt exists in my mind that this is the most unforgiving and downright miserable place on our entire planet. These islands are part of Alaska, included in the original purchase from Russia, known as "Seward's Folly." Attu is the only significant island owned by the United States and occupied by the Japanese during World War II. The U.S. took it back from them, in a short, bloody battle, prior to *Wren's* arrival.

*Wren* arrived at Kuluk Bay, Adak, in about the middle of the Aleutian Chain, at 1035, August 19. Our ship was assigned to Division Two, Destroyer Squadron 57, Task Force 94. Commanded by Captain H.L. Thompson, which included the destroyers; USS *Rowe*, DD564, *Watts*, DD567, *Smalley*, DD565, *Stoddard*, DD566, and USS *Wren*; DD568, Division one included; USS *Bearss*, DD654, *Jarvis*, DD799, *Porter*, DD800, *John Hood*, DD665, *Kimberley*, *DD521*, *Young*, DD580, and *William D. Porter*, DD579, USS *Concord*, CL10, *Trenton*, CL11, and *Richmond*, *CL9*, were older four-stacker cruisers, also part of Task Force 94. The fleet trained at Adak for the next month and a half.

Signals given by the flagship must be executed simultaneously. Like a huge drill team, their movements are rehearsed until flawless. Every ship in a task force must learn to function, as one. Each potential situation is anticipated and different alignments and configurations are carried out on a signal from the flagship. It is imperative that those changes are executed smoothly to provide maximum effectiveness in different combat situations. Total firepower could be greatly reduced if ships got in each other's way during surface attacks. Considerable time must be spent rehearsing maneuvers before a task force is ready to deal with all combat problems.

*Signalman on the bridge*

Only signalmen, and related bridge officers, understood the maze of signal flags and their meanings. Ships relied almost totally on flags and signal lights, with little or no voice communications while in war zones. Rear Admiral J.L. McCrea, aboard his flagship *Richmond*, was assigned the responsibilities for this considerable achievement. His efforts were complicated by the always present rough Aleutian waters.

At 0710 October 2, Task Force 94 got underway for Attu, but the cruiser, *Concord*, remained at Adak. While en route, the training and antiaircraft drills continued, as the ships fired at towed sleeves and the wakes of other ships.

At 2226 hours *Wren* crossed the 180th meridian for the first time and Task Force 94 entered Massacre Bay, Attu on October 3.

R.J. "Mother" Miller was an electricians mate first class and I soon learned why they called Rufus, Mother. He was truly a kind and gentle man, sporting a full beard, neat and trim, like many of our crew in the Aleutians. He had been interested in becoming a priest before joining the Navy and continued to be a devout Christian, setting a good example for younger shipmates. Rufus, serious-minded, obviously cared deeply for the well-being of everyone he came in contact with. Mother lived like a Monk.

*R. J. "Mother" Miller*

"Mother" Miller was a very unusual letter writer. I can still remember him, usually in a corner by himself, writing. We often wondered what he was writing about, but now years later I have finally found out. Although Rufus passed away before I started writing this book, I now have many of his letters, thanks to his wife, Dorothy. He wrote two long letters everyday, one he mailed whenever possible, the other he held until he got home. The second letter, like a diary, would be delivered in person after the war.

In one of these letters written the morning of October 13, 1944 Rufus said: "It's Friday the thirteenth, I'm not superstitious, but I have had a strange feeling for the last few days that something is up. I haven't been able to talk to anyone about it, for fear of causing them undue anxiety, but it's there. When we got underway at 1359, I looked back over the stern at the mountains on Attu, they were snow capped and beautiful. I paused for awhile, as the now distant mountains seemed to slip into the sea, and wondered just what we were in for on this trip.

"My anxiety soon became confirmed, as they called us to quarters and our division officer laid down the law, 'Check your life belts and have all machinery and equipment in good working order.' I knew then that I had not been wrong, something is up—we're going on a raid. I had a sick feeling as I looked back one more time and watched the very tip of the mountains slip into the sea. My thoughts were of you, my darling, and I prayed we would return safely.

"The attitude of every man seemed to change, as we headed towards our still unknown destination. The ship became lively and each man put his heart into his work. This was the real thing. What we had been trained for.

"The men were standing around in small groups, each expressing his own thoughts and feelings. As for myself, I felt scared and darling I know what battle means, death and suffering. But those who are eager know nothing about war. In the early days I, too, felt euphoric, but now I feel nothing but -- remorse and sick. I just want to be with you and our new baby, if only I could be there when she is born, my darling. Knowing we are going into battle, a million thoughts run through my mind and they are all of you. It's difficult for me to even write this letter, feeling as I do.

"Well darling, it's 1800 and the captain has just announced our destination; we're going to bombard a Japanese home island called Matsuwa. It's right in the Jap's own back yard. Tension builds among our crew as every hour brings us closer to the enemy. They just announced over the PA system that the next general quarters alarm will not be a drill. At 2000 the word came down to darken ship and the smoking lamp is out.

"At 2200 I sat down and wrote my darling wife a letter assuring her I was safe. It's difficult for me not to be able to share my experiences with you as they are happening, but we do have the censor. The fear of what's ahead is overwhelming. We'll be attacking an airfield. We will have no air support. We're all the way out on the end of the limb and so far from home. Believe me, we'll need plenty of luck and the help of God, to get through this one alive. Every man is sleeping with his clothes on, as speed in manning our battle stations is very essential.

"Well, darling, it's 0530 October 16, I'm writing this letter on watch in the forward engine room and this is the day we're supposed to arrive at our destination. We're steaming on all four boilers towards our rendezvous with destiny. We're due to start our raid about 0200 tomorrow morning.

"Well, dearest, twenty-four hours have gone by and we're just as far from our target as we were yesterday. For some reason they have postponed the raid. Our radar picked up an enemy scout plane this afternoon; we're not sure if they have detected us or not. We have now secured two boilers and are heading away from the target area, so I don't know what is up. Well, they have just handed down the word, the raid has been canceled because the weather is too clear."

Mother's letters describe feelings we all had during those hectic times.

Without air support they felt we needed stormy weather for our first bombardment. After all, we were attacking a Japanese home island and we knew little about their strength in this region. Who would think we could have had so many postponements due to good weather in this part of the world. While we kept busy trying to accomplish our first bombardment, major events were about to unfold in the South Pacific.

American superiority in the air and on the sea was taking its toll on the Japanese Navy and Air Force. Japanese occupation forces in the Philippines uneasily anticipated an American invasion. Admirals Toyoda, Yamamoto, Kurita, and Ohnishi burned midnight oil struggling with their dilemma. How could they stop the certain onslaught? The tide of war had turned in favor of the Americans. Those Admirals had learned about the U.S. resolve to fight this war. Their defeats taught them how wrong they had been thinking the Americans had no will or courage to fight a war against the Japanese.

*Buried Quonset huts on windswept Attu*

*Wren's crew arrives in the Aleutians*

# FIVE
# THE NIGHTMARE BEGINS

Vice Admiral Takijiro Ohnishi had one last big trick up his sleeve that could turn the war around for Japan. Being a Samurai warrior he knew there was no way out of this war for him, but death. If he could convince other Admirals of the validity of his ill-conceived plan, he seemed to think: "If an aircraft can be guided directly to its target by the pilot, all chance and skill will be eliminated. We can destroy the entire American Navy."

One pilot, one aircraft; that's a good trade-off for one American ship, Ohnishi theorized. Once before a divine wind rose up to save the Empire from defeat. Japanese history called this divine wind, "Kamikaze." "Could still another Kamikaze save our beloved Empire?" Ohnishi wondered. Japanese history, religion and culture seemed to indicate that this idea could be sold to their people en masse.

*Vice Admiral Takijiro Ohnishi*
*Kamikaze Pilots are given a farewell saki toast.*

The code of Bushido, or the way of the warrior, tells how a warrior dies seven times, each time dying in battle for the Emperor. He then enters the Yasukuni Shrine, where he guards the Empire of Japan for all time, as a "War God." What greater aspiration could their pilots achieve than to be so enshrined? Admiral Ohnishi sold this doctrine to his young pilots.

Up to this time many acts of self-sacrifice had been reported by both sides. Those deeds of heroism were glorified, but were they suicide? It's the kind of things movies are made of. During the battle of Midway, June 5, 1942, U.S. Marine Captain Richard E. Fleming crashed in flames into the Japanese cruiser, *Mikuma*. He received the Congressional Medal of Honor, posthumously.

August 8, 1942, during the battle of Guadalcanal, the SS *George F. Ellott* was crashed into and sunk by a Japanese "Betty" bomber. She became the first ship, of many to follow, that covered the floor of "Iron Bottom Sound."

On October 26, 1942, during the battle of Santa Cruz, two apparent suicide planes, one flown by LT Commander Mamoru Seki and the second by LT Jiichiro Imajuku, struck the carrier USS *Hornet*, CV8. Commanded by Captain Mitche, *Hornet* received heavy damage and the Japanese destroyers *Makikamo* and *Akigumo* later sank her.

Our research indicates that the Japanese did successfully test the idea of suicidal attacks before their first all-out use on October 25, 1944.

### USS FRANKLIN, CV13, OCTOBER 13, 1944:
As flagship for Task Force 38.4 *Franklin* operated in the Palau area on October 9, where they launched air strikes in preparation for the invasion of Leyte. Four days later, 12 days before the all-out suicide attacks on our Taffy fleets, *Franklin* was struck and damaged by a Japanese aircraft. It is not known if this attack could have been deliberate suicide, but it appeared to be. *Franklin* stayed in action until October 30, when she fell victim for the second time.

### USS RENO, CL96, OCTOBER 14, 1944:
Ten days before the first all-out suicide attacks occurred, an apparent Kamikaze struck the *Reno*. While with Task Force 38, off Formosa, the cruiser came under heavy air attack. Although *Reno* shot down six enemy aircraft in the heat of battle, a torpedo plane crashed and exploded on her main deck, aft. The cruiser stayed with the task force until November 3, when she was hit by a torpedo fired from the Japanese submarine I-41. They towed *Reno* 1500 miles to Ulithi for temporary repairs; then she returned to Charleston Navy Yard, under her own power, for extensive rebuilding.

### USS SONOMA, ATA175, OCTOBER 24, 1944:
*Sonoma* entered San Pedro Bay, Leyte Gulf, October 20; the morning of the 24th she came under suicide attack. The tug cast off her moorings from the freighter, SS *Augustus Thomas*, and opened fire with her deck guns. In flames, the enemy bomber crashed into *Sonoma's* starboard side amidships and exploded on contact. USS LCI72 and USS *Chickasaw*, ATF83, came to the tug's rescue as she started to sink, fast. After casualties were removed, *Chickasaw* tried unsuccessfully to beach the tug on Dio Island, but she sank in 18 feet of water.

When Americans performed those individual acts, we rightfully called them maximum acts of heroism. When the other side carried out similar acts, we explained them away by saying they had already died, their controls probably jammed, or they were just fanatics. We had considerable difficulty believing that an individual would actually, deliberately, destroy himself and his aircraft. Did he have such low self-esteem? Did he hate his enemy so badly? Did he have no hope for survival? Or did he just have such an overwhelming desire to be a dead hero?

These thoughts can be pondered, but could an entire nation through its military leaders, with all of their intellect, make a unanimous, conscious decision to use suicide as an ultimate weapon of war? Could this actually happen? This seemed like sheer madness to Americans, as we fight wars to win and live. However, ideas like death before dishonor, death to save face, the Emperor and Empire above all, have been instilled in the minds of Japanese for centuries. Admiral Ohnishi's idea could indeed be sold.

*Japanese Kamikaze pilots are briefed*

October 17, Admiral Ohnishi took command of the Two Hundredth Air Fleet of land-based aircraft, for defense of the Philippines. Two days later he arrived at Clark Field, near Manila, to assume command. On arrival, the Admiral reviewed his twenty-three non-commissioned pilots with an eye towards their demise!

He apparently found It quite easy to convince all of them to enter the code of Bushido. Thus, the seeds were planted that would grow into the worst nightmare -- Naval fighting men have ever faced. Never before, to the best of my knowledge, had any nation been prepared to commit mass suicide and use it as a serious weapon.

At the same time U.S. ground forces had decided to test Japanese strength and resolve in the Philippines. Two small islands at the mouth of Leyte Gulf, Suluan and Dinagat, were invaded October 17th, and quickly fell to U.S. forces.

*Kamikaze pilot salutes as he receives orders.*

Admiral Ohnishi continued brainwashing techniques on his Kamikaze pilots, telling them: "You are already War Gods!" -- as he presented them with their hachimaki, the white head band of determination.

On October 20, U.S. invasion forces hit the beaches of Leyte, the second largest island in the Philippines. Three days later, MacArthur waded ashore making good on his promise -- "I shall return."

Admiral Ohnishi declared, "It is time to unharness our second divine wind." The twenty-three suicide recruits were split into three groups and escorted to their target by trained fighter pilots. October 21, the first group took off in search of a target, but bad weather forced them back. Other attempts were made; however a suitable target could not be located.

The Admiral kept busy recruiting additional volunteers for his suicide squadrons, and at the air base on Devo a second continuum formed. This group would draw the first American blood and usher in the nightmare called -- "Kamikaze."

Three small fleets operated in support of U.S. invasion forces at Leyte. Each consisted of six small escort carriers, three destroyers and three to four destroyer escorts. They were referred to by their radio call letters, as Taffy 1, 2, and 3.

"Taffy 1," commanded by Admiral Thomas Sprague, operated in the southern position off the coast of Mindanao. "Taffy 2," commanded by Admiral F. B. Stump, operated off the entrance to Leyte Gulf, and "Taffy 3," commanded by Admiral Clifton Sprague, operated off Samar Island. Thus began the infamous battle of "Samar."

On October 25, at 0645, a time and date that Admiral Clifton Sprague would never forget, Taffy 3 ran directly into the Imperial Japanese Navy! They faced four battleships, eight cruisers and twelve destroyers at battle range. Lookouts reported antiaircraft fire to the northwest. Then minutes later pilot ENS Hans L. Jensen's excited voice came over the radio: "A strong force of heavy enemy ships is heading straight for Taffy 3!"

As the distinctive pagodas of Japanese battleships started to appear on the horizon, Admiral Sprague knew his Taffy 3 fleet was in deep trouble. His three destroyers and four destroyer escorts were no match for that formidable array of battleships, cruisers and destroyers. Gunfire from the fourteen-to eighteen-inch guns could reach the small escort "jeep" carriers, but the Japanese remained out of range for retaliation. Frantic cries for help flooded the airways from Taffy 3 -- but they had no surface help. Taffy 2 ships were about twenty miles south, while Taffy 1 operated one hundred miles beyond them.

The Japanese fleet steamed at thirty knots and jeep carriers only at eighteen, so running seemed hardly an option. Admiral Sprague had no choice -- stand and fight! He called for air attacks from all Taffy carriers: "Please arm all available Avengers with torpedoes and go after them," he ordered. For Taffy 3 carriers to launch into the wind, they had to head towards the Japanese ships. They did!

The future of U.S. carriers as landing strips seemed very much in doubt, so planes of Taffy 3 were ordered to land, fuel and rearm at the Tacloban airstrip on Leyte. While launching their remaining aircraft, all Taffy 3 ships were measured by the Japanese with smoke shells from their heavy guns. Red, green and yellow smoke puffs started popping between the ships, marking their range. As carriers completed launching they headed south, away from the Japanese. Huge geysers, reported to be higher than the masts of destroyers, erupted around the rear carriers.

At 0706 Admiral Sprague ordered his escort ships to lay down a smoke screen and attack Japanese ships with everything they had. The gallant carriers desperately maneuvered in the smoke, towards a rain squall, for any shielding they could find. At 0750, the USS *Kalinin Bay*, CVE68, commanded by Captain Charles R. Brown, took her first of fifteen direct hits. The USS *St Lo*, CVE83, took heavy, but inaccurate shelling.

### USS GAMBIA BAY, CVE73, OCTOBER 25, 1944:

The escort carrier, commanded by Captain Walter V. Vieweg, came under heavy attack from Japanese cruisers that had flanked the carriers from the east. She stubbornly fought back with rapid fire from the lone 5-inch gun -- but they were doomed from the start!

The destroyer, USS *Heermann*, defended *Gambia Bay* with gunfire while laying down a smoke screen to her east, but to no avail. As she lay dead in the water, three Japanese cruisers closed in on *Gambia Bay* to point blank range -- for the kill! At 0907 *Gambia Bay* could take no more. With fires raging throughout, Captain Vieweg gave the order -- "Abandon ship." *Gambia Bay* capsized and sank!

*Gambia Bay* was a small aircraft carrier, but a very large ship. Five hundred twelve feet long with a 65-foot beam, her flight deck rose about 75-feet above the water. The hangar deck, a huge open area, full of planes, jeeps, tools and equipment of every conceivable kind, had aviation gasoline everywhere. To her crew of 860 men she was home. If your home suddenly became up-ended and submerged under the sea, it would be a horrible experience.

Imagine it -- For the crew to get from the bowels of the ship, engine rooms, etc., many ladders and other hazards had to be negotiated. The hysteria of an abandon ship order plus the pre-capsizing list, made the trip perilous, indeed. Fires raged throughout, equipment flew all over the place and many casualties occurred during their flight to escape.

When, or if, you reach a point where you could abandon ship, what would you do? The water was already full of debris and men, while the enemy continued to fire. If you jump, will the ship roll over on you? If not, what will happen when she does roll over? Yes, they went through hell!

## USS HEERMANN, DD532, OCTOBER 25, 1944:

The destroyers USS *Hoel, Heermann, Johnston* and the destroyer escort USS *Samual B. Roberts*, steamed undauntedly toward the huge guns of their Japanese attackers. As *Heermann* started closing in on the cruisers for a torpedo attack, the now familiar dye-colored shells started dropping close around her. They opened fire on the heavy cruiser, *Chikuma*, while setting up to fire torpedoes at the *Haguro*. As they launched the second torpedo, *Heermann* came under fire from four battleships. DD532 redirected her fire to the lead battleship *Kongo*. *Heermann* launched three torpedoes at her, then quickly closed on the battleship *Haruna*, the target of her last three torpedoes.

Gunnery officer, Lieutenant William W. Meadows, describes the inbound action:

*"I watched the massive Haruna fire her first two turrets, followed with two more, then all four."* As those rounds, each fourteen inches in diameter, weighing nearly two thousand pounds, hissed over his head, Lieutenant Meadows said: *"I was fascinated as they roared over like an airborne freight train. I took my five-inch director and raked our fire up and down her superstructure. Much to my surprise, our fire must have done something to their fire control system, as they stopped shooting at us. For about four minutes we were able to continue our run on them, firing all the way, without retaliation."*

They launched from only 4,400 yards. Believing some torpedoes had found their mark *Heermann* retreated at flank speed. Huge shells dropped around her, as the destroyer maneuvered to become an elusive target.

Many ships had been slowed down, even the giant battleship *Yamato* was forced out of action by the combined efforts of all ships and planes of Taffy Fleets. The fighters, bombers and torpedo planes had to use what they had already loaded in defense of their fleet. U.S. ships should have had armor-piercing bombs and torpedoes; however they only had fragmentation bombs and depth charges.

Laying additional smoke, *Heermann* sped back to protect her charge of carriers. She once again exchanged fire with four cruisers and received heavy damage to her bow from hits by eight-inch guns. Her forward compartments were flooded so badly that her anchor dragged in the sea. Efforts of *Heermann* along with the continued pounding of carrier planes, caused the retreat of the cruiser *Chikuma*. While turning north *Chikuma* sank. Captain Amos Hathaway declared, "Well done," to the cheers of his crew.

## USS SAMUAL B. ROBERTS, DE413, OCTOBER 25, 1944:

The destroyer escort with Commander Robert W. Copland, as her Captain, made a torpedo run on the cruisers. As she advanced against those overwhelming odds, she scored at least forty gunfire hits and one torpedo found its mark. A salvo of fourteen-inch shells from a battleship, blew a forty-foot long by ten-foot wide hole in her port side. With number two engine room flooded *Samual B Roberts* -- quickly sank. One hundred crewmen were left clinging to three life rafts -- for fifty hours.

## USS HOEL, DD553, OCTOBER 25, 1944:

The destroyer also took her orders to attack, very seriously. Headed straight at the battleship *Kongo*, she opened fire from 14,000 yards. The speed and maneuverability of destroyers and the ability of their captains to watch and time incoming salvos, made them a very elusive target. *Hoel's* Captain, Commander Leon Kintberger, was a master at dodging salvos. In spite of the captain's skill, *Kongo* scored hits on the elusive ship. A fourteen-inch projectile hit the bridge, knocking out all voice and radio communications. But Captain Kintberger continued to press the attack. Despite severe damage, he launched five torpedoes at 9,000 yards. Even though all torpedoes missed their mark, they succeeded in forcing her away from the engagement. *Kongo* avoided her own destruction -- she ran north.

Minutes later, *Hoel* took many additional devastating hits. She had only two of her five guns, no fire control or radar and had lost her port engines. Unable to steer from the bridge, it would seem she was finished. But no Way! *Hoel* went on the attack! She charged the lead cruiser, *Haguro*. As the badly crippled destroyer closed to six thousand yards, they fired their remaining five torpedoes. This time several found their mark. With the battleship, *Kongo,* then only 8,000 yards off her port beam and the heavy cruisers 7,000 yards off her port quarter, the end seemed inevitable. Or was it? *Hoel* drew the fire of all ships to herself. While leading the Japanese ships away from her charges, *Hoel* survived for one more crucial hour.

Before she became dead in the water, this mighty ship sustained over forty hits from heavy guns. At 0830, with her engine rooms flooded, Captain Leon S. Kintberger reluctantly gave his final order -- "Abandon ship." The Japanese continued to fire at her fleeing crew, until 0855. Then *Hoel* rolled over and sank! Among her crew of 339 -- only 86 survived.

## USS JOHNSTON, DD557, OCTOBER 25, 1944;

Commander Ernest Evans, skippered the *Johnston*, the first Taffy 3 ship to respond to the attack. Before any orders had been given, her captain reacted instinctively. Captain Evans laid a smoke screen between the carriers and advancing enemy ships, but he made sure this chore directed him towards the enemy. After he completed the smoke screen, Captain Evans sped at flank speed to attack the rapidly closing enemy. Under heavy fire, while trying to get in range for his own guns, Evans maneuvered to avoid being hit. Eruptions of steel, smoke and water dwarfed the little ship. But Captain Evans closed the gap.

For twenty long minutes Captain Evans dodged 2,000-pound projectiles, before he could return fire. *Johnston*, the first American ship to open fire on the Japanese, scored several damaging hits. The first Japanese ship to feel the wrath of Evans' guns, was a cruiser.

Gunnery Officer Lieutenant Robert C. Hagen, had red dye splashed in his face from a near miss by one enemy cruiser. Wiping the dye from his face, he remarked:

"Looks like someone is mad at us." In the ensuing five minute period, Johnston pumped 200 rounds of five-inch shells at the enemy, in furious retaliation. Commander Evans ordered: "Fire torpedoes!" They fired all ten then turned away and headed for a heavy smoke screen nearby. A few minutes later the Japanese cruiser, *Kumano*, could be seen burning from torpedo hits -- she ultimately sank.

However, *Johnston* took fourteen-inch shell hits from a battleship and three, six-inch shells from a light cruiser. It was like taking a sledge hammer to an ant! She lost power for steering and three of her five-inch guns, then took temporary respite in a smoke-filled rain squall, sent by providence. They used the time to make temporary repairs. Then at 0750, Admiral Sprague ordered further torpedo attacks, but *Johnston* had already spent all of hers.

The courage of captains and crewmen of all Taffy ships was astounding, but *Johnston* stood all alone, out in front. At 0820, with only one engine and blind manual steering, she came out of her smoky hiding place. Captain Evans ordered *Johnston* to attack. Then, a huge 30,000-ton Japanese battleship of the Kongo Class, stared them in the face. Off *Johnston's* port bow a scant 7,000 yards away, the battleship's pagoda loomed over her like a medieval structure. She opened fire, at point blank range, on the already stricken *Johnston,* but scored only near misses.

Captain Evans then noticed enemy cruisers going after USS *Gambia Bay*. In the true fighting spirit of the man and his ship, Captain Evans ordered the attack directed at the lead cruiser. *Johnston* scored four hits. A squadron of destroyers attacked *Gambia Bay,* so Captain Evans directed his attention to the lead ship. He attacked until they miraculously broke off the engagement. As the enemy destroyer retreated, he fired his remaining torpedoes in a desperate attempt to hit *Gambia Bay. Johnston* then opened fire on the second destroyer, out-fighting them, until they also broke away and headed north.

In the brief engagement, *Johnston* took still another hit that flattened the bridge and put two forward guns out of commission. Captain Evans then shifted his command to the fantail. He yelled: "More shells -- keep firing," through an open hatch to the men who turned her rudder by hand. The Japanese destroyers realized *Johnston* was finished. They moved in for the kill! They surrounded her and kept firing until the last engine and fire-rooms were knocked out. By 0930, this remarkable ship stood dead in the water. At 0945, their skipper shouted his last order, "Abandon ship!" *Johnston* rolled over and sank!

A Japanese destroyer came up to within a thousand yards and pumped one last salvo into her on the way down. Survivors reported seeing the Japanese Captain salute the gallant ship -- as she slipped away. I know this incident sounds like Hollywood, but I have verified it in at least six different places in <u>The Dictionary of American Naval Fighting Ships.</u> I believe the Japanese Captain slipped on through her crew in the water, as he left.

From her crew of 327 men -- only 141 were saved. Fifty were killed outright by enemy action, 45 died in rafts from battle injuries and ninety-two, including Captain Evans, were alive in the water but never seen again!

*Gambia Bay*, *Hoel*, *Johnston*, and *Samual B. Roberts* were sunk. *Fanshaw Bay*, *Kalinin Bay* and *Heermann* were badly hit. Then the Japanese did a stupid thing. They disengaged the battle and ran full steam north. Silence fell over Taffy 3 ships. The crews stood in amazement. A signalman aboard one carrier broke the silence by shouting: "Damn it, they got away."

At 0750, during the heat of battle between U.S. destroyers and the Japanese heavy ships, a second battle began. Ships of Admiral Sprague's Taffy 1, about 120 miles south, were feverishly landing, fueling, arming, and launching planes.

### USS SANTEE, CVE29, OCTOBER 25, 1944:

Captain Robert E. Blick, skipper of the escort carrier *Santee*, had just launched his second strike of five Avengers and eight Wildcats, when four planes suddenly appeared high overhead. Occasionally enemy planes mingled, unannounced, with U.S. returning flights. Taffy 1 ships identified the intruders as enemy aircraft and opened fire. Without warning, or a moment's hesitation, Admiral Ohnishi's first suicide pilot made good his pledge, "I will die for the Emperor!"

A single engine Zeke went into a power dive, straight for *Santee* and crashed on her flight deck. Debris, gasoline and body parts spread over a wide area. The bomb went through her flight deck, exploded on the hangar deck, creating an inferno. Sixteen minutes after the first suicide plane struck *Santee*, a Japanese sub sneaked in with the fleet and succeeded in hitting the already stricken ship with a torpedo. Although heavily damaged, after temporary repairs, *Santee* managed to return to Los Angeles.

Simultaneously, two of the original four planes dove for USS *Sangamon*, CVE27, and USS *Petrof Bay*, CVE8. Both planes were shot down, to crash near their target ships.

### USS SUWANEE, CVE27, OCTOBER 25,1944:

At 0759, nine minutes after the first sighting, suicide aircraft number four dove for Captain William D. Johnson Jr.'s, carrier, *Suwanee*. Coming out of a cloud at 8,000 feet, the pilot had already chosen his target ship. Despite heavy antiaircraft fire, this fourth pilot also made good on his death pact with Admiral Ohnishi. He struck *Suwanee's* flight deck about 40 feet forward of the after-elevator.

*A bomb laden Zeke (Zero) takes off for the Taffy Fleets*

Once again, the bomb penetrated the flight deck and exploded on the hangar deck, causing a 25 foot gash. The Zeke collided with a torpedo bomber, which exploded along with nine other planes. Tremendous fires engulfed the flight deck. While attempting to save the heavily damaged ships, U.S. airways kept busy with information about the deadly new weapon Admiral Ohnishi had unleashed. The U.S. high command responded with doubt, disbelief and denial. But Taffy 1 crewmen knew better.

*A Kamikaze crashes into the flight deck of USS Suwanee, in the distance.*

At 1050, far to the north with ships of Taffy 3, six Zekes appeared. As if they didn't have enough for one day, now this. One here and one there, the planes continued to return from Tacloban. While attempting to get them back aboard, two suicide planes headed for the USS *White Plains*, AFS4, commanded by Captain Dennis J. Sullivan. For the first time this day, 40 and 20mm gun crews had their chance, as diving aircraft were taken under fire. On fire, one plane veered off and crashed into Capt. Francis J. McKenna's USS *St Lo*, CVE63. The plane skipped along the flight deck and went overboard, but the bomb went through and exploded on the hangar deck. Huge fires and explosions rocked *St Lo*. USS *Dennis*, DE405, rescued 434 men.

**USS KITKUM BAY, CVE71, OCTOBER 25, 1944:**
Approaching from the stern the second aircraft continued his dive on *White Plains*. This Zeke, taking continuous hits finally rolled and crashed into the sea, a few yards behind the carrier. A third Zeke crossed ahead of *Kitkum Bay*, climbed strafing on his way in and dove straight for the island. He missed it, but struck her port catwalk.

Repairs were made at Manus, in the Admiralty Islands. *Kitkum Bay* returned to service only to be hit a second time on January 1, 1945, by an "Oscar." With one engine heavily damaged, they were forced back to the states for repairs.

### USS KALININ BAY, CVE68, OCTOBER 25, 1944:

The other three Zekes of Admiral Ohnishi's second strike force dove for *Kalinin Bay*. Already heavily damaged by gunfire earlier that morning, she managed to recover aircraft. One Zeke was shot down by intense gunfire, but the other two got through to crash the already crippled ship. Even though heavily damaged, *Kalinin Bay* managed temporary repairs sufficient to stay in service. Although CVE68 suffered 60 casualties, miraculously only five were killed.

### USS ST LO, CVE63, OCTOBER 25, 1944:

Escort ships remained behind to search for survivors of USS *St Lo*, CVE63 -- which was not so lucky. Shortly after the first sighting at 1050, *St Lo* took a hit from a Zeke that exploded her torpedo and bomb magazine. Billows of smoke erupted from her flaming hulk. She sank thirty minutes later.

*USS Suwanee, CVE27, note men cautiously climbing up to her flight deck.*

Four out of five carriers remaining in action, after the Japanese fleet retreated, were hit by Admiral Ohnishi's second suicide strike. The only aircraft carrier remaining intact out of the original six of Taffy 3, was the USS *Fanshaw Bay*, CVE70. Many Presidential Unit Citations were given to the brave men and their ships.

Admiral Ohnishi did not achieve his goal of one pilot and one plane for one American ship. But six hits out of ten planes wasn't bad! This threat against our war effort would have to be recalculated.

What would the US be getting into if they sent thousands of Kamikazes? US Admirals would ponder those and many other questions concerning this irrational enemy we were facing.

*USS Suwanee , CVE27, note men cautiously inspecting the damaged elevator.*

# SIX

# WREN'S FIRST ACTION

On October 26, *Wren* arrived off Matsuwa for the second time; because of clear weather in the target area, operations were canceled again. *Wren's* crew was like a tightly wound rubber band, and frustrated. Practicing continually for months, they felt as though they had been training forever. When would *Wren* receive her baptism under fire? Each time our ship returned to base without attacking, the crew felt relieved, but disappointed.

In another of 'Mother' Miller's letters to his wife, Dorothy, dated October 25, 1944, he writes: "Darling I'm praying for your sake we can complete our mission and return safely. I know your time is near for delivery of our first child and I hate being away at this crucial time. Darling, if I was single I'd be craving action, but now I feel afraid. Afraid I might not get back to you and our baby! I'm glad you don't know the danger we're in tonight. My darling, this may be my last letter to you until all of this bloody mess is over. I pray I'll come through all right." Once again this caring and loving man shares his innermost feelings at a very uncertain time.

October 29, 1944, *Wren*, along with the other eight destroyers and three cruisers of Task Force 94, sailed back into Massacre Bay, Attu. I watched from my barracks, on shore, with much anxiety. This was my first look at the ship I would call home for the rest of this war. A fleet of warships entering a small harbor seemed an awesome sight to me, as the ships looked so big compared to the harbor.

Assigned to the *Wren* late in July, 1944, I left Alameda Naval Air Station, where I had been for about a year, for Bremerton by train. Upon arrival, I was told our ship operated out of San Diego. After being placed in charge of a draft of men, seeking other ships in our squadron, we were sent back down the coast to Camp Pendleton. We repeated this yo-yo procedure six times, before the Navy finally figured out where our ships were.

Our draft increased to a sizable number as we reached Bremerton for the last time. If they had boxed us all up and mailed us to our ships, we would have gone straight to them. It always amazed me how mail found us in the most remote areas. Ultimately, we were assigned to the merchant ship, SS *Henery Failing*, for transport to Attu. The search for my ship still did not end, as all passengers and crew of *Failing* were under quarantine on Attu, because of scarlet fever. While still confined, we watched as the fleet sailed out of Massacre Bay. How far would we have to travel and how long would it be, before we caught up with our ships again?

I felt relieved November 13, when the Task Force came back. Off quarantine at last, I would go aboard my ship. After living out of a sea bag and having no money for about three months, I could call anyplace home.

In the short-day long-night fashion of the Aleutians, early darkness had already engulfed Attu. We had just settled in for the night when Torpedoman First Class Bud Brennan, who was returning to the *Wren*, called: "Bill, grab your sea bag and come on, our whaleboat is at the dock." Bud and I became acquainted on our way up from the States. He is a real gentleman.

*L to R--Bill Sholin, unknown, Bud Brennan*

Although we arrived at the boarding dock in the dark, we could still see the bay was rough. "Bill, we're in for a wet ass on this trip," Bud commented.

Not being permanently stationed on Attu, I had been unable to obtain a single item of clothing necessary for life in the Aleutians, except the one knit sweater given me by the Red Cross. As soon as we left the dock in the open whaleboat, capping swells started breaking over our bow. Everything I owned got soaked. I was freezing! "Bud, why didn't we just swim out?"

"We might just as well have," Bud responded. "Hang on, Bill!"

After twenty to thirty minutes we finally arrived at *Wren's* sea ladder and Bud led the way up in the dark. The OD stood in a sheltered part of the quarter deck, where he had limited use of a flashlight. Bud snapped a salute and said, "This is Bud Brennan, sir, do we have permission to come aboard?"

The OD returned Bud's salute and said, "Welcome back Bud, we're glad to see you."

I followed Bud's lead, and said, "Bill Sholin, sir" I saluted and gave him my orders.

"Welcome aboard, Bill, just find an empty bunk anywhere for the night and report to the electric shop in the morning."

"Aye, aye, sir," I responded and followed Bud below decks.

In darkness while hatches were open, the dim lights of compartments turned off automatically. This maintained blackout conditions required in wartime. Before entering the Navy, I worked as an electrical supervisor at Seattle-Tacoma Shipyard, where *Wren* was built. I was very familiar with destroyers, but not from this perspective. After some confusion, in the dark, I finally located an empty bunk and crawled up into it for the night.

Next morning I joined the early coffee brigade in the electric shop, where they always had a pot brewing, and began to meet the people I would be working with. First and foremost I met R.J. "Mother" Miller, introduced in the last chapter, then Electrician's Mate Second Class Aaron "Hefty" Howard, who was very knowledgable having served on destroyers before the *Wren*. Aaron seemed to be the character of our crew, very likable and easy to get along with. Not in for the duration, First Class Electrican's Mates Charles Schriner and Clayton Schwalen were the "Old salts," USN. Richard Shermer, Charles "Feet" Fullen and Calvin Fifer were the kids. First Class Electrician's Mate Williams, was

*Electricians*
*L to R --1st row--Ruby, Miller, unknown, Williams*
*2nd row--O'Neil, Schriner, Howard, Pauletti*
*3rd row--Fifer, Thedford, Fullen*
*Not shown-- Chief Cannon, Schwalen, Shermer, Sholin*

our "Politician," John Thetford ran movies for the officers and crew, Eugene "Frenchy" Lamere, Jerry O'Neill, and Ruby rounded out the electrical gang. Chief Electrician's Mate Joe Cannon was chief.

Electricians were busy people on destroyers, standing switchboard watches four hours on and eight off and doing maintenance chores between. During general quarters we did everything from switchboard-watch to repair party duties. Some had various communications and ammunition handling jobs.

A ship has an extensive electrical and communications system, with two steam turbine generators capable of supplying a good-sized city. Her power was supplied by steam, but all complicated systems were electrically operated.

I soon learned that my first cruise on *Wren* would be her first combat duty. We were going back to bombard Matsuwa. November in the Aleutians almost guaranteed that the weather would be bad and we could complete our mission. November 17, *Wren* took on ammunition and the 18th we left.

Shortly after leaving the harbor I heard the shrill, rhythmic, sound of our general alarm -- "ping, ping, ping" -- which would soon become awesome. Over the public address system a voice said, 'Now hear this...General quarters, general quarters, all hands man your battle stations.' This drill would be repeated many times and our survival over the next few months depended on our ability, as a crew, to respond quickly.

The reality of going to war closed-in. I felt the tension of shipmates I hardly knew. Never had I felt the surging power of a fast ship under my feet, or walked the decks of a rolling, catapulting, vibrating destroyer. I felt inadequate and unprepared. I had never heard the guns fired -- yet we were on our way to bombard a Japanese home island. Feelings of anxiety and fear were crushing in that hostile environment. What had I gotten into?

I attempted to sleep in a top bunk that insisted on throwing me out on the deck with every roll and surge of the ship. To get from the after crew's quarters, where I had been assigned, to the mess hall in the bow, became another major undertaking. We had to walk on the open deck exposed to rough, cold, Aleutian waters. Each time it was an adventure. When the ship rolled the decks were suddenly under water.

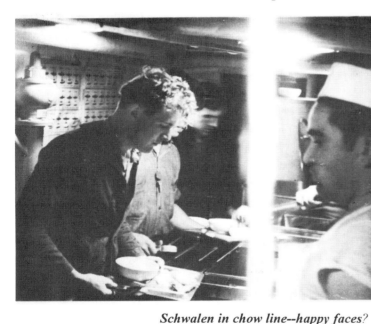 

*Schwalen in chow line--happy faces?*

The chow line itself, was a hostile place. Being the "New kid on the block," it seemed every mess cook vented his anger against me. They threw the food from large containers onto my tray, put the gravy on top of the pie or other dessert, and scowled while they did it.

Large coffee pots swung from the overhead in the mess hall. Table tops had large ribs around the outside, were welded to the decks and the benches were chained to the table legs. As the ship rolled while we ate, slack in chains allowed the benches to attempt to go under the table. We held on to keep from being knocked off. With the next roll, the guys on the opposite side had the problem. Sitting at the table was almost impossible.

Many of us stood up to eat. We tipped our trays back and forth to keep food on and took a good wide stance, in an effort to remain upright. It seemed like trying to stand on a roller coaster that was also going from side to side. We could not keep food on our trays. They were frequently dropped, not to fall on the deck, but rather they took off across the room. I soon learned why the Navy called this the mess hall. After every meal the decks became slippery with greasy food. Eating utensils and trays were strewn everywhere. This was the scene in the mess hall, more often than not, in the rough Aleutians.

Those mess hall conditions were in normal Aleutian weather. During storms, described in chapter 7, regular meals could never be prepared on destroyers.

Shipboard routine on *Wren* was difficult. Climbing swells often as high as fifty to sixty feet from the top to the valley, the ship catapulted upward. We could hardly lift our feet from the deck. It felt like they were stuck in mud. Then, without warning, the entire bow dropped like a rock and often our feet actually left the deck. As the ship bottomed-out we felt bone-jarring jerks.

Many experiences have been discussed by destroyermen about everyday foul weather life on those ships, some humorous, some tragic. Frank Bohn, a tall, blond machinist mate aboard the USS *Williamson*, DD244, relates one such story.

*"Willy,"* as she became affectionately known by her crew, was an older four-stack destroyer with a long distinguished service record. The engineering crew bunked aft, and tables were set up in conjunction with their bunks, so they had meals in their quarters. With the galley being off the main deck, amidships, much like *Wren's*, they had to carry food a great distance over weather decks. They were in the Aleutians during the invasion to reclaim Attu from the Japanese and Frank recalls this story.

*"I was still a fireman second class drawing mess cook duty -- the Navy equivalent to KP. All non-rated men had to serve on this well named and much dreaded job, from time to time. We helped the cooks serve food and cleaned up afterward.*

*"I decided to help a mess cook, named Bourland, transport two large containers of hot soup for the engineering crew. Those were definitely two-handed containers and presented quite a problem. Bourland said, 'Thanks, Frank, we'll have our hands full getting this down there.' We took a good wide stance setting ourselves firmly on the deck, as the ship leveled off momentarily, we scooted aft, fast. We learned to anticipate timing of the roll. While in the holding position I heard Bourland yell. I looked over my shoulder and saw the soup fall on his head.*

*"After reaching the crews quarters and securing the soup, I returned to find Bourland sliding back and forth between the deck house and life net -- screaming for help. The decks were slippery with greasy soup. I couldn't stand up either. I yelled hold on to something, Bourland, I'll try to get to you. Crawling on the deck and holding on to the life net, I finally reached him. I managed to slide him aft, out of the soup, and got him on his feet. Finally, we made it to sick bay where he spent the next week or so being treated for cuts, bruises, facial and hand burns."*

*Wren's* crew became tense and anxious about the mission we were going on in two short days. We had no idea what the Japanese had in the Kurile Islands. Three B-24s were hardly capable of defending us against air attack, still that's the only air support we had and they left us about 100 miles from the target. The U.S. command hoped to use the raids to keep the Japanese off guard, so they wouldn't know where we might start our next invasion. Of course, this had a demoralizing effect on the Japanese.

Admiral McCrea planned to make the bombardment in a storm; thus preventing our discovery and air retaliation. *Wren* arrived off shore at Matsuwa the afternoon of November 20. We originally intended to attack about midnight; however weather conditions were unfavorable, so they postponed the attack for another 24 hours. *Wren* steamed eastward until the early hours of the 21st, when we headed straight for Matsuwa. Now that the final word was -- go for tonight -- *Wren's* crewmen were really up-tight.

The wives of two electricians were expected to deliver babies, one on this date the other at any time, but they were not sure about being alive to see them. The atmosphere on *Wren* became tense, with a lot of nervous small talk.

## BOMBARDMENT OF MATSUWA

"Mother" Miller's letter to his wife dated November 21,1944 describes his feelings, knowing he will see action this day: "It's going to be rather hard for me to write, because we are weathering our worst storm of this season. All four boilers are on line and we are on our way in for sure, this time. Our target is the island of Matsuwa. We went to general quarters at 2245. We became very nervous when arrangements were made for handling possible casualties." Rufus then went to his battle station.

Coming in we completely surprised the Japanese. When *Wren* approached our target area all ships fanned out, side by side -- headed straight for Matsuwa. The cruisers *Richmond* and *Concord* were in the middle, about 3,000 yards behind the line of eight destroyers. Porter, acting as picket for the fleet, steamed about 3,000 yards behind the *Richmond*, Rear Admiral John L. McCrea's flagship. This operation was code named "Greyhound."

At 2330 *Richmond* signaled a 55-degree starboard (right) turn, which put the entire fleet in a column, with our target 12,000 yards off our port quarter. *Richmond* and *Concord* were off our starboard bow about 15,000 yards from the target; *Watts* cruised in front and the *John Hood* directly behind *Wren*. The destroyers -- *Rowe*, *Smalley*, *Stoddard*, *Jarvis* and *Bearss* -- were at the front of the column of ships.

At 2245 the Admiral gave the commence-fire order. Nothing can describe the fury of a Naval bombardment! Like all ships, *Wren's* five-inch guns fired at 12-second intervals. Those of us on weather decks -- were stunned. We felt like we had been pelted with hundreds of sand bags. I was an ammunition handler for a 40mm gun, which did not fire, so had a bird's-eye view of everything.

The blackness instantly became daylight and the noise deafening, as all ships fired their first salvo at the same time. *Wren*, and Task Force 94 had arrived. We delivered the war to Japan's doorstep.

Over 67 guns being rapid-fired by our ships, caused lightning-like flashes to appear faster than our eyes could see. They bounced off the low clouds and danced among the ships. With each gun flash a deadly package left on its way to the enemy. We could see the tracers streaking through the sky, each followed the path of the one ahead. It seemed an eternity before the first projectiles exploded on their targets. Within two or three seconds of the first impact, the entire 67 rounds from the first salvo exploded.

The airfield, ammunition dumps, radar installations, and anything else within the impact area -- had been flattened. Every twelve seconds this devastation was repeated. Each ship had its assigned target area. The gun directors raked their fire back and forth to saturate their target. We were scared -- waiting for that big explosion that would throw us all into the icy sea.

During the 18 minutes of firing, the nine destroyers fired a total of 4,500 rounds of five-inch and the two cruisers fired 1,400 rounds of six-inch ammunition. Captain Mac said, *"We were unable to get seven rounds off because projectiles in handling rooms jarred out of their ready racks. This resulted from firing our guns in such heavy seas."*

Task Force 94 completed its bombardment and another 90-degree starboard turn took us away at 25 knots. Large fires and many secondary explosions could be seen on the island, as we withdrew. We had delivered a devastating blow to the enemy. But, could we be lucky enough to get away with it? This thought preoccupied our minds -- for retaliation seemed inevitable.

Continuing our high-speed departure, two small "Skunks" (surface craft) were picked up on radar by the *Concord* and later by *Wren*. They disappeared from the screen, then reappeared briefly. They were probably PT boats, suicide boats, or just radar ghosts. Aircraft were also picked up by radar, but no contact made. The storm we headed into was probably our ally. Could we be that lucky?

We return to Rufus Miller's letter to his wife, this day, as he ponders what had just happened "Darling, it's hard to explain the totally sick feelings and thoughts I had during that next hour. We were out to kill men as much alive as I am and there was a chance we could be killed, too. It's very unwise to think of such things, still we do.

"I know I love you, more than I'll ever be able to tell you. My every prayer, my every heart beat and my every breath were thoughts of you and the baby. I was scared darling. There's no getting away from it. At 2235 we started firing our big guns and the entire ship shook with every salvo. After completing our bombardment we sped away at 25 knots, leaving fires and explosions raging on the island. I now feel wonderful to have this ordeal behind us."

On our return trip we listened to Tokyo Rose, who commented about the Ninth Fleet and the insignificance of our mission. She talked about how we shot up a few canneries and killed women and children. We laughed off her comments about whom our wives and sweethearts were probably out with and what they were doing, but we enjoyed the good old American music she played. Sentimental songs like -- It's Been a Long Long Time, I'll Be Seeing You, It all Comes Back to Me Now, It Had to be You, Sentimental Journey, Serenade in Blue, Once in a While, Our Love, It's Always You and I Cried for You -- were sure to bring a tear to our eyes.

All of these events onboard the *Wren* have vividly occupied a place in my subconscious mind. I now relive them with some remorse for the Japanese who most certainly died without knowing what hit them.

*Above--Directing delivery of ash cans.*
*Below--Deep ash can seeking its target*

*Above--Captain Mac, uptight as usual*
*Below--Happy mess cooks.*

# SEVEN
# WREN'S FIRST BIG STORM

Leaving Matsuwa at 25 knots all hell broke loose. Our men could not stand against swells, driven by high winds, that broke over the bridge. It seemed like the ocean was out to get us! The main weather deck and high catwalk were awash with 30-mile-an-hour-water. Movement on weather decks was impossible, and people trapped on the opposite end of the ship could not get to their bunks.

The crew huddled behind anything that would act as a break against the wind, spray, and ocean. We took refuge in narrow passageways behind the officer's quarters and pilot house, unable to venture either to the port or starboard side without being washed overboard. The *Wren* was under siege!

Bill Ferguson, gun captain, 5-inch mount one, "On the open bow, the only way we could think about getting out of our mount was for Captain Mac to change course and slow down long enough for us to do so. Even at that we had to move fast."

Clay Harris, first class machinist mate, throttleman, "While returning to my bunk from GQ I was ordered by the OD to head a party to remove empty powder casings from the bow. They were everywhere after the bombardment. He gave me a bunch of young kids to help stow those casings, but I smelled trouble immediately. I told them, if you want to live, watch when he turns this ship into the storm and get up that ladder to the higher deck, as fast as you can. The words no sooner left my mouth when he turned into the storm and we scrambled, just in time. Waves broke over the bow and slammed casings everywhere. Casings, life lines, stanchions and life nets, all washed overboard. We all could have been lost!"

Bridge, Lowell Clark, JR-OD, "We dealt with one wave at a time. *Wren* climbed the mountainous waves, breaking all the way over our mast, then dropped like a rock. She shook, vibrated and dove into the next wave, as tons of water broke over our bow. Visibility on the bridge was zero.

"While operating with the fleet we couldn't change course or speed without orders from command. Occasionally we could see a cruiser mast, but visual communication was not possible and no one wanted to break radio silence.

"The command realized they could not continue at that high rate of speed, but not before our ship had been damaged. Mount one was knocked partially from its mounting, life line stanchions were torn from the deck leaving holes which flooded some forward parts of the ship. We knew we had a real challenge just to get the *Wren* through this storm."

After running at 25 knots for about an hour, they reduced speed to 10 knots to ride out the storm, and crewmen started the hazardous trip over open decks to their quarters. The danger increased because oil and blue dye were on the weather decks, making them extremely slippery. Five gallon cans of blue dye had been lashed underneath the catwalk ladder, but they were pulverized and dye mixed with oil and sea water spread throughout the after crew's quarters. The dye was used to color our very visible white hats that the Japanese snipers shot at.

On the fantail at the entrance to the crew's quarters, oil up to a quarter-inch deep and empty 5-inch shell casings were piled on the open deck. (They had attempted to keep those expensive brass casings for reloading.) With each roll and surge the casings slammed back and forth. Life nets "snaking" around the open decks temporarily prevented some of them from washing overboard.

Entering the after cabin we could see it was also a disaster. The deck was filled with empty shell casings, ankle-deep oil, dye and water covered everything. The casings slammed from side to side as we attempted to get through to our bunks. Our clothing, bedding and everything else was soaked, but too tired to care, we simply crawled into them and attempted to sleep. Trying to stay in my bunk was a losing proposition. It had two straps that were supposed to solve the problem, but the rough ride could not be resolved so easily. I wound up on my stomach, with arms and legs draped over the sides, engaged in my own private battle to stay there. The duty watch struggled to keep the ship afloat as the storm continued to build during the night and following day.

Rufus Miller, in a letter to his wife wrote: "After we slowed down, I ventured back to my bunk for writing material and some rest. To say the trip was a little hazardous would be putting it mildly. My rest was cut short, since I had to return to the forward engine room at 0400 to stand watch. I stayed there for the next fourteen hours before relief got to me."

LT jg Jack Clemens, engineering officer: "After reviewing a letter to my parents dated December 18, 1944, I recalled my brush with disaster during the storm. It dropped our barometer -- twenty hundredths in one hour. I was in the after engine room and the noises above, on the main deck, indicated more than empty shell casings were loose, so Machinists Mate Edward Delage and I went up to investigate. The rolling and pitching of our ship was significant. The 5-inch powder casings could not be retrieved, as they ricocheted with substantial speed over the deck. At that time we also believed a depth charge was loose.

"Once topside, we were continuously beaten by the sea. A huge wave came over the ship, throwing Edward and myself against the outboard life lines and starboard depth charge "K" guns. I can still recall the water completely covering me and thinking I would wind-up overboard -- never to see the *Wren* again.

"After the wave receded I could hear Edward's call for help. When I located him, he told me he couldn't move, so I pulled him about 60 feet to the starboard door of the after deck house. Because of the rough sea, I was unable to hold the door open and lift him over the step to put him inside, so I got help from the crewmen below. Once Edward was inside, a pharmacist gave him an injection of morphine to ease his pain.

"In the incident, my right shoe was ripped off and disappeared. My right pant leg was torn from the bottom, completely up to the waist and my cap washed overboard. Blue dye was coming through the door and flowing down into the living compartment, an added item of inconvenience. I didn't go back again to look for loose depth charges."

Edward Delage also recalls his time of disaster. "When we got up on deck, the sea was behaving. I hung out over the top life line trying to cut away a life raft that had been broken in two. The raft was banging around, hitting depth charges and K guns on the starboard side.

"Jack Clemens yelled when he saw the first big wave coming -- but too late. I had my leg through the lifeline and it snapped like a twig when the wave hit me. My inflatable life-belt was ripped off. Jack got me untangled and started dragging me aft when the second big wave hit us both. We held on to anything we could get a hold of to keep from being washed overboard. They finally got me inside the after deck-house, but not aware of the blue dye they laid me in it. I was covered. The corpsman verified my broken leg, gave me a shot of morphine, then took me below on a wire stretcher and put me in a middle bunk. Next day Dr. Romig put one of those long wire leg braces on me. (crafted from a stretcher)

"They transferred me to Adak and in a few days sent me on to Kodiak Naval Hospital on an inner-island tug. Eventually they flew me to Seattle for continuing treatment. I spent 33 years in the Navy -- but didn't return to the *Wren*."

While standing watch in the forward engine room I spent a lot of time with Wally Rupe. He stood evaporator watch next to the switchboard, and through our conversations we learned we were both from Tacoma, Washington, where we had worked next door to each other.

Wally Rupe, machinist mate second class, "I came to *Wren* after completing a special training program aboard the *Twiggs*, at Norfolk. As an engineering student for Fletcher class destroyers, I had to learn about all specialized equipment and machinery unique to the *Wren*. This was in spite of the fact that I had just spent two years on the *Perkins*, a Mahan class destroyer. I became 'water king' on the *Wren* and responsible for maintaining enough water and keeping the evaporators in good repair.

"I was aboard the *Perkins* when she sank on November 29, 1943, in a collision with the Australian troop transport, *Mercantile Duntroon*. It happened at night and I spent three hours in the water before being taken aboard the Australian ship. We were rammed just off Buna, New Guinea and abruptly wound up in the ocean. I was scared out of my wits, but flabbergasted to learn most of the Australians didn't even know they hit us, until they saw us in the water next morning."

Wally talks about his personal encounter with the storm. "I returned to my bunk in the after crew's quarters, from GQ in mount-5 magazine, but found it a mess. A mixture of oil, salt water and blue dye up to two inches deep covered the deck. Hearing an awful racket, I looked through the hatch into the crew's quarters, where you were, Bill. The empty shell casings and powder cans were slamming from side to side with each roll of the ship. In spite of the circumstances I tried to sleep in my wet bunk. Banging noises started coming from the overhead, directly above me, as depth charges had broken loose from their storage racks.

"I had to relieve the 0400 to 0800 watch, but no way! Travel on weather decks from the after living compartments was impossible. After dark, the following night, I decided to try again. Going up the narrow port side main deck, a wave hit me. Falling to the deck I saw the life lines were all down. With nothing to hold onto, I desperately dug my fingernails into deck rivets. As the ship rolled to starboard, I ran as fast as I could to shelter amidships. Managing to get to the forward engine room, I learned only two of us made it. After hearing our stories everyone else stayed put. It still scares me to think about what almost happened."

Seaman First Class Al Copson recalls the loose depth charges and blue dye incident during this storm. "I had returned to my bunk in the after crew's quarters right after the bombardment. All of a sudden there was a hell of a noise up on the fantail over my head. We knew there were loose casings rolling around, but this seemed more than that. Going up to investigate, we saw huge swells breaking over the fantail. Five gallon cans of blue dye, dozens of empty 5-inch shell casings and 600-pound depth charges were slamming all over the place. Most of our life lines were down and the stanchions were ripped from their welds.

"Another shipmate, the first to get there, was hit and knocked over the side. His leg got tangled in the life net, breaking it, but that probably saved his life. Several other men were there and we eventually got him into the entrance to the crew's quarters. His leg appeared to be badly broken, so we laid him on the enclosed deck. One of the officers called the bridge, but they didn't even know we were having a problem. The following day Dr. Romig somehow managed to get back aft, over the catwalk, to set his leg. He was transferred off at Attu and Dr. Romig was commended for his super effort."

Chief Carpenter's Mate Joseph Martino, along with 20 or 30 other men, came onboard the *Wren* before commissioning. They had survived the sinking of the *Bristol*, DD453, torpedoed in the Mediterranean, en route to Oran for replenishing.

Joe, a damage controlman on *Wren*, describes his duties and experiences that night. "The 7 foot wide and 20 foot long carpenter shop just under the fantail in the stern of the ship, located directly over the propellers next to steering aft, was probably the noisiest place on the ship. Plywood, sheet metal, angle bars, nuts, bolts, coffee and hot plate -- would shake, rattle and roll. No matter how we secured the shop for rough seas, we came back to a mess.

"I was in charge of number 3 repair party and our 12 man crew patrolled the after part of the ship during GQ. We were the 'roving line-backers,' from the after engine room bulkhead to the fantail. We closed hatches, vents, doors, responded to any emergencies and assisted gun crews. We were trained in firefighting and reported the condition to bridge officers.

"During the big storm, after our first bombardment, they announced 'Man over-board' on the public address system. Fire and rescue teams went into action. It seemed as if the entire ocean was coming over the after part of our ship, so I went to number 3 damage-control locker for an emergency life line. We had a hell'uva time securing it from the depth charge racks on the stern to a cleat on the bulkhead forward of mount 5. We had to wait on the lee side of the superstructure until the stern rose to the top of a big swell, then run like hell. We tried to get a safety line attached before the next wave hit.

"I wrapped a security line around my waist and attached it to the emergency life line. As I started searching the darkness around the depth charge racks, sure enough we found an injured shipmate clinging to the underside. Holding on for dear life, his screams could hardly be heard over the noise of the sea. The waves were crashing into depth charges knocking them from their damaged security racks. With the help of several others, we assisted him to safety."

In less severe Aleutian weather the seas often washed over, momentarily flooding *Wren's* fantail. With heavy life nets encircling the stern, our ship could conceivably become a fish-trap. Joe talks about occasionally having his own private source of fish under the depth charge racks; however without nets he caught no fish this night. Based on all of my interviews with shipmates, I think at least two men were injured that night.

Clay Harris recalls, "I think the second guy was trying to get something out of the after life raft, when a big wave hit and washed him under the depth charge racks."

John Powell describes his encounter with the storm and some of its damage: "Rivets were pulled from the lower bulkhead attachment at the after deck house and the sea pushed it in, causing flooding into the crew's quarters. The bullworks up forward were pretty well beat-up and had to be modified or replaced in some areas. Both whale-boats were knocked off. We also lost the reels that held mooring lines, leaving them trailing over the stern. We were scared to death that the wire and hemp lines would get tangled in our screws. If this happened -- we'd still be there. It probably would have pulled the struts off and caused a hell of a mess. Some lines were gone, others we managed to recover. I don't know how many, but quite a few depth charges broke loose, going through the snaking and over the side.

"Dr. Romig wanted to get back to the after crew's quarters the following day to check on Delage, but he was unable to move on the weather deck, so I took him back late in the afternoon.

"I was off watch standing near the torpedoes watching the waves go by. The water would slam back and forth across the open section between the deck-houses, and I knew we weren't going to go over the main deck, so I took him over the catwalk. The main problem was at the forward torpedo mount. The hoist to load torpedoes, a heavy piece of machinery, is usually depressed and secured. Unfortunately, it broke loose and was damaged, banging back and forth it became a real problem.

"The 'I' beam part of it was about 6 inches wide and we only had about 10 feet to go. While we were watching it seemed like it had jammed, so I jumped on and ran across. Dr. Romig had to wait for the ship to stop bucking before he could follow. As he started across, the thing started wobbling again so he said, 'I'm not going to walk on it.' Sitting down, he started scooting across the beam and it swung out with him on it. I was afraid he might get knocked off when it banged against the deckhouse. As he got closer to my side, I was able to put a foot on the beam to help hold it until he reached the catwalk. From there we went down through mount 3 into the handling room and out in the crew's head, putting us inside the after deck-house.

*L to R--Unknown, Danny Wann, Barney Pullen*

"Dr. Romig made a splint out of a stretcher, laid Delage's leg in and filled it with plaster. When we returned to Attu, they removed Delage from *Wren* attached to the stretcher. We later received a message from Seattle saying, 'The setting is fine.'"

Seaman Daniel Wann lied about his age to join the Navy at sixteen. At seventeen he was on *Wren* for the commissioning. Dan was a small, blond-haired kid, doing a man's job this night. He, Barney Pullen and Jim Pridmore shared lookout duty on the flying bridge, the highest point on Wren where sailors stood watch. Al Copson stood watch about ten feet below on the port bridge. They had a real bird's-eye view of Wren's struggle against the most severe challenge she faced so far. The lookouts dressed in full foul weather gear, with head and face protection, wore goggles over their face gear to protect the only exposed part of their bodies. As the temperature dropped, the raging sea often hit them in the form of ice. That's the most grueling duty on any ship. Captain Mac, being mindful of their danger, often called them to the bridge for shelter.

Dan tells about standing lookout during our first challenge to survive the wrath of an Aleutian storm. "I was scared," he confides. "The seas were so much bigger than we were, and the director deck (Flying-bridge) was about fifty feet above the water level. When we were in the valley, tops of approaching waves were like huge mountains. They towered another full ship height, up to a hundred feet, over our heads. We looked straight up to see the angry capping tops of those waves. We felt so -- insignificant in comparison.

"Each approaching wave seemed to attack our ship with its individual ferocity. Wren would climb each wave almost vertically to the top, hesitate momentarily, then slam back down to the valley below. She shook severely each time, threatening her continued existence. I think I could have actually reached out and touched those waves from where we were. From time to time it became too dangerous to be there, so we were called down from our watch.

"While on the bridge during that same storm, they called me to relieve the helmsman. Steering our usual zig-zag course was extremely difficult. We were directly affected by each wave and had to stay with it to prevent broaching. A huge wave hit us in just the wrong way. Every man on the bridge thought we were going over! The OD and I both observed the clinometer indicate 74 degrees and no one really knew how far we could heel-over -- and still come back."

Ensign L. D. Criswell remembers: "During the 'Okinawa typhoon' I was on the bridge looking right at the clinometer, when it indicated an unbelievable 74 degrees. We were virtually on our side! *Wren* nearly foundered. Everyone on the bridge -- thought we were going over."

John Powell says: "As the ship starts to roll back, momentum of the pendulum effect sometimes causes a slight override and the clinometer will over-indicate."

To determine how far a destroyer can heel over and still come back, one must refer to those that did not. The destroyers *Hull, Spence* and *Monaghan* were pushed too far over in the typhoon of December 18-19,1944. All three sank with a loss of 790 men. An extensive search failed to recover more than a few survivors.

LTjg A. S. Krauchunas was the sole surviving officer from the *Spence*. In telling his story for Theodore Roscoe's book "U.S. Destroyer Operations in World War II" published by the U.S. Naval Institute, he states:

*"The ship was caught in huge swells. The first huge swell rolled the ship 75 degrees, from which it recovered, but the next one rolled her over, trapping all of those below the main deck, passageways, radio shack, CIC, wardroom, and so forth. Fifty to sixty men managed to get off into the water from their stations topside."*

In excerpts from a story told by Second Class Water Tender Joseph C. McCrane, the highest ranking of six *Monaghan* survivors, he stated:

*"I went back to the engineer's compartment and the ship was rolling so heavy that all of us decided to go topside into the after gun shelter.... I managed to work myself to within about ten feet of the door on the port side. There were about 40 men in the shelter. One of the fellows was praying aloud. Every time the ship would take about a 70 degree roll to starboard, he would cry out, 'Please bring her back dear, dear Lord, don't let us down now.' We must have taken about seven or eight rolls to the starboard before she went over on her side."*

*While rescuing survivors of the Hull and Spence, the DE Tabberer reported heeling over 72 degrees.*

Rosco further describes this storm. *"American Battleships rolled like canoes in rapids. The light carriers Montery and Cowpens were heaving like hammocks and suffered damage when aircraft broke loose. Fires broke out on the flight deck of the CVE Cape Esperance. CVE Kwajalein lost steering control. CVE Rudyard Bay went dead in the water.*

*"Rough on battleships and carriers the typhoon was unmitigated hell for destroyers. During the storm a number of DDs were rolled on their beams and pinned down with their stacks almost flat against the sea. The destroyer Dewey laid over in a cant which registered 75 degrees on the inclinometer. The Aylwin rolled 70 degrees."*

Everyone on *Wren* agrees on two points. The waves were about as high as they could be and we heeled over about as far as we could and still come back.

"The bridge was a very eerie place for me," Dan Wann recalls. "The dim lighting at night, along with the constant ping of our sonar and the scary seas, seemed right out of Frankenstein's Castle."

To estimate the true height of waves in a storm has always been a challenge for seafaring men. People like Dan, Barney and Jim Pridmore certainly had many hours of the best possible perspective. We rode out two typhoons in the south Pacific, so I asked Dan to describe the difference. "I think the waves were higher and certainly closer together in the Aleutians," Dan said.

Lt Ray Copeland was a TBM pilot. (The TBM like the TBF is an Avenger, the TBM was manufactured by Martin and the TBF by Grumman.) Ray, stationed aboard the carrier *Essex*, CV9, during the typhoons of December 19, 1944 and June 5, 1945, remembers. *"A huge wave came clear over our flight deck, one hundred twenty-nine feet above the water. The force broke tie-down cables as it washed the aircraft overboard."*

The third day, while *Wren's* cleanup crew turned to in our crew's quarters, I went out on the weather deck. The first thing you must do before going out of the hatch is to peek, to determine the lee side of the ship. In a storm like this you are going to get wet, even at best, but you never go out on the windward side. The main deck was divided by superstructure that ran through the center of the ship. On top of that, was the catwalk deck. This cabin offered some protection for the narrow main deck on the lee side. We learned to anticipate the roll. When *Wren* rolled towards the windward side, we had a few seconds to run up the deck to about amidships; then at that point hesitate for another favorable roll. If the decks took water, an exhaust vent for the after engine room curved aft and provided enough room to take cover in. I made my way forward behind the officer's quarters, where it was dry and watched the wild seas in action. I knew there were eleven ships out there, but none could be seen. After standing switchboard watch in the engine room, it was refreshing and fascinating to spend time on deck.

Dan Wann said, "We thought we were all alone even from our vantage point on the flying bridge. As we rose to the top of an extra big swell, occasionally we could see the ghostly tip of a cruiser's mast, seem to emerge from the sea."

I think Al Copson, Joe Martino, Edward Delage, John Powell, Jack Clemens and all others who risked their lives that night to save our ship, deserve a medal for their effort. It's easy now to look back and wonder, but if one depth charge blew, we could all be history. Shipmates like those who performed instinctively, without regard for their own safety, epitomized the true destroyerman.

That entire trip back to Attu turned out to be a real survival test for all destroyers. Task Force 94 continued traveling at a snail's pace. *Wren's* crew licked their wounds and shored up against storm damage.

At 1154 hours November 25, *Wren* dropped the hook at Massacre Bay, Attu. Our first encounter with the Japanese was behind us, and we had survived the big storm. During the eight days since we left Attu our crew had very little good rest. We had not been able to lie in our bunks without holding on. We had no decent place to sit. Sitting was only possible if we could wedge ourselves in place and brace against the ship's roll with our legs. The weather had been our worst enemy! Now we were back in the harbor and could all get lots of good rest. Wrong! Anchored in Attu harbor, *Wren* still rolled up to 20 degrees.

I probably have the dubious distinction of being the only sailor in the U.S. Navy to survive such a first week at sea. The first time I heard the big guns fired, we bombarded Japan. Then the big storm hit. More importantly I survived the mess cooks, chow line and did not get sick.

# Eight
# Dutch Harbor

During our two days anchored in the harbor I became acquainted with Reno Pellegrini, who came from the town I was born and raised in, Aberdeen, Washington. We had a lot in common, when we were together it was like a contest to see who could get into what, first. We went ashore at Attu, had a few 3.2 beers, reminisced about home and compared notes on people we both knew.

At 0936 November 28, Task Force 94 got underway for Adak. Next day at 1115 -- *Rowe, Wren, Watts, Smalley*, and *Stoddard* -- left the formation for Dutch Harbor.

At 2300 on the 29th, the seas were still rough and the night coal black, when suddenly, unidentified blips appeared on *Wren's* SG radar. General quarters sounded with unidentified surface craft off our starboard bow. Captain Mac pondered the identity of the ships when a star shell popped directly over *Wren's* bow, exposing the five U.S. destroyers. *Wren* returned fire exploding several star shells directly over the intruders. Bright flames floated gently down on parachutes and turned the blackness into daylight. The light exposed three Russian freighters.

Captain Mac, "squad dog" for all five destroyers on this trip, furiously shouted on the radio: "How dare you fire on us. Get your proper IFF on or we will sink the lot of you." Allied ships were given a radio code each day for identification; after delivering his tongue-lashing we continued to Dutch Harbor. With the wind still blowing and the seas rough, we were unable to enter port, so we steamed off shore until the following day.

*Wren* went directly to the submarine base at Cliuliuk Harbor to exchange damaged torpedoes. The storm had taken its toll on our munitions, as well as the ship. *Wren* remained at the facility to receive badly needed repairs, then transferred to a drydock for underwater work. We stayed there until December 13, where we received supplies, ammunition, and fuel.

During this time our crew invaded the notorious Unalaska bars. It had been a long dry spell and we were like race horses at the starting gate. To get to Unalaska we had to cross the channel on a barge attached to both shores with cables, and a winch pulled it back and forth. The operator of the barge, a soldier also from Aberdeen, spent the entire war on that job. It so happened we had trained together as boxers and he became the military heavyweight champion of the Aleutian Islands.

Seaman First Class Jack Jarc, a husky-built ex-Chicago cop, with a long Aleutian beard, got off the barge onto the snow-packed streets with Reno and me. It felt like stepping into an old Hollywood western set. The entire town consisted of a few unpainted, ransacked, old buildings, spread out over two short blocks. With no outside lighting the place looked like a ghost town.

"Reno, what the hell are we doing here?" I asked.

"How the hell do I know. There's supposed to be some bars over here, somewhere."

*Seaman First Class Jack Jarc*

Coming over the barge was crammed with sailors, but now the streets ahead were deserted. We moved on down the dark street to the first building that appeared habitable; then we pushed the door open and stepped inside. Sure enough -- it was a bar.

The bar itself ran unbroken from the left side of the door to the far end of the long, narrow room. There were no tables, chairs or bar stools. Already lined with sailors, the ten feet of standing room between the wall and bar soon became jammed. The entire bar top was covered with shot glasses, some empty, some full. The three bartenders had a bottle in each hand and poured liquor until they were empty. We selected our drink by color only and tossed our fifty cents on the bar.

When the fleet was in, the bars were only allowed to remain open between four and six PM. But, us guys were ready. Without knowing what we were drinking, sailors grabbed right and left-handed drinks. With no music the crescendo of our voices rose by the minute. The room became so jammed with sailors we could hardly put our arms down at our sides. By the end of the first thirty minutes the tempo increased, but after an hour shot-glasses, beer cans and bottles flew around the room. It was impossible to talk with anyone. We could only shout and get drunk.

Just before closing time tempers raged and fists flew. I looked over my shoulder to see Reno, who stood about a head taller than most of the crowd, take a punch from behind. He spun around and popped the guy on the nose with a long left, over the heads of others. Jack and I tried to work our way through the crowd to help him, when a shore patrolman raised his club. Jack is the strongest man I have ever known and when he grabbed that shore patrolman's arm, it was like being caught in a vice. "Try to use that club and I'll run it right up your ass. I carried one of those for four years in Chicago, as a cop, and I know what they'll do. We're all friends and we don't need that here," Jack yelled.

By that time the masses moved toward the door and before we knew it we were back on the street. Sailors silhouetted against the mounds of snow that lined the streets, became easy targets. Hitting Reno from behind proved a big mistake for that sailor. Reno went looking for him! After finding his man relieving himself against a snow bank, Reno spun him around with his left hand and hit him with a devastating right cross, from left field. That sailor went down -- and stayed there. "Hey Bill," Reno yelled, -- "Did you see what I did to that guy?"

Well, that was just the beginning. The walk to the warming shed at the barge became littered with blue jackets in the snow. Jack, Reno and I were jumped twice by cruiser sailors. Each time they outnumbered us. We left them all -- reclining in a horizontal position!

By the time we got to the barge -- I felt like fighting! The warming shed, an open room about 25 or 30 feet square, had a potbellied stove vented straight through the high roof. I stepped inside, knocked the chimney across the room with a left hook and yelled, "All right, any of you fucking cruiser sailors that wanna fight, step up. Well, where the hell are all of you yellow-bellies that have been picking fights? Step up, one or a dozen!" No one did. It sure is strange how tough we were -- after two hours in Unalaska bars.

As each section had its turn at Unalaska liberty, our ship became a disaster area when they returned. Their behavior ranged from fighting to consoling, laughing to crying, arguing to singing as they snuck aboard, crawled aboard and were carried aboard. But, that was *Wren's* crew at Dutch Harbor. I'm sure psychologists have a long explanation for this behavior. But, I simply call it mass venting of anger and frustration among friends.

Our five destroyers got underway at 1057, December 13. Forty-eight hours later we were back at buoy 1, Sweepers Cove, Adak. In five days, with the other ships, we got underway for Attu. *Wren* returned to berth D-15, Massacre Bay at 1617 on the 21st, where we stayed until after the Christmas season.

During this time, Lieutenant Commander Dan E. Henry, executive officer, transferred to his own destroyer command; Lieutenant Commander Robert H. Pauli, replaced him. *Wren* was lucky to get such an experienced replacement.

Robert Pauli XO: "I graduated in 1940, and was immediately assigned to the *Mississippi,* going aboard as a Jr officer at Pearl Harbor. Battleships were good training grounds at that time; because they moved me to different jobs, including engineering, air defense, and communications, every few months. *Mississippi* eventually left the Pacific for Iceland, where I transferred to the USS *Schenck,* an old four stacker converted to a three stacker, which had only one 3-inch gun.

"After going aboard as a Jr. officer I soon became a 'Top Watch Officer,' with only 15 officers *Schenck* offered good opportunities for learning and advancement. I became the first lieutenant and gunnery officer. We were on escort duty in the north

Atlantic when the war broke out. With only one diversion for the invasion of north Africa, we remained there until 1943, when I contacted mononucleosis and they transferred me to a land based hospital.

"After recovery, I went to Bremerton where they assigned me to the *Howorth*. After shakedown we joined MacArthur's fleet in the Philippines, and took part in the invasion of Hollandia and Leyte. Shortly before the Lingayen Gulf invasion, I transferred to the Aleutians as XO of the *Wren*. Before leaving, I turned my job over to Pete Hamner. That's the last time I saw him. Shortly after I left -- *Howorth* was hit by a Kamikaze that killed Pete.

"My orders were to proceed and report, which meant I had four days travel time, so I decided to make the best of them. My wife and I lived in Chicago and I had not seen our new born baby. I decided to go for it. A call to Washington, D. C. netted me three additional days. It was great! I reached *Wren* at Attu just in time for her next trip to bombard Suribachi."

Our lives settled into the boring routine of Aleutian duty. Christmas was a particularly difficult time for all of *Wren's* crew. Captain Mac always did his best for our morale, with movies, the best possible food and occasionally special entertainment. Christmas eve was one of those occasions. We had a party in the crew's mess hall. The program consisted of a sing-along of Christmas carols, a narration of the Christmas Story, an officer's quartet, enlisted men's quartet and a special message from Captain Mac-Donald, followed by refreshments.

We made a Christmas tree out of spiral lathe turnings and kept music flowing out to the crew from the electric shop. Even with our limited supply of records, our phonograph was a popular item with *Wren's* crew. One of my favorite pastimes, while off duty, was playing music for them. We kept it lighthearted -- Will Bradly's, Down the Road a Piece and Peggy Lee's, Why Don't you Do Right, were popular, but we also played Bing Crosby's, White Christmas and I'll Be Home For Christmas -- during this season.

In the forward fireroom Hap Rogers had been making his own plans for a little Christmas spirit. Hap recalls, "As oil king I was responsible for the quality and freshness of boiler water, so periodically we had to run tests to verify the alkalinity and salinity. We accomplished this by mixing a solution of green soap and pure medical alcohol into a vial of boiler water and shaking it together. For some strange reason our medical alcohol -- continually evaporated.

"Reno Pellegrini and Dr. Romig, in sick bay, seemed to have the same problem with this 180 proof alcohol. Our frequent requisitions did not help their cause. Dr. Romig suggested we get our own, directly from Adak. One of our engineering officers provided me with a requisition for a gallon to be kept in a special locker in sick bay and designated for fireroom use.

"Armed with the request, signed by an engineering officer, I proceeded to the special Quonset hut that dispensed medical supplies. But, they told me two things were wrong. First, the alcohol only came in five gallon containers and second, it had to be signed for by an officer. While heading back toward the dock I came upon a new ensign, from *Wren*. He cheerfully agreed to help me with my problem and changed the requisition to five gallons, then signed for it.

Hap continues: "Bringing the five gallons aboard I found a one gallon container for the sick bay supply. After all -- we couldn't trust them with the entire five gallons. After diluting the remaining four gallons, 5 to 1 with water, we had a potent mixture of 20 gallons to be mixed with fruit juice. Our fireroom became the most popular place on *Wren* over the Christmas holidays. The trade value was great!" It's easy to see how Hap got his nickname, and why he became so popular onboard *Wren*.

*USS Wren at Dutch Harbor*

# NINE
# WHAT EVER HAPPENED TO
# "LIL ABNER?"

As we counted our blessings for *Wren's* safe return to Attu, Admiral Ohnishi's suicide pilots were getting into full swing in the Philippines. Fleet carriers experienced the wrath of deliberate suicidal attacks, with eight ships hit during the first 30 days.

## USS FRANKLIN, CV13, AND BELLEAU WOOD, CV24, OCTOBER 30, 1944:

Both carriers were in action east of Leyte Island, when suddenly, three Kamikaze bombers appeared. One splashed near *Franklin's* starboard side, with a tremendous explosion. The second aircraft crashed into her flight deck and exploded on the galley deck below. The third Kamikaze, after being hit by *Belleau Wood*, narrowly missed *Franklin*, but ultimately managed to crash into the *Belleau Wood*. Ammunition exploded and intense fires spread throughout.

*Franklin* had 56 men killed and 60 wounded. *Belleau Wood* sustained 92 killed or wounded. Both ships

*USS Franklin and Belleau Wood*

sailed together to Ulithi for temporary repairs; then *Franklin* went to Bremerton and *Belleau Wood* to Hunter's Point, California for extensive rebuilding.

## USS INTREPID, CV11, OCTOBER 30, 1944:

While the carrier's planes attacked Clark Field, a flaming Kamikaze hit the port gun tub killing 10 and wounding 6 crewmen. *Intrepid* stayed in action until November 25, when they were hit for the second time.

On November 1, 1944, U.S. destroyers were pulled into the rapidly expanding conflict -- in a big way.

*Chief Electrician's Mate Lloyd Megee*

Lloyd Megee, without a doubt, could have been one of the most unlucky sailors in the U.S. Navy. ( Judge for yourself.)

On December 7, 1941, Lloyd served aboard the destroyer USS *Shaw*, DD373, in drydock at Pearl Harbor. The Japanese sank the drydock and *Shaw* along with it. *Shaw*, eventually salvaged, had a long, impressive war record. Lloyd swam ashore amidst the raging battle. He tells his story for our book.

"After checking in at the post office, where survivors were supposed to report, I volunteered to work on the *Tucker*, sister ship of *Shaw*, also being repaired in the harbor. When that work was finished, later the same day, I stayed aboard as a crewman.

"On August 4, 1942, *Tucker* struck a mine, broke in two and sank. After ten hours in the water we were finally picked up and eventually given a 30 day survivors leave, which I enjoyed. After that, several others from the *Tucker* and I were assigned to the new construction Fletcher class destroyer, USS *Abner Read*, DD526.

"We joined the crew at San Francisco and put *Abner Read* in commission on February 5, 1943. After a pre-trial cruise and shakedown, we joined the invasion to retake Attu.

Lloyd continues: "On August 18, 1943, either a mine or torpedo blew *Abner Read* in half. We suffered heavy losses, with 71 dead or missing and 34 wounded, but the front part of our ship was still floating. After a great deal of thought, discussion and confusion, they decided to try salvaging the forward part. The tug *Ute*, was called and they towed *Abner Read* to Adak.

"Our starboard shaft protruded intact, with no support, directly from the after engine room; after some emergency patchwork it was secured. The tug USS *Oriole*, towed us to Bremerton. A new after section had been prefabricated and they installed it. *Abner Read* was whole again! We were given our second life.

"From April to late October, 1944, we operated in the southwest Pacific; then *Abner Read* left for the invasion to recapture the Philippines from Japan"

November 1, 1944, just seven days after the first organized suicidal attacks against the U.S. Fleets at Samar, USS *Claxton*, DD571; *Killen*, DD593; *Ammen*, DD527; *Abner Read* DD526, and *Anderson*, DD411; patrolled Leyte Gulf near Samar.

### USS CLAXTON, DD571, NOVEMBER 1:

While operating in Leyte Gulf, supporting troops on shore, a suicide aircraft narrowly missed her starboard side. The tremendous explosion opened her after crews' quarters to the sea. It killed 5 and wounded 23 men. With *Abner Read's* medical and damage control assistance, *Claxton* was able to et underway by 1350 hours. After temporary repairs at Tacloban, they continued on to Manus for extensive rebuilding.

*Forward part of USS Abner Read*

### USS KILLEN, DD593, NOVEMBER 1, 1944:

About a minute after *Claxton* suffered her near miss, *Killen* was hit by a bomb. The Kamikaze crashed into the sea. Before getting hit she splashed four of seven attacking aircraft. Fifteen men were killed. After temporary repairs at San Pedro Bay and Manus, the destroyer returned to Hunter's Point for repairs. *Wren* and *Killen* trained together on shakedown at San Diego.

### USS AMMEN, DD527, NOVEMBER 1, 1944:

While the destroyer patrolled off Leyte Gulf, she was crashed into by a Japanese dive bomber. The Kamikaze killed 5 and wounded 21. Severely damaged, *Ammen* returned to Mare Island Navy Yard for battle repairs.

## USS ABNER READ, DD526, NOVEMBER 1, 1944:

*USS Abner Read -- exploding*

Chief Electrician's Mate Lloyd Megee, recalls the tragic events of that day: "During the early morning hours, while patrolling in Leyte Gulf near the island of Samar, we came under air attack. Being in the repair party I could roam freely to observe the action. While firing at several Kamikazes, one dove out of the clouds straight at us. The aircraft was hit and seemed to explode over the *Claxton*, some 1000 yards away. After the shooting stopped, our repair parties and medical personnel went aboard her to lend assistance. *Abner Read* stood by and screened *Claxton* until about 0130, when they were able to get underway.

"As we left to rejoin the fleet, two Japanese aircraft came at us from the bow. One came in on our starboard side and our skipper swung the ship around to bring all guns to bear on the targets. I stood on the quarter-deck and watched that thing come in. The "Val" dive bomber came straight at us. They shot a wing off about 200 yards out -- but he kept coming, right on in! I thought he would hit in my area, but he crashed about 20 to 30 feet away, between the after stack and torpedo mount. We didn't see the bomb drop from the plane, as it must have shaken loose just when he hit us.

"The bomb went through the after deck house and exploded in the after fireroom. It blew out the bulkhead in the after engine room and destroyed our fire main. We could not get enough pressure to fight fires, but we did manage to get a couple of handy-billies going. I headed towards the emergency generator room and ran a power line down the starboard side to get a portable pump going. Then -- number 3 magazine exploded!"

Lloyd continues: "I found out that gasoline from the suicide aircraft ran down into the handling room, through the hoist and into the magazine, causing the explosion. A crewman from the tug coming along side told me, 'It looked like that 5-inch mount blew 150 yards, straight up in the air.'

"Our ship was pretty well blown in two, but she didn't separate. We listed to starboard and started taking on water fast. I helped evacuate the wounded. Our life rafts had been painted so often we couldn't get them to release; the stainless steel cables could not be cut and the starboard whaleboat had the stern blown out. All we could do was put life jackets on the wounded -- and throw them over the side.

"A lot of us gave our life jackets to the wounded, so we had to abandon ship without one. When she listed about 45-degrees, a motor machinists mate named Clarence McCormic and I left the ship together. We left over the high port side, shedding our clothing, as we walked down into the water.

"I swam as fast as I could, then looked back to see our ship's stern settle into the sea. After we were a couple of hundred feet away we treaded water and watched. She paused, with her bow straight up in the air, for what seemed like two or three minutes. Still burning, our ship seemed to desperately gasp for lifesaving air. Then, as if giving up, she expelled and the turbulent, bubbling sea engulfed her. 'Lil Abner' sank!. She continued to creek and moan, while being pulled to the depths. *Lil Abner* screamed her death cries! We waited for the depth charges to explode. But someone had set them on safe. Our home, sanctuary, many friends and *Lil Abner* -- were gone forever!"

Lloyd continues: "After about 15 minutes in the burning water, we were the first two of about 30 survivors picked up by a boat from the USS *Richard P. Leary*. As I boarded *Leary* from the whaleboat, Torpedoman Second Class Ernest Zingy needed help getting up the sea ladder. When he left his station in number-2 torpedo mount, his entire body was on fire. After helping him board, most of the flesh on his hands came off in mine. He died within an hour! *Leary's* whaleboat made about six trips picking men out of the ocean. There must have been a hundred of us sitting all over her deck. Some were badly wounded. Many died right away!

"After they took the whaleboat aboard, we headed towards the hospital ship USS *Pinkney*, and *Leary* fought off still another suicide plane. I don't know where they took the other survivors picked up by the tug and *Claxton*."

*Lil Abner*, the first of many destroyers that felt the ultimate sting of Admiral Ohnishi's wrath, had 24 men killed and 54 wounded. Some of her injured died later from their wounds.

Lloyd Megee, also slightly injured, stayed aboard the *Pinkney* for a few weeks; during that time they continued to pick up survivors of suicidal attacks, until they were loaded. *Pinkney* then sailed to Oro Bay, New Guinea, where Lloyd transferred to the SS *Lurline* for transport to San Francisco. He then had his third 30 day survivors leave. Returning to duty, Lloyd describes his next ship.

"They sent me to Lingayen Gulf and assigned me to the USS *Laffey*, DD724, a 2200 ton Sumner class destroyer. I stayed onboard until April 15, 1945, when 6 Kamikazes crashed on her after deck, at Okinawa."

**Was Lloyd the most unlucky sailor in the U.S. Navy?**

## USS ANDERSON, DD411, NOVEMBER 1, 1944:

The fifth and final destroyer to fall victim to the Japanese suicidal madness, on this day, operated near Ponaon Island when three suicide planes attacked. One of the enemy fighters crashed into her port side aft, causing heavy damage. *Anderson* had 16 men killed and 20 wounded. She eventually returned to San Francisco for battle repairs, arriving December 9, 1944.

During the months of November and December 1944, before the invasion of Lingayen Gulf and Iwo Jima, the following number of ships were hit by Kamikazes: Nine fleet carriers, 11 escort carriers, 2 battleships, 3 cruisers and 19 auxiliary ships -- including 12 that were scrapped or sunk. In addition, 22 destroyers fell victim, including 4 either sunk or scrapped. The story of each ship is in chapter ten.

Even though *Wren's* Aleutian duty was nerve-racking and grueling at times, in retrospect -- it was not so bad.

***Pictured below, Abner Read after she was blown in two, at Attu.***
*Looking back from the crew's quarters to the missing after compartment, where the off-duty watch were all killed in their bunks. Like Abner Read, Wren was a Fletcher class destroyer. If that had been Wren, most of my friends and I -- would have perished!*

# Ten

# Philippines -- November And

# December, 1944

### USS LEXINGTON, CV16, NOVEMBER 5, 1944:

While patrolling off Luzon, an aircraft crashed near her island, destroyed most of that structure, and spread fire in all directions. On November 9, *Lexington* went to Ulithi for repairs. "Radio Tokyo" claimed she had been sunk.

*Japanese Kamikaze, in a steep dive for USS Lexington's island, moments later he struck home.*

### USS INTREPID, CV11, NOVEMBER 25, 1944:

Less than a month from the first time the carrier was crashed into by a Kamikaze, she took a second hit. While *Intrepid's* planes attacked airfields in the Philippines, the Japanese retaliated against her. Within five minutes, shortly after noon, two Kamikazes crashed into *Intrepid*. Explosions and fires killed 65 officers and crewmen. The following day she sailed to San Francisco for repairs.

*USS Intrepid, at the moment of impact November 25, 1944*
*Intrepid was hit for the third time April 16, 1945, at Okinawa.*

### USS CABOT, CVL28, NOVEMBER 25, 1944:

Japanese retaliation to air strikes continued. After fighting off several attackers, *Cabot* was hit by a flaming suicide plane. The flight deck, port side 20mm gun continued firing -- as the plane crashed into it. A second burning Kamikaze crashed just off the port side. Bomb fragments, aircraft debris, and gasoline were strewn everywhere. *Cabot* -- suffered 62 men killed or wounded. She returned to Ulithi for repairs.

### USS COLORADO, BB45, NOVEMBER 27, 1944:

The battleship supported U.S. troops on Leyte, when two Kamikazes crashed her decks. They considered *Colorado's* damage moderate, but she suffered 19 men killed and 72 wounded. BB45 returned to Manus Island for repairs.

### USS ST LOUIS, CL45, NOVEMBER 27, 1944:

The Cruiser arrived in Leyte Gulf on the 16th, where she patrolled the Gulf and Surigao Strait. At 1138 on the 27th a "Val," hit and on fire, crashed into her port quarter-deck and exploded on impact. All crewmen of 20mm guns 7 through 10 were killed instantly. A moment later, a second suicider crashed 100 yards away. At 1151 two more attackers penetrated the cruiser's defenses; the first exploded against the hull at the port quarter, the second nearly hit the starboard side. A number of holes blown in the cruiser's hull stripped away 20 feet of armor. She took a port list from flooding which was soon controlled; then *St Louis* returned to California for battle repairs. The cruiser fought off a total of 22 suicide aircraft, but she had 16 men killed and 43 wounded.

### USS ESSEX, CV9, NOVEMBER 25, 1944:

This carrier led a charmed life, until a Kamikaze hit the port edge of her flight deck and crashed among aircraft already fueled for takeoff. Fifteen men were killed and 44 wounded.

*USS Essex, CV9, note the gunfire and debris hitting the water*

### USS ROSS, DD563, NOVEMBER 28, 1944:

In drydock at Mariquitdaquit Island for repairs caused by a mine, *Ross* came under suicide attack. A "Tojo" crashed into the drydock and damaged it, delaying *Ross'* return to action.

### USS MARYLAND, BB46, NOVEMBER 29, 1944:

Shortly after sunset, as she patrolled the southern approaches to Surigao Strait, the battleship became the victim of a diving suicide plane. The aircraft hit between number 1 and 2 turrets -- 31 sailors died in the explosion. *Maryland* returned to Pearl Harbor for repairs.

### USS AULICK, DD569, NOVEMBER 29, 1944:

While operating with the Leyte defense forces, the destroyer came under attack by Japanese planes. One suicider sideswiped her bridge and crashed on the bow. He exploded on impact! She sustained 32 men killed, 60 wounded, and heavy damage. They returned to San Francisco and were repaired in time to be a survivor of the Okinawa Picket Line.

### USS MISSISSINEWA, AO59, NOVEMBER 21, 1944:

Anchored in Ulithi Harbor the tanker became the first victim of the "Kaiten" manned torpedo. Her crew had just filled all of her tanks with aviation gasoline and diesel fuel, when a manned suicide torpedo struck. A huge fire with billowing smoke could be seen for miles. Her survivors abandoned the lost ship. At 0900, *Mississinewa* slowly rolled over and sank! Sixty crewmen died with her.

**Miscellaneous ships crashed into during November**. SS *Matthew P. Deadly*, November 4; USS *Egeria*, APL8, and the USS *Achillies*, ARL41, on the 12th; USS *Alpine*, APA92, and another APD, name unknown, on the 20th.

Reading this account, as in writing it, the stories seem repetitious, but this is the monumental insanity of what the war had become. The month of December was relatively quiet in the south Pacific, if you consider only 24 ships hit by suicide aircraft, quiet. Most heavy fleet ships were spared during this time, but destroyers and landing craft caught the brunt of -- Admiral Ohnishi's attention.

### USS DRAYTON, DD366, DECEMBER 5, 1944:

Escorting a convoy of LCM's and LCI's to San Pedro Bay, she came under attack by a twin-engine bomber who scored a near miss. The explosion caused some damage, killed one and wounded seven. Later the same morning 10 to 12 enemy fighters attacked, and one crashed into a 5-inch mount starting raging fires. *Drayton* successfully delivered her charges to San Pedro, then went to Manus for repairs.

### USS LAMSON, DD367, DECEMBER 5, 1944:

*Lamson* was screening a convoy off Ormac Bay, when she splashed two "Dinahs" before a third crashed into her superstructure. The USS *Flusser*, DD368, escorted her back to safety for temporary repairs. *Lamson's* severe damage forced her return to Puget Sound Navy Yard for extensive repairs. *Lamson* -- suffered 25 crewmen killed and 54 wounded.

### USS MUGFORD, DD389, DECEMBER 5, 1944:

Written about in the book, The Ship that Outlasted Time, *Mugford* suffered a hit this same day, killed 8 and wounded 14. She had sped to protect landing craft being attacked by Kamikazes in Surigao Strait, when a "Val" crashed into her, causing extensive damage. *Mugford* returned to Mare Island, California for repairs.

### USS MAHAN, DD364, DECEMBER 7, 1944:

Shortly before 1000 the USS *Walke*, DD416, *Ward*, APD16, and *Mahan* patrolled between Leyte and Ponson, when a swarm of suicide aircraft attacked them. *Mahan* shot down three, but the other three crashed into her. Fires soon spread out of control to her magazines. They abandoned the stricken destroyer! One hour later her companion ship, *Walke*, sank the *Mahan!*

### USS WARD, DD139, -- APD16, DECEMBER 7, 1944:

A fast destroyer transport became the next ship to fall victim to the twin-engine Bettys from Leyte. Her crew observed gray and black smoke from *Mahan* off in the distance, as U.S. P38's and P40's came to her rescue. Suddenly, three Bettys headed straight for *Ward*. At 0956 *Ward's* gunfire hit number two aircraft, but he came on in to crash into her starboard side at the waterline and exploded. The bomber passed through the forward part of the boiler room and lower troop space, as one of the planes engines exited the outer port side hull. Betty number one crashed into the sea about 600 yards away and the third some 200 yards from *Ward*. At 1130, unable to extinguish fires -- the crew abandoned ship. After her crew successfully left, the USS *Obrien*, DD725 -- sank the flaming hulk! *Obrien's* captain, Bill Outeridge, carried out this order with deep remorse -- *Ward* was his old command. She fired the first shot of World War II., and sank a two man Japanese submarine outside of Pearl Harbor, on December 7.

*USS Ward, DD135, December 7, 1944*

### USS LIDDLE, APD6, DECEMBER 7, 1944:

Hit on the bridge and seriously damaged, the converted DE went to San Francisco for repairs. *Liddle* lost 38 officers and crewmen in the attack.

### USS HUGHES, DD410, DECEMBER 10, 1944:

Badly damaged by a suicide plane, with one engine room demolished and most of her machinery wrecked, she was towed to San Pedro Bay, Leyte for temporary repair. Captain E.B. Rittenhouse took his ship on to Pearl Harbor and San Francisco for complete rebuilding. Eighteen were killed and over 20 wounded.

### USS REID, DD369, DECEMBER 11, 1944:

The destroyer patrolled Leyte Gulf, when suddenly, a Kamikaze crashed into her. Two minutes later -- she heeled over and sank!

### USS HOWORTH, DD592 DECEMBER 12, 1944:

One man died when *Howorth* was struck by a Kamikaze. This man replaced Lieutenant Commander Robert Pauli, when he transferred to *Wren* as XO. On April 1, *Howorth* received many casualties, when once again, a Kamikaze hit her.

### USS CALDWELL, DD605, DECEMBER 12, 1944:

*Caldwell*, while escorting a convoy of landing craft to Ormac Bay, came under attack by suicide aircraft. Bombs dropped close by spraying the entire ship with fragments, then a Kamikaze hit her bridge. Thirty-three men were killed and 40 wounded, including her CO Lieutenant Commander J. F. Newman, Jr. After temporary repairs at San Pedro, they had a long, slow, voyage home to San Francisco for rebuilding. *Caldwell* returned to the war April 15, 1945.

### *USS HARADEN, DD585, DECEMBER 13, 1944:*

*Haraden* fell victim to a Kamikaze while escorting "Jeep" carriers in the Sulu Sea. Attacked by four aircraft the combined force shot down three, but the fourth, trailing smoke, hit *Haraden* destroying the forward engine room and severely damaged her main deck. After caring for 14 killed and 24 wounded, she sailed to Bremerton for repairs.

### USS NASHVILLE, CL34, DECEMBER 13, 1944:

*Nashville* was crashed into while en route to Mindoro. Off Negros Island the attacker dropped two bombs about ten feet over her deck. They exploded in mid-air, then crashed into her port 5-inch gun. Exploding ammunition and burning gasoline, turned *Nashville's* midships into an inferno. With 133 killed and 190 wounded she sailed to Puget Sound Shipyard for repairs.

THE U.S. LSTs, 472, 738, AND 748 WERE SUNK BY KAMIKAZES, DECEMBER 15

### USS MARCUS ISLAND, CVE77, DECEMBER 15, 1944:

While supporting the Mindoro invasion forces, *Marcus Island* came under heavy Kamikaze attack. One aircraft narrowly missed her port bow, and a second the starboard bow of the Jeep carrier. The near misses caused the carrier some damage and loss of life.

### THE USS LSTs, 460, 479; AND THE SS JOHN BURKE, DECEMBER 21, 1944:

All ships, crashed into by Kamikazes, were sunk. *John Burke* had no survivors!

### SS WILLIAM SHARON, DECEMBER 28, 1944:

*William Sharon* was crashed into by a Kamikaze.

### USS PORCUPINE, IXI26, DECEMBER 30, 1944:

No, "Holiday Spirit" was shown by Admiral Ohnishi's relentless suicide pilots. They sank an additional four ships on December 30.

The tanker *Porcupine*, off White Beach, Mindoro was hit by a "Val" dive bomber. The explosion blew a long hole under the waterline. On fire, in danger of blowing up from her aviation gasoline, they gave an emergency order to the USS *Gansevoort*, DD608, "Blow her stern off." Despite the effort to save her, *Porcupine* burned to the waterline.

### USS GANSEVOORT, DD608, DECEMBER 30, 1944:

*Gansevoort*, took a near fatal hit later that same day, when a suicide pilot crashed into her main deck. Unable to stop flooding, they beached *Gansevoort* to prevent her sinking. The destroyer tender USS *Piedmont*, later refloated the derelict ship and repaired her. *Gansevoort*, sustained 34 crewmen killed or wounded.

### USS ORESTES, AGP10, DECEMBER 30, 1944:

*Orestes*, a motor torpedo boat tender, became the third ship to feel the sting of deliberate suicide on this day. Heading towards Mindoro with 30 PT boats and 50 other vessels, a Val bomber came in low on the starboard side and crashed into her amidships. Accompanying LCI's brought the fires under control, but she had to be beached. *Orestes* lost 45 crewmen to this suicide attack. The USS LST,788, later towed her back to Leyte, where temporary repairs were made. She returned to San Francisco, where it required 202,500 man hours to restore the PT boat tender.

## USS PRINGLE, DD477, DECEMBER 30, 1944:

As *Pringle* escorted a convoy to Mindoro three Kamikazes attacked. She shot down two, but the third hit and destroyed her after deckhouse and one 40mm mount. Two after 5-inch mounts were badly damaged, and 11 men were killed with 20 injured. After repairs *Pringle* returned to action in February 1945. However, the destroyer paid the ultimate price April 16th -- at Okinawa!

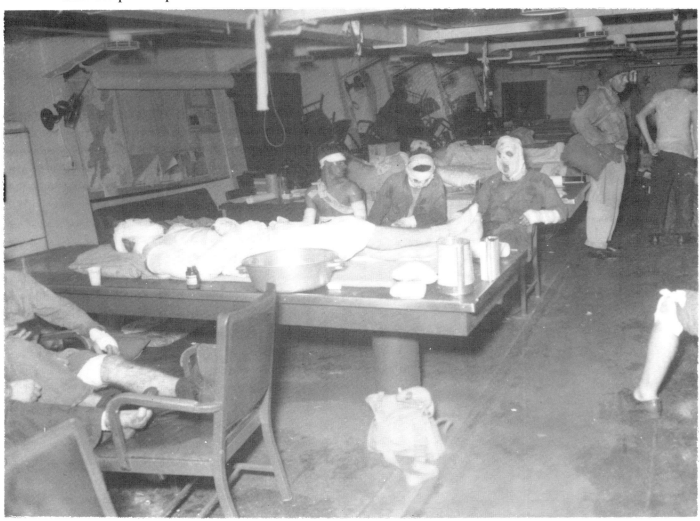

*Wardroom of the Suwanee, CVE27, becomes a sick bay and operating room.*

# ELEVEN

# THE FIRST DAYLIGHT NAVAL BOMBARDMENT OF JAPAN

At 1006 January 3, Task Force 94 cleared Massacre Bay for our fourth crossing. Full of fuel and ammunition we headed for Suribachi, Kurile Islands. For the first time we had all three cruisers with us on a raid. With Cruiser Division 1 the USS *Richmond, Trenton*, and *Concord*, Squadron 57 included -- USS *Rowe, Wren, Stoddard, Smalley, Watts, Bearss, Jarvis, Porter* and *John Hood* -- our task force was full strength.

Suribachi, on the southern tip of Paramushiro, is the most northern island in the Kuriles. It's a desolate part of the old USSR, located just off the southern end of Kamchatka Peninsula.

After getting off watch, usually at night, Reno and I often met on the weather deck to just shoot the bull or plot our next boredom-relieving escapade. During the Aleutian winter, with dark days and pitch black nights, we had to spend an hour or so on deck before we could see.

One night, Rodgers the cook, came out of the galley in his white uniform, next to where Reno and I were standing. He stepped out of the lighted compartment into the blackness and felt his way along the bulkhead with his left hand -- like he was blind. While making his nightly trek toward the bridge with his prize cuisine, he carefully juggled a tray of goodies in his right hand. Reno whispered, "You grab his leg when he goes up the ladder and hold on." Reno quickly went up the ladder ahead of him and waited on the catwalk above. When Rodgers went up the ladder, I grabbed his leg from behind and held it fast. He squealed like a stuck pig. Even though he could not see us, he suspected. "Reno, you bastard knock it off," he yelled. I let Rodgers go, after Reno relieved him of some of his choice -- bribes.

We stayed on the weather deck partaking our ill-gotten gains, when Rodgers suddenly appeared again. This time he came over the catwalk from the port side, carrying a bucket of water. As he groped across the catwalk, we backed off to the outside rail and watched him dump the water over the heads of two unsuspecting shipmates. They, too, had not been on deck long enough to be able to see. During the shouting, cursing and confusion, Reno and I slipped off in the darkness.

Our crossing to Suribachi was quite uneventful; after the usual rehearsal, the task force moved towards our bombarding position.

Bridge January 5, Lowell Clark general quarters JR-OD: "I had relayed the order to come from 325 to a 90 degree heading. Our guns were trained over the port side during that moment of 'quiet before the storm.' Captain Mac sat in his chair, unperturbed, as usual. No matter how hectic things got -- he never stopped projecting that image.

"I observed mount one and two below us, from the front bridge windows, and their gun barrels made short, jerky moves, both up and down as well as sideways. No matter how the ship rolled and pitched under them, those 5-inch guns remained trained on their respective targets. We were poised -- waiting for that 'commence firing' signal.

"This being the first daylight raid against Japan, officially thirty minutes after sunset, we expected to have air retaliation. The ear-piercing ping of our sonar was the only sound on the bridge during those final tense moments. It searched the surrounding waters for unwanted undersea intruders. Our radarmen stared at both air and surface screens for any sign of enemy activity. *Wren's* lookouts watched for air or surface targets that might slip through radar.

"At 2040 this peaceful prelude ended. The 'commence firing, commence firing' order came down. All hell broke loose! Words just cannot adequately describe the fury created by that order. All guns fired at once. It felt as though *Wren* jarred sideways in the sea. Windows and bulkheads on the bridge were hammered from direct concussion. Our heads felt as if they would burst!

"Between rounds the noise level continued. Shell casings flew from the three mounts that surrounded the bridge, slammed on the deck and bounced to a stop. During the next twenty minutes everyone was on the cutting edge. It seemed like the shelling would never stop. With each salvo anticipation and anxiety grew among our bridge crew. Captain Mac's calm example was a confidence builder. But, what chance would any of us have in those icy waters -- if we were sunk?

"Forty 5-inch and thirty-six-6-inch guns brought the war to the very threshold of Japan. It had seemed a long time since December 7, and Pearl Harbor, but this became our own little vindication. *Wren* did especially well, we fired 537 rounds at about 10-second intervals. The *John Hood* stood screening station on the disengaged bow of the cruisers, so they did not fire.

"At 2058 we relayed the cease fire order. All ships adjusted course to 90 degrees and sped away at 25 knots. At 2117 *Wren* secured from GQ and at 2145 we reduced speed to 15 knots. Although three star shells came our way, this bombardment seemed uncontested," Lowell concluded.

It's a simple matter for us to talk about how many rounds we fired in a given amount of time, but it took a lot of doing. Many anxious people perspired, in magazines in the bowels of *Wren*, without ventilation. Others dealt with live ammunition in handling rooms and gun mounts; each performed their job in the manner they had practiced for weeks. Just to have been there, they were all heroes. Wally Rupe spent his entire GQ time, both on the *Perkins* and *Wren*, in magazines. Surrounded by all of those explosives, it must have been terrorizing! But, they kept busy and were very special people.

Wally describes the scene in mount 5 magazine during this bombardment: "As soon as we got down in the magazine we turned off the ventilating system. The hatch to the ammunition hoist, normally located in the projectile room, was un-dogged and the only ventilation we had came down through the hoist opening. Each magazine had one or more projectile rooms and a powder room. During GQ, hatches leading to the other projectile rooms were left open, but we kept the powder room door dogged-down. A self-closing trap door, within the main hatch, allowed the powder casing to be passed through to the hoist man. The walls, ceilings and decks were insulated against moisture, creating a quiet, claustrophobic atmosphere.

"Four men occupied our magazine during GQ. One fed powder casings and projectiles into the hoist, another passed powder casings through the trap door, and I handled projectiles. I carried a knife to cut the canvas protector from the back of the projectile, before I passed it to the elevator man. Continuing requests for specific numbers of rounds were shouted down the hoist opening and over the inner communication system.

"Each time they let go with that first salvo, we got that sick feeling of anticipation. We hit the Japanese home islands, in daylight. Would that big one -- be headed our way? We had little time to dwell on being scared, or for that matter to think about anything during a bombardment. We practiced every move until it became automatic. Our entire purpose for being there, was to keep the handling room supplied with ammunition. Of course we never forgot where we were and what would happen if we took a round in the area of our magazine. We were always damn glad to get out of that hole." Wally concludes.

Twenty men, including Jim Pridmore and Ralph Langford, shared this hazardous duty with Walley.

Lowell Clark, Bridge: "Tension and anticipation remained high on the bridge during withdrawal. We set our zigzag course back to Attu, wondering just how hard we had hit them. Did we get their radar and airfield? Could they still launch aircraft? The usual fires and explosions could easily be seen, but just how effective had we been? With no available air cover those thoughts weighed heavily on our minds. As blackness quickly replaced the northern dusk, the odds started moving back in our favor. Our task force ran silent and slow to minimize phosphorescence. We all held our breath!

"Relieved from my GQ station by the regular duty watch, I went below leaving the questions behind. Next morning we were over 200 miles away and our B24 air cover had returned."

Even in relatively calm Aleutian seas, *Wren's* cooks and mess cooks had a chore getting the many containers of food to the mess hall three times a day. The galley was on the main deck and the mess hall two decks below. The serving containers were large, deep stainless steel kettles, with two handles, so they had to negotiate the ladder with no hands. The kettles dropped into holes in the steam tables, where they stayed warm.

Reno Pellegrini recalls an incident on this trip: "While heading up the ladder, returning to sick bay, Rodgers, the cook came down. He carried a big kettle of mashed potatoes. I stood there and waited for him to negotiate the ladder. The ship suddenly dropped and Rodgers lost his footing, he fell to the deck below. Fortunately, the mashed potatoes remained upright. A third shipmate, heading for the ladder, came lumbering down the deck from the mess hall -- timing Rodgers mishap perfectly. The jolt caused him to lose his footing so he fell forward. He regained his balance, but wound up with one big wet boot planked right in the middle of Rodgers' kettle of potatoes.

"Rodgers said, 'What the hell are you doing? You've wrecked my potatoes. What am I gonna serve?'

"The third shipmate, very helpful and apologetic said, 'It's OK Rodgers.' He pulled his foot out of the potatoes and smoothed them over with his hand, saying, 'Nobody will ever know the difference.' Rodgers went ahead and served the potatoes to our crew," Reno concluded.

In spite of the powdered eggs, half-rotten chicken and bugs in our bread and biscuits, the food was pretty good. On the few rare occasions when we had fresh eggs, our shipmates always woke us up for breakfast, even if we stood the midnight to four AM watch. Even though the eggs were green, more often than not, we always got up for this kind of breakfast.

We dropped anchor back at berth D-15, Massacre Bay, Attu, at 1142 January 7. My 21st birthday.

*Wren's mess cooks were always smiling, until the new kid came down the line.*

# TWELVE
# BACK TO DUTCH HARBOR

After fueling at Attu we laid over until the next day, then got underway for Adak. We arrived on the 10th, replaced ammunition fired at Paramushiro and left for Dutch Harbor at 0833 on the 13th. At 1416 January 14, we tied up to the USS *Salinas* in Iliuliuk Bay, Dutch Harbor, until the 25th. Could we stand it? More accurately, could the people of Unalaska and the land based military withstand the onslaught of the entire 9th Fleet, for 11 days? This would test everyone's endurance. The impact on this community of a dozen or so permanent civilian residents must have been devastating. They were braced for our arrival; however, headlines in their local newspaper told of Task Force 94's recent raid. Following is that article.

## *TARGET PARAMUSHIRO*
## *TASK FORCE HERE BLASTED JAPS EARLIER THIS MONTH....*

*The jabbering little sons of the Rising Sun have suffered consequential losses in Pacific waters from the heavy guns of the task force now located temporarily at Dutch Harbor. A colorful history of courageous ocean fighting has been earned by the brave men who man the ships of this hard-hitting American force.*

*In the first naval bombardment of the Kurile Islands conducted in daylight, Pacific Fleet units under the command of Rear Admiral John L. McCrea smashed Japanese coastal defenses, fish canneries, shore installations and an airfield at Suribachi Wan on Paramushiro's coast early in January 1945. A total weight of 181 tons of shells were hurled at the Nip station during the 20-minute bombardment. Admiral McCrea disclosed this result upon the task force's return to Attu.*

*Although the evidences of damage as seen from the bombarding warships were difficult to assess, a number of fires could be seen gathering headway among the blasted Suribachi installations as the task force withdrew. Return fire from the Japanese coastal batteries was ineffective and none of our ships suffered any damage.*

*By approaching Suribachi Wan and conducting its bombardment in full daylight, the task force risked early discovery and possible attack by Jap aircraft based on Paramushiro and other nearby islands of the Kurile chain. However, complete surprise apparently was achieved, the task force steaming to within range of the shoreline and opening fire before there was any indication that the Japanese defenders were aware of the attackers' presence.*

*American naval commanders were themselves 'surprised,' and pleasantly so!, by the comparative ease with which their warships were able to make their undetected approach, especially so since they were in range of Japanese radar stations on the island's east coast. Darkness soon cloaked American ships as they turned from the islands at the end of the bombardment and withdrew eastward at high speed. If any Japanese aircraft took off in pursuit, they were unable to find our ships. Daylight on the following day found the task force well off the enemy shore and the weather, which had favored our forces during the approach, again produced frequent snow and rain to hide the American ships from searching Jap aircraft.*

*As yet there has been no report from the photo reconnaissance plane, and until one is received it will be difficult to determine the extent of all damages, but Tokyo Rose charged the U.S. forces with killing 410 'innocent civilians' and rendering hundreds of others homeless. She indicted that damage to food processing factories was extensive and claimed that the American task force had been 'driven off by superior shore defense batteries and aircraft.'*

*We salute these heroic fighting men who are blotting out the symbol of the Rising Sun and bid them a warm welcome to Dutch Harbor.*

"Kiska" Pat, the only known female at Unalaska during that time, was tough as nails and you did not have to do much to provoke her anger. Being the only woman sailors came in contact with, she enjoyed the attention so they put up with her guff, laughing off her foul mouth and argumentative personality. With tables, chairs and a sit down counter, her restaurant-bar was much larger than the one we stumbled into last time we were there.

Reno Pellegrini and several other shipmates were in her place during the non-alcoholic hours, drinking coffee, he recalls: "I flipped my spoon from the counter top and it landed in a bucket on the back-bar, so I quickly replaced it with that of Louis Tasson, sitting next to me. Pat didn't see who did it, but she heard the bucket rattle and searched for a missing spoon. She angrily accused Louie because he had no spoon and ordered him out. Louie did not like being accused of something he didn't do. He was pissed! Finally, with the help of some cruiser sailors, she threw him out."

Naturally, Reno took exception to those "cruiser guys" picking on his buddy, so he went outside and cold-cocked a couple of them. Reno was lanky, wiry and quite capable on those snow-covered streets.

It sounds like "true confession" for me to even mention my liberties while onboard the *Wren*, especially those on this trip, at "Dutch." If there were no cruisers the destroyer sailors fought each other, but this time -- we had cruiser sailors. Everyone knew that any sailor who would stoop low enough to ride one of those "floating hotels" -- was not really a sailor at all. Under that forgone conclusion, the Ninth Fleet invaded Unalaska and the infamous watering holes.

Reno, Al Trombie, several other shipmates and I ventured over to Kiska Pat's. I guess the Navy thought they limited potential for disaster on the beach with restricted drinking hours. Only two hours a day. Wrong! Even with three-section liberties there had to be a minimum of 2,000 sailors in that little town, from 4 to 6 pm. -- over half were cruiser sailors.

After blinking our eyes a few times, the two hours passed and we were all out on the darkened street again. Now those cruiser sailors were "real bad" and they wanted to fight, but we destroyer sailors were "peace loving and pacifistic." We found groups here and groups there all making the same inquiry from us. "What ship are you from?" Well, it didn't make any difference what we said, or what ship we called home. This challenge meant "Fight!" And fight we did.

Closing bars at Unalaska, rang the bell for the biggest gang fights I have ever seen. No one was mad at anyone. The sheer pride in our ships, fueled by alcohol, started the fights. The greatest insult to a sailor is to bad-mouth his ship by calling it a scow, old tub, bucket of bolts or perhaps something even less flattering. Destroyer and cruiser sailors in such a small place, who were allowed such a short time for drinking, created a sure formula for "Land war"!

*L-R Tiger Hall, Bill Sholin, Dickey McCabe, H. Truitt Picture taken in San Diego after the war, note, the new battle stars, but the old battle scars. (Missing tooth)*

We battled our way to a relatively deserted area near the water's edge. Unconscious people were all over the place, in the snow. Several Dutch Harbor Shore Patrolmen came along in jeeps and asked, "What's going on here?"

Trombie perked up and said: "Oh, nothing. We're all from the same ship just having a little fun." They drove off and let us go at it. All three of us were still on our feet when it was over -- but that's not saying much.

*Wren's* OD and accompanying quarter-deck personnel had their hands full checking us all back on board. Next morning my dress blues were laying in a heap on the deck, next to my bunk. They looked like a pile of unrecognizable gray substance. As I lifted my battered face from the pillow -- I knew we must have had a good time. But I did wish I still had my front tooth. The Navy has a universal saying that seems to define this condition best -- all fouled up.  When you were -- f..... up, you were f..... up, no need to deny it.

One of our officers must have had a good sense of humor; because a few days later I was back in the same bar, as Ship's Shore Patrol and I had to watch the spectacle, without drinking.  The first 30 minutes were relatively quiet, but the second half-hour cans and bottles started flying.  The noise level resembled a ball game with the score tied, in the last of the ninth, when the umpire made a bad call.  The second hour, fighting started and the place became a total disaster area.  Rivalry existed between battleship, cruiser, and destroyermen -- but this was total unprovoked mayhem.  Could we blame it on the war, rough water, confinement, isolation, youth -- or alcohol?  Well -- what else?

January 25, at 0845, the 9th Fleet left Dutch Harbor and headed back along the Aleutian Chain.  Each time we headed back toward our enemy, those nagging feelings of uncertainty returned -- and we wondered if we would make it back.

Next day at 1431 we tied up alongside the USS *Cuyanna* in Kuluk Bay, Adak.  After an hour or so we moved to dock 9, Sweepers Cove, where we tied up to the starboard side of the *Porter*.  *Wren* would remain dockside for eight days, a real treat for us.  We could go on liberty without getting wet in a whaleboat and our bunks remained upright.  Adak had become our favorite port, even though it had no town, few civilians -- and no women.

Captain MacDonald continued his liberal policy of providing two-section liberty while dockside.  This meant we could go on shore every other day if we wanted, and liberties on Adak were serene after Unalaska.  They usually involved eating gee dunks and pogey bait (ice cream and candy) and a movie at the PX.  Often we just ran free in the hills, playing like kids.  It felt good just to blow off steam.

On one of those liberties Jesse Long, Leonard Lamoreaux, and I ran over the barren landscape playing chase or tag.  Jesse got the bright idea of putting a rock on a heavy piece of cord and swinging it overhead like a lariat.  On the snow-covered hills it became an effective way for him to make us "eat dirt."  Their stories in my scrap book still remind me of those simple, fun times.

Task Force 94 left for Attu, February 3, 1945.  Next day at 1219 the cans (destroyers) patrolled outside of Massacre Bay, screening for the entrance of our three cruisers, until 1412 when we moored to buoy 4.  The fleet remained at Attu until February 9, 1945.  Then we left for our fifth crossing to bombard Japan.

# THIRTEEN
# WREN'S FIFTH AND SIXTH CROSSINGS
# TO BOMBARD JAPAN

Seven destroyers and three cruisers of Task Force 94 got underway, leaving *Rowe* and *Stoddard* behind. Our destroyers took up AA screening positions around the cruisers; as always we steered a zigzag course and varied speed while underway with the fleet. Gunner's skills were being sharpened during simulated air attacks, as they fired 902 rounds of 40mm and 1200 rounds of 20mm ammunition at towed sleeves.

During that AA practice, Ken Kutchin was loading his 40mm and recalls a mishap. "I was a loader, pouring clips into mount 43 on the starboard side -- when suddenly the gun exploded in my face! What happened, I wondered! Were we hit? The next thing I knew, Doc Romig was picking a piece of metal out of my left eye with an instrument that resembled a nutpick, and I had powder burns all over my face. The round jammed in the breach and exploded the powder prematurely. Fortunately, the projectile didn't explode or that would have ended it for me. I started to think they were out to get me! While negotiating the sea ladder from the whaleboat, I fell in the icy bay and now this! At least that time I was given a shot of brandy."

*Quartermaster Third Class Ken Kutchin*

Seaman Second Class Joseph Gordon, seriously injured in this same accident, was sent to the medical facility at Attu and later on to Seattle for treatment. The war ended for Joe, when he was eventually discharged.

February 10, Task Force 94 rehearsed for another Matsuwa bombardment. Next day we took up bombarding positions, but operations were canceled again due to clear weather and increased enemy air activity. With the heavy losses U.S. forces had been experiencing to the new Japanese suicide weapon, this decision seemed prudent. We sped away at 25 knots for Attu, arriving in Massacre Bay at 1116 on the 14th, where *Rowe* and *Stoddard* rejoined the Task Force.

Two days later the fleet sailed, this time for Karabu Zaki, Paramushiro. Once again, destroyers took up defensive AA screening of the cruisers and practiced firing at towed sleeves. At 1512 the following day, Task Force 94 came to bombarding position for rehearsal of our next attack.

Lowell Clark, bridge GQ: "At 2036 we were on a southeasterly course of 135 degrees, pondering the go, no go decision, when an excited voice came over the JV phone from the fantail, 'Torpedo wake, torpedo wake,' he shouted. Every man on the bridge saw the torpedo running on an 80 degree heading. It narrowly missed our stern. Since sound waves sent out to detect submarines also had a way of announcing our presence, we ran sonar silent on those raids. From that point, *Bearss* remained behind the Task Force to cover our flanks during final approach. At 2255 the 18th, we increased speed to 25 knots. It became fingernail-biting time, once again."

Reno Pellegrini had his battle dressing station in mount 4 handling room; the hatch opened to the main deck and his first-aid cabinet hung on the "bulkhead" (wall). Reno recalls a frightening incident before and during the bombardment. "Getting to my battle station, I was shocked to find the handling room deck covered with 5-inch projectiles. The protective caps had been removed from the fuses and they were ready to go. I didn't know what the hell they were doing! Checking my supply was like moving through a mine field."

Why did they find it necessary to over-supply the handling room? One could speculate concern about possible suicidal aircraft retaliation, and the Japanese did know we were coming. With continuing bits and pieces about our enemy's new suicide weapons reaching our crew, we all realized that we could be in real danger. Mass Kamikaze attacks in those icy waters, with no chance for air support, would spell disaster for many of our ships.

Jim Hutzel and his mount 4 gun crew were the most "Gung Ho" gang on the ship. *Wren* was poised -- our guns were trained out. In number 4 handling room Reno checked his supplies and Fred Stec passed powder casings up to Harold Branson. Harold, in the cage suspended from the rotating part of the gun above, passed the powder casings through the trap door to Dick Williams, the mount 4 powderman.

Lowell Clark, bridge GQ: "At 2326 I relayed the order to come to a 250 degree heading and reduce speed to 18 knots. Our southwesterly bombarding course took us cross wind, so we picked up a little turbulence as we prepared to open fire."

Reno describes what happened. "We were waiting for the order to commence firing when the ship started to roll. Those projectiles slammed back and forth on the deck. We almost had a heart attack! I grabbed right and left-handed life jackets and started stuffing them in around the projectiles. Then they opened fire. I was relieved when those projectiles were shoved into the hoist for the short trip up to mount 4."

Gunner's Mate Second Class Jim Hutzel, was gun captain in 5-inch mount 4. The other four mounts had boatswain's mates as captains, and Jim was proud of the fact that he was the only gunner's mate to be captain. He describes the feverish pitch in mount 4 during this bombardment.

*Gunner's Mate Second Class Jim Hutzel*

"We had our first round in the breech, *Wren* was poised like a rattlesnake, ready to strike. Williams had taken a second powder casing from Branson, who passed it from his rotating cage in our handling room below and placed it in the tray. Al Trombi, who had a grip like a vise, placed another projectile into the hoist, which carried them from the handling room up to the mount. Bob Malik, who could pull a 54-pound projectile from the hoist with one hand, had gently placed the next projectile in the tray ahead of the powder casing.

"Frank Munoz, to my right in his sight-setting seat, stared at the now-slowly-moving dials. As they moved indicating gun elevation and wind deflection, Frank quickly matched pointers. Tom Hall my pointer, sitting straight ahead of me, did likewise since we were on remote fire. Tom had been on a cruiser before *Wren* that had been shot up pretty badly, so he would mumble to himself when he had a target in his sights.

"Russ Russell my trainer, sat poised at his station. Our 'hot-shellman,' Johnson, had his asbestos gloves on, and stood next to the breech, anticipating that first hot powder casing he would be handling. As those casings slammed out of the breech, his job was to grab them and throw them down a chute to the open deck below. From my platform I looked out of the top of our mount.

"We practiced this procedure until it became automatic. We worked like a well-oiled machine. Each man was a professional. I had confidence in my crew, and always thought we were the best.

"Suddenly I heard the first two short warning beeps followed by a long one, as all of our guns were fired at once. This was our 'go' signal! Our crowded enclosure now became a smoke-filled, dimly lit, potential entrapment. Not a place for the weak or claustrophobic!

"Our hoists rumbled carrying a continuous flow of projectiles to our mount, as one was removed another took its place. Each time the arm slammed closed, sliding its powder and projectile into the breech, Bob and Williams would replace them on the tray.

As the breech opened, Johnson grabbed the hot shell casing. We repeated the process over 100 times. Being that busy left little time for fear until the firing stopped.

"Watching from the top of my mount it seemed like forever before the 76 rounds from the fleet's first salvo exploded on shore. After the first round hit it looked like an eruption, and the rest followed like a huge package of firecrackers. During the next twenty minutes we threw out 102 rounds. The 'cease fire' order was welcome. These memories have vividly remained with me for a lifetime," Jim Hutzel concluded.

Jim had the right to be proud of his crew and the job they did on *Wren*. Their capability of firing 20 or more rounds in a minute had a lot to do with *Wren's* survival at Okinawa.

Seventy men in five gun mounts shared the responsibility of moving 5-inch ammunition from magazines in the bottom of the ship and delivering it to the enemy. The horror stories told about entire 5-inch mounts being blown 150 feet into the air when a magazine exploded is grim evidence of their hazards. Dacre Dunn and John Powell still have nothing but praise for all of *Wren's* gun crews.

Lowell Clark, bridge: "Our task force opened fire at 2330, and continued until 2350, then left on a course of 180 degrees at 25 knots. Many fires could be seen at Karabu Zaki as we made good our withdrawal. At 0009 we secured from GQ and reduced speed to 18 knots. I was relieved from GQ, but lingered on the bridge for a few minutes. At 0017 the task force came to a heading of 090 degrees and set up an AA defensive screen around the cruisers.

"At 0151, some 45 miles from the enemy island, *Wren* picked up two Bogies closing on our formation. GQ sounded, so I was glad I stayed. At 0207 the fleet increased speed to 25 knots, then three minutes later to 28. One enemy plane, on a zig-zag course, closed to three miles. Orders came down to open fire if we could get a satisfactory resolution on the targets.

"We wondered -- is this it! Had they located our position in the darkness? Were we about to be swarmed by enemy planes? On our bombardments, we usually knocked out their shore radar, but if those aircraft found us we could have been smothered by -- suicide planes. The decision to open fire was a big one. Our position would be divulged. To the aircraft, our wakes were not as visible in the rough, northern waters as they were down south. We held fire until the aircraft's range opened, much to the credit of our individual commands. At 1055, we set a zigzag course for Attu. *Wren* arrived February 23, 1945."

Two days later we left for Adak, arriving February 26, and remained until March 8. We spent a day in drydock and replaced our ammunition. The next few days at Adak were spent in various training activities in the area, then we left for Attu, arriving at buoy 4 at 1952, March 9, where we stayed four days.

# Fourteen
# Lingayen Gulf And Iwo Jima
# January, 1945

Admiral Ohnishi's suicide squadrons scored big during the battle of Lingayen Gulf. Following is that story in detail.

The new year started with the U.S. on offensive. Task Unit 77.4.3, the Lingayen Transport Cover Group, bound for the invasion of western Luzon, had a long, arduous three day trip from Manus in the Admiralty Islands, by way of Leyte Gulf.

They traveled through the Surigao Straits into the Mindanao Sea, then south-westerly into the Sulu Sea and northwest along the western edge of Mindoro, into the South China Sea. Coming to a northern heading the route took them off Manila Bay and Clark Field, still occupied by the Japanese. The fleet's location was no mystery and easily plotted. The Japanese were waiting! This was a bold move by U.S. Forces and alarmed the Japanese. When the fleet bypassed Manila they were on a course that could take them to Formosa, or even Japan.

After passing through the Surigao Straits, Task Force 77 encountered a series of air attacks, but air cover destroyed seven Japanese aircraft before they could reach the fleet.

**USS KITKUM BAY, CVE71, JANUARY 1, 1945:**

At 1857 an Oscar broke through air cover and intense AA fire to crash into the carrier. For the second time *Kitkum Bay* fell victim to Kamikazes. This one hit her port side, amidships, at the waterline. At almost the same instant they were hit in the same area by a "friendly" 5-inch shell. In spite of dealing with their casualties, 16 killed and 37 wounded, her crew managed to control the fires.

January 2, *Kitkum Bay*, listing with only one engine, left for two months of battle damage repairs at San Pedro, California. The USS *Kadashan Bay*, CVE76, replaced *Kitkum Bay* on the 3rd.

**USS ORCA, AVP49, JANUARY 2, 1945:**

She was showered with steel and bomb fragments when a Kamikaze crashed close aboard, wounding 6 men.

The same day an unknown minesweeper was sunk near *Orca*, and the Liberty Ship SS IX-225, hit with a bomb and beached to prevent her sinking. In San Pedro Bay, the tanker USS *Cowanseque*, AO70, was crashed into violently, but fortunately the bomb did not explode. They dumped it harmlessly overboard. The tanker lost 2 men killed and 2 wounded. Also, an unknown merchant ship hauling ammunition exploded and disappeared.

**USS OMMANEY BAY, CVE79, JANUARY 4, 1945:**
**BURNING IN THE SULU SEA OFF LUZON, A DESTROYER STANDING BY**

While operating in the Sulu Sea with other ships of Task Force 77 the carrier was attacked by an undetected suicide bomber. He dove for *Ommaney Bay's* island structure, bounced off and crashed into the starboard side. Two bombs were released just before the crash, one penetrated her flight deck and exploded below among fully fueled aircraft. The second passed through the hangar deck, ruptured the fire main on the second deck and exploded near the starboard side.

Under the threat of secondary explosions from bombs and torpedoes, her men struggled against overwhelming fires. With no communication or water to fight fires *Ommaney Bay* was obviously lost. The carrier's topside became an inferno, and her torpedoes were in danger of exploding. Captain H. L. Young's order to "Abandon ship" was passed at 1750. At 1945 *Ommaney Bay* was sent to the bottom with a torpedo fired by the destroyer USS *Burns*, DD588. Two crewmen of assisting destroyers and 95 of *Ommaney Bay's* crew were killed.

Next day the Japanese began to realize where the invasion fleet was headed, and they intensified their efforts to stop them.

**USS LOUISVILLE, CA28, JANUARY 5:**
While in the vicinity of Task Force 77, en route to Lingayen Gulf, two Kamikazes successfully crashed into the cruiser. Fifty men, including her skipper Captain R. L. Hicks were wounded. Despite heavy damage, *Louisville* shelled the beaches of western Luzon and shot down several enemy aircraft before returning to Mare Island for repairs. The cruiser HMS *Australia* was hit in the same action.

**USS MANILA BAY, CVE61 JANUARY 5:**
Shortly after *Louisville* and HMS *Australia* were hit, two Kamikazes dove at *Manila Bay*. At 1750 the first aircraft hit her flight deck, to starboard abaft of the bridge. The second aimed for the bridge, but missed the island and crashed off the fantail. Fires, including two fueled and burning torpedo planes, were soon under control.

*USS Louisville, CA28, January 5, 1945, at the moment of impact.*

In spite of heavy damage and loss of life, the crew managed to patch up CVE61, enough to keep the carrier in action through the invasion of western Luzon. January 17, *Manila Bay* steamed along with a convoy to Leyte, Ulithi, Pearl Harbor, and on to San Diego for repairs. They lost 14 men killed and had 52 wounded.

USS *Savo Island*, CVE78, was also slightly damaged when a Kamikaze grazed her about the same time as *Manila Bay*.

**USS STAFFORD, DE411, JANUARY 5, 1945:**
The USS Goss, DE444, and USS *Ulvert M. Moore*, DE442, were screening the carrier USS *Tulagi*, CVE72, when eight "Zekes" came in low, out of the sun. All ships opened fire at about 8,000 yards, then four of the suicide-bound intruders peeled off to the right and disengaged. The others made their runs on the carrier. Each escort shot down one plane, but the fourth crashed into *Stafford's* starboard side, amidships. Dead in the water and flooding, all but a skeleton crew were transferred to the *Ulvert M. Moore*. After *Stafford* became stabilized by her remaining crew, she stayed in the area until January 11, when her full crew went back aboard. She joined a slow convoy back to Leyte for temporary repairs, then started her long trip home to Mare Island Navy Yard.

Five additional auxiliary ships are known to have been crashed into during the four days of movement towards the U.S. landing at Lingayen Gulf.

Fast fleet carrier squadrons had carried out raids on Luzon, and heavy fleet ships were in place to bombard shore installations on January 6. The destroyer minesweepers started sweeping operations, and the cruisers, battleships and destroyers bombarded. The Army and Marines stormed ashore, on January 9, 1945.

January 6, major fleet units gathered in Lingayen Gulf, where pre-invasion bombarding had begun, and Japanese suicide attacks intensified.

*USS COLUMBIA, CL56, JANUARY 6, 1945:*
*EXPLOSION ON THE MAIN DECK FROM A KAMIKAZE AT 1729*

The cruiser, included among the heavy fleet units, began to bombard when the suicide attacks started. In a short time, CL56 was badly damaged by the crashes of two Kamikazes. The first hit close aboard, followed by a second that crashed into her port quarter. That plane and its bomb penetrated two decks before it exploded with a tremendous impact. Damage was extensive. Her after turrets were put out of action, the ship was on fire, and 13 crewmen were killed with 44 wounded. Decisive damage control efforts saved the ship from further secondary explosions, as two magazines were promptly flooded to extinguish fires. *Columbia* remained on station, bombarding with her two operative turrets.

January 9, the morning of the invasion that would complete the Philippine liberation, the cruiser headed towards shore. Surrounded by landing craft, with limited maneuverability, she came under attack again. For the third time she was hit by a Kamikaze. Six gun directors and one mount were destroyed and the ship was ablaze. Twenty-four men were killed and 97 wounded, leaving *Columbia* short handed, but they saved their ship. That night CL56 sailed for San Pedro Bay, guarding empty transports; after temporary patchwork, she sailed to the west coast for permanent repair. *Columbia* received the -- Navy Unit Commendation -- for this operation.

### USS NEW MEXICO, BB40, JANUARY 6, 1945:

During pre-invasion bombardments the battleships were under continuous suicide attacks. Captain R. W. Fleming was killed when a Kamikaze hit the bridge. After temporary repairs, they remained on their station until the invasion January 9; then she sailed to Pearl Harbor for further repairs. Twenty-nine men were killed, along with their captain and 87 were wounded. The battleship returned to service during the Okinawa Campaign, just to be crashed into again on May 11, 1945.

### USS CALIFORNIA, BB44, JANUARY 6, 1945:

While bombarding shore installations with other heavy fleet ships at Lingayen Gulf, the battleship was also hit by a Kamikaze. Forty-four of her crew were killed and 155 wounded, but they extinguished fires, made repairs and continued to bombard. January 23, *California* sailed to Bremerton Navy Yard where permanent repairs were completed. BB44 returned to action at Okinawa June 15, 1945.

### USS MISSISSIPPI, BB41, JANUARY 6, 1945:

The battleship was the third to be hit while bombarding Lingayen beaches, on this day. The suicide pilot made good his pact with death when he crashed near the waterline. Despite damage, she stayed in action only to be hit again, at Okinawa, on June 5th, 1945.

January 6, as usual, destroyers were in the middle of the action and six were crashed into by suicide planes.

### USS O'BRIEN, DD725, JANUARY 6, 1945:

The destroyer, while screening the invasion fleet and fighting off numerous aircraft, was crashed into on the port side of her fantail. *O'Brien* stayed on station for several days then sailed to Manus Island, for repairs. February 10, found *O'Brien* back in action. But, her war would end at Okinawa March 27, 1945 -- after a second Kamikaze crashed her decks.

## USS ALLEN M. SUMNER, DD692, JANUARY 6, 1945:

While en route to join the Lingayen invasion force, a suicide plane crashed into the destroyer's after funnel and torpedo mount. With heavy damage, 14 killed and 29 wounded, they stayed in action until January 14. *Allen M. Sumner* then returned to San Francisco for battle repairs.

## USS WALKE, DD723, JANUARY 6, 1945:

American minesweepers started the necessary, but dangerous job of clearing mines before the Luzon invasion. *Walke* was called upon to protect them. No sooner had they started sweeping when the minesweepers came under suicide attack. Four enemy "Oscars" came at *Walke*, low on the water, from her starboard side. The first two were quickly splashed as the 2200 ton Allen M. Sumner class destroyer opened fire, but despite many hits, the third suicide pilot pressed home his attack and crashed into her port bridge. With her superstructure ablaze, *Walke* was without communication, radar, gyro repeaters, and electricity; however she fought on. The 250-pound bomb passed completely through the CIC room and exited the starboard side without exploding. *Walke* had heavy damage. Her gun and torpedo directors were gone and the bridge severely damaged.

The fourth Oscar followed on the tail of his leader. He dove at *Walke* without mercy. The starboard 40 and 20mm guns along with mount 3 firing locally, saved the ship. They splashed the Kamikaze close aboard.

Despite serious injuries and extensive burns, Commander George F. Davis moved control of his ship to a secondary conn, (control station) aft. He remained in command until he was sure *Walke* would stay afloat; then turned the conn over to his executive officer. He died shortly thereafter. The captain received the Medal of Honor, posthumously. The USS *Davis*, DD937, was named after him -- for his heroism on that day. No other casualty figures were provided in the ship's history.

Walke remained with Task Unit 78.4.2 until January 10, then left for the long voyage home to Mare Island Navy Yard. The destroyer returned to action May 10, at Okinawa.

January 2, the Task Force fought off suicidal air attacks in the Mindanao Sea. They were at the entrance to Lingayen Gulf in early morning on January 6.

## USS LONG, DMS12, JANUARY 6, 1945:

After undergoing a period of repairs and training at Manus Island, *Long* joined the command ship USS *Hovey*, DMS11, *Southard*, DMS10; *Palmer*, DMS5; *Brooks*, DPD10; *Chandler*, DMS9, and *Howard*, DMS7, then got underway for the Luzon invasion. Theirs would be the dangerous task of clearing mines from Lingayen Gulf, ahead of the invasion force.

The minesweepers started their hazardous job at daylight. At 0800 the Kamikazes attacked. While defending themselves, they managed to complete their first sweep.

Shortly after noon, just after starting the second sweep, two "Zekes" headed straight at *Long*. After slipping her sweeping gear, *Long* came to 25 knots and opened fire. As if defying her gunfire, the suicide pilot stayed on his direct course for *Long's* port side. He crashed one foot above the waterline, below the bridge, causing a huge explosion. With secondary explosions and raging fires amidships, *Long* was a tangled inferno. Without power, internal communications, and unable to fight fires, Commanding Officer LT Stanley Caplin gave permission for the men trapped on the forecastle to leave the ship. Due to a misunderstanding the crew aft also followed the abandon ship order. *Hovey*, stood by and quickly retrieved *Long's* crewmen.

Still believing his ship to be salvageable, LT Caplin, now aboard the tug USS *Apache*, ATF67, prepared to lead a salvage party. However, continuing air attacks prevented all attempts to save her. Later the same afternoon, a second suicide plane crashed in the same spot. This Kamikaze demolished the bridge and broke her back. *Long* -- capsized and sank the following morning.

*Hovey* picked up 149 survivors from the veteran ship. Casualty information was not available in her ship's history.

### USS SOUTHARD, DMS10, JANUARY 6, 1945:
While sweeping mines under the protection of *Ward*, the destroyer minesweeper came under suicide attack. Late in the afternoon while fighting off suicide planes one broke through her defenses and crashed into the after stack. The engine embedded itself and the fuselage tore a six-foot-wide gash in the deck as it exited the opposite side of the ship. Quickly, *Southard's* crew cut her sweeping gear loose and retired to carry out emergency repairs. Within 14 hours the DMS resumed her duties for 5 more days, before getting underway to Pearl Harbor for much needed repairs.

*Southard* returned to her sweeping duties at Okinawa the latter part of May. She narrowly missed destruction for the second time -- when a Kamikaze crashed 15 yards ahead of that plucky DMS.

### USS BROOKS, APD10, JANUARY 6, 1945:
The ship had been drawing double duty as a fast transport and destroyer mine-sweeper. While assisting the other ships clearing Lingayen Gulf, a Japanese Kamikaze crashed into her port side. Three of her crewmen were killed and 11 wounded. The forward engine room was flooded, severing auxiliary steam lines, and fires were out of control. Dead in the water, the SS *Watch Hill* towed her to San Pedro, California. *Brooks* was considered a total loss, decommissioned and sold for scrap.

### USS HOVEY, (DD208) DMS11, JANUARY 7, 1945:
While *Hovey* led sweeping operations on January 6, the USS *Chandler* and *Hovey* splashed one suicide plane at about 0800. Shortly after 1200, having observed the destruction of the last two ships of the sweeping column, *Hovey* slipped her gear and went to the rescue of *Brooks* and *Long*. As *Hovey* attempted to move alongside of the badly

damaged *Long*, they were greeted with raging fires and many secondary explosions. Efforts to assist were impossible. *Hovey* stood helplessly beside her stricken sister ship. She did, however, pick up 149 survivors. As darkness settled in, the destroyer mine-sweepers retired to patrol the entrance of Lingayen Gulf.

At 0425 the following day, enemy aircraft were picked up on radar, and it started all over again. Within 30 minutes a Kamikaze headed for *Hovey*. Flying low on the water from her starboard quarter, he passed by ahead of *Hovey*. Another aircraft made a determined effort to get her, but gunfire from *Chandler* set him ablaze. He passed by very low overhead and crashed on *Hovey's* starboard beam.

At 0455, the instant the burning plane crashed, *Hovey* was struck on the starboard side by a torpedo. (Possibly dropped by the aircraft.) The torpedo entered and exploded in the after engine room and lights and power were lost instantly. The veteran destroyer's back was broken. Two minutes later the bow rose vertically and stern first -- she sank! *Chandler* stood by to assist and recovered 229 men from the stricken *Hovey*. Twenty-four of her crewmen were killed along with 24 survivors from *Brooks* and *Long*, picked up the night before.

Sinking of the *Hovey* and *Long* hit close to Captain MacDonald's heart. *Long* had been his first destroyer and *Hovey* his first destroyer command, Captain Mac took their loss very hard. He left *Hovey* around April 5, 1944, just after completing the Solomon Islands Campaign.

### USS PALMER, (DD161) DMS5, JANUARY 7, 1945:
At about 1545, while preoccupied in sweeping operations and under almost continuous air attacks, a violent explosion knocked out her port low-pressure turbine; they brought in the sweeping gear. It's not known what caused the explosion since no aircraft were observed at that time; however since almost all Japanese retaliations were suicidal, it could possibly have been a suicide boat, or submarine. Built from wood and riding very low in the water, suicide boats were difficult to detect. In slight swells, they could ride the valleys on a crisscross course and get through undetected. *Palmer* left the formation to make repairs.

At 1840, a twin-engine bomber singled out the already crippled destroyer mine-sweeper, for destruction. Flying low overhead, he dropped two bombs hitting *Palmer's* port side. *Palmer* sank in six minutes, as fires billowed smoke skyward. Two crewmen were killed, 26 missing, and 38 wounded. Survivors were picked up by her sister ships.

### USS KADASHAN BAY, CVE76, JANUARY 8, 1945:
The escort carrier had just arrived at Lingayen Gulf. Her aircraft had been launched on an early morning strike, when she was hit directly below the bridge. The Kamikaze caused heavy damage, fires, and flooding. The ship's repair party quickly responded, then they sailed to Leyte. Twenty-nine men were killed and 22 wounded.

After additional temporary repairs, *Kadashan Bay* left for San Francisco for complete rebuilding.

### USS CALLAWAY, APD35, JANUARY 8, 1945:

As they approached Lingayen Gulf from the south with the Blue Beach Attack Group, the force came under heavy Kamikaze attack. Despite heavy AA fire, a suicider determined to die, crashed on the starboard wing of the troop transport's bridge. Her damage control party kept material damage to a minimum and fires were extinguished. Despite 29 men killed and 22 wounded, *Callaway* carried out her mission before retiring to Ulithi for repairs.

### USS LEROY WILSON, DE414, JANUARY 10, 1945:

When on antisubmarine patrol near the entrance to Lingayen Gulf, the destroyer escort came under Kamikaze attack. A twin-engine bomber came at her bow, 25 feet above the water, and his wing crashed into the port side. The explosion killed 6 and seriously wounded 7 gunners. Maximum efforts by her gunners managed to divert the suicide pilot and saved the ship from total destruction. Heavily damaged, *LeRoy Wilson* stayed on patrol until relieved later the same day, when she sailed to Manus for badly-needed repairs. They returned to fight the Kamikazes again at Okinawa.

### USS WAR HAWK, AP186, JANUARY 10, 1945:

At 0410, under cover of darkness, a suicide boat snuck in on the still partially-loaded transport and crashed into her port side at number 3 hold. The ship shuddered under the tremendous explosion, which blew a 25 foot hole in her side. With 61 men killed, no power, and the engine room flooding, her crew fought desperately to save their ship. With only dim emergency lighting and without ventilation, the temperatures rose to an unbearable level. But, the huge gash in her side had to be repaired.

While fighting off air attacks, the crew disembarked her remaining troops and unloaded their mechanized equipment. Her crew nicknamed their ship "Sitting Duck" as she sat off Lingayen Gulf until the next day. On January 13, while en route to Leyte, her gunners shot down still another would-be suicider. The Kamikaze crashed close aboard and sprayed her bow with gasoline.

After temporary repairs at San Pedro Bay, *War Hawk* sailed for Manus, arriving January 30. After entering drydock her port side was sufficiently repaired to make the long voyage home, to San Francisco, for extensive repairs.

### USS DUPAGE, APA 41, JANUARY 10, 1945:

The transport had landed her troops near San Fabian, then casualties were taken aboard from the beaches and other ships. By the evening of January 10 they were reloaded with wounded and ready to leave the area when they came under attack. Despite heavy antiaircraft fire a Kamikaze crashed into the port side and severely damaged *DuPage*. Five crewmen were blown overboard and quickly retrieved by escorting destroyers. Raging fires were extinguished, but persistently reignited.

Despite her losses of 35 killed and 136 wounded, APA41 managed to fulfill her duty as guide ship. She arrived at Leyte three days later. While making emergency repairs, *Dupage* transferred the casualties to other ships. They landed additional troops at Zambales, Luzon, and left for San Francisco by way of Manus and Pearl Harbor, arriving March 10. *Dupage* disembarked marines picked up en route, then she entered drydock for extensive battle repairs.

### USS BELKNAP, (DD251) APO34, JANUARY 11, 1945

*Belknap* operated as a reconnaissance ship and performed selective bombarding missions during the initial landings. Then an aircraft hit her number 2 stack and knocked out both engine rooms. Despite 38 killed and 49 wounded, her crew managed to extinguish fires and prevent their ship from sinking. Over the next seven days, while dead in the water, her crew continued making as many temporary repairs as possible. January 18, the USS *Hidatsa*, ATF102, towed *Belknap* to Manus, Admiralty Islands, for temporary repairs. Then APD34 got underway for the Philadelphia Navy Yard, where she was sold for scrap. The crew received the -- Presidential Unit Citation.

### USS GILLIGAN, DE508, JANUARY 12, 1945

During screening operations for "Attack Group Able," the destroyer escort came under attack by a Kamikaze. <u>As the suicider closed on DE508, one of her crewmen panicked. He jumped on the 5-inch director and threw it off target</u>. The DE was only able to fire 14 rounds of 5-inch, so the pilot had a relatively easy time getting through to crash directly into the muzzle of number two 40mm. **The above underlined statement is highly contested by *Gilligan's* Captain, Officers, and Crewmen. THIS AUTHOR HAS CHECKED ALL LOGS AND HAND WRITTEN NOTES AND I FIND NO MENTION OF A BLUEJACKET JUMPING ON ANY GUN DIRECTOR!**

While extinguishing raging fires, *Gilligan's* crew managed to keep the ship seaworthy; however 12 men were killed and 12 wounded. After temporary repairs at Leyte, the DE left for Pearl Harbor.

### USS SALAMAUS, CVE96, JANUARY 13, 1945:

The escort carrier, originally named *Angula Bay*, ACV96, and reclassified July 15, 1943, arrived at Lingayen Gulf on January 6. Her planes blasted the beaches before and during the invasion. Just before 0900 on the 13th, a Kamikaze bomber carrying two 250kg bombs crashed into the carrier's flight deck. The flight deck, hangar deck, and spaces below, became an inferno. One bomb failed to explode, but punched a hole through the starboard side at the waterline. With 15 killed and over 80 wounded, her surviving crewmen fought to save their ship. They had no power, communication, or steering control, one engine room was flooding and her starboard engine knocked out. They had to fight for survival. Heavily damaged, CVE96 continued to defend herself and shot down two additional Kamikazes.

Eventually the carrier's fires and flooding were under control. After temporary repairs she sailed to San Francisco, arriving February 26. *Salamaus* returned to Guam May 20, then became damaged again in the Okinawa typhoon on June 5. That forced her back to Guam for repairs.

## USS ZEILIN, AP9, JANUARY 13, 1945:

The transport arrived off San Fabin beachhead January 11th for the second phase of the assault on western Luzon. On the evening of the 12th, they had successfully disembarked her troops and off-loaded subsequent equipment, then grouped with a fast transport convoy, she headed for Leyte the same evening.

The following morning a single Kamikaze closed the convoy from cloud cover and headed straight at *Zeilin's* port quarter. The suicide pilot quickly changed direction, momentarily and headed for the *Mount Olympus*, then back toward *Zeilin*. Successfully getting through AA fire, the Kamikaze's right wing struck the port kingpost and boom that served number 6 hatch. The fuselage crashed into her superstructure and blew it away, along with several staterooms. The plane's engine entered then exited the superstructure, winding up in a landing craft. Ten of *Zeilin's* crewmen were killed and 30 wounded. After temporary repairs at Leyte, they sailed to Ulithi for more patchwork. In March, *Zeilin* returned to San Francisco for permanent repairs. Her war ended.

## USS MADDOX, DD731, JANUARY 21, 1945:

The destroyer had completed her duty in Lingayen Gulf with Task Force 38.1, then carried the war closer to Japan and operated in the South and East China Sea. While off Formosa, *Maddox* took a suicide plane aboard. The ship returned to Ulithi for repairs, then returned to action off the Japanese Home Islands on March 14. *Maddox* survived the Okinawa operations as a bombarding ship and plane guard for the carriers.

## USS TICONDEROGA, CV14, JANUARY 21, 1945:
## LISTING AND ON FIRE AFTER KAMIKAZE CRASHES

After carrying out raids along the Chinese coast and Hong Kong, Task Force 38 turned its attention to Formosa. While CV14's aircraft raided the Pescadores and Sakishima Gunto, the fleet came under suicide attack. A single-engine Japanese plane scored a hit on the *Langley* with a glide-bomb. Seconds later, a second Divine Wind intruder swooped out of clouds and crash into *Ticonderoga*. He hit her flight deck next to number 2, 5-inch mount. The bomb penetrated her deck and exploded just over the hangar deck. Fires ignited among planes stored on the deck. Death and destruction flourished. Captain Dixie Kiefer, ordered immediate flooding of all magazines and other compartments to prevent secondary explosions.

They corrected a 10 degree port list with flooding, then induced a 10 degree starboard list which allowed firefighters to wash much of the fire debris overboard. Fires were extinguished by heading downwind to prevent fanning of the flames.

Smoke and flames from the crippled *Ticonderoga* were like a magnet for other Kamikaze pilots in the area. They swarmed like vultures to the attack. Three were quickly shot down by the carrier's gunners, but the fourth struck home. Heavy damage and loss of life was inflicted, once again. The plane smashed into her starboard side near the island. Ensuing fires and explosions killed or injured another 100 crewmen, including Captain Kiefer. In spite of overwhelming odds, her crew fought to save their ship.

*USS Ticonderoga, CV14, January 21, 1945*

Shortly after 1400 the following day, escorted by USS *Halsey Powell*, DD686, *Ticonderoga* painfully retired. The carrier arrived at Ulithi, January 24, then four days later they left for the Bremerton Navy Yard and extensive battle repairs. June 1 found *Ticonderoga* back in the center of action off Kyushu. *Wren* joined her and the other Third Fleet carriers, after Okinawa, for 91 days off Japan.

Reliving those individual life and death stories, we begin to realize the devastation, hysteria, and the courage of each man on every ship. Imagine! What would you do first? Attend the wounded, put out fires that were consuming everything, try to keep water out of the ship -- or perhaps jump over the side to save yourself?

Trying to do anything -- they walked through body parts of the dead, listened to agonizing cries of wounded friends and expected to die themselves at any instant. Fortunately the Navy had men trained in firefighting, flood control and emergency medical procedures. Think of their agony and trauma. They were -- scarred for life.

## IWO JIMA

The chain called the Volcano Islands, isolated by the vast Pacific Ocean, proved to be one of the most grueling and fierce land battles of the Pacific War. The Japanese suicidal attacks were severely handicapped during this battle. Iwo Jima had three airports, and near by Chi-Chi Jima had at least one, but anything that even resembled an airfield, within flying distance, had been pulverized by the U.S. Japanese air retaliation to the invasion seemed almost nonexistent. February 19, the 4th and 5th Marine Divisions landed on the southeast end of the island.

On February 21, at 1700, the only day of significant Japanese air retaliation, sixteen Kamikazes, mostly all carrier based "Jills," attacked. Nearly all suicide attacks up to this time came from land-based aircraft, and the Japanese were not known to have any carriers in the area. Still, at least three of the attacking Jills -- crashed into American ships. Where did they come from? Were they all considered suicide planes?

### USS KEOKUK, CMC6, FEBRUARY 21, 1945:
The net-cargo ship, reclassified AKN4, crashed into by a Jill sustained heavy damage, and 17 men were killed with 44 wounded. *Keokuk* was hit in the first strikes at 1700. She went to Leyte for repairs.

*USS Saratoga, CV3, February 21, 1945*
### USS SARATOGA, CV3, FEBRUARY 21, 1945:
The second and last attacks known to this author came the same night at 1900 when a bomb hit the carrier. For the sixth time this day -- *Saratoga* had been hit. Severe damage to the "Fighting Lady" caused the loss of at least 123 men, and forced her back to

Bremerton for repairs.  Still, from the ship's history, it is not clear if her attackers tried to crash dive on the carrier.

**USS BISMARK SEA, CVE95, FEBRUARY 21, 1945:**
In the same action, the *Bismark Sea* was crashed into by two Kamikazes.  She sank in 90 minutes!   At least 318 men were killed.

*USS Bismark Sea, CVE95, February 21, 1945*

## USS LUNGA POINT, CVE94, FEBRUARY 21, 1945:

The escort carrier came under attack, but believe it or not *Lunga Point* sustained only slight damage, while shooting down three Jills.

*USS Lunga Point, CVE 94, February 21, 1945*

*The Australian Cruiser, Australia, was also hit in Lingayen Gulf.*

# Fifteen
# Wren's Seventh And Eighth
# Crossing To Bombard Japan

As the battle to liberate the Philippines wound down, so did *Wren's* Aleutian duty.

March 13, at 0831, we got underway for our seventh crossing to bombard Matsuwa. Task Force 94 cruised on a heading of 230 to 240 degrees while continuing our usual zigzag, variable-speed, course. *Smalley* was 16,000 yards ahead of the formation as picket ship, while the others conducted various training exercises. At 0912 the following day we went to GQ, for "abandon ship" and bombarding drill..

When *Wren* approached radar range from Matsuwa, they dispatched *Porter* to investigate a surface contact. It turned out to be a rain squall.

At 2125 March 15, *Wren's* radar picked up Matsuwa fifty-eight miles away, and two minutes later we started our high-speed approach. At 2145, radar picked up a second surface contact six miles away. We went to GQ, then proceeded to the target without incident. At 2230 our Task Force headed straight at Matsuwa.

LT Howard Cook, bridge: "It was a black night, cold and damp, with limited visibility. Our fleet was fanned out on final approach to bombard. We were to execute a PARA (pre-arranged bombardment course) of 035 at a specific time. This involved a starboard turn, which would put our fleet cruising in a column.

"For some reason still unknown to me, I walked out on the open bridge where a voice tube provided communication between there and the pilot house. I gave the order for the course change. A few moments later, as we turned, it became apparent that the destroyer to our starboard failed to execute her turn.

"All of a sudden she appeared, broadside, directly in front of us. *Wren* was about to ram her! I shouted the order, 'Reduce speed, all ahead one third.' Our man on the engine order telegraph responded immediately.

"Captain Mac strode out to the open bridge and asked, 'What are you up to this time?' There wasn't enough time to answer so I made a sweeping gesture and pointed at the ship crossing our bow, about a hundred yards away. The other destroyer was still apparently unaware that she had missed the course change. The Captain emitted a friendly growl and stalked back into the pilot house. *Wren's* engines churned back to fleet speed."

This was an excellent call by Howard. If he had overreacted by calling an emergency stop, we could have been hit from behind. I also saw that near miss from my repair party station. I thought for sure, we were about to ram one of our own destroyers.

While counting down the time before our bombardment, weather lifted in the target area and visibility improved.

Lowell Clark describes the action from the bridge: "Suddenly, at 2233 the black sky became like daylight. Ear-piercing concussion followed as the big guns of our Task Force let go with their first salvos. Sixty-seven blinding flashes penetrated the smoke filled darkness, as deadly messengers were sent to their slow but sure -- rendezvous with death. Each destructive projectile moved slowly, like a tiny star, followed by another every ten seconds. Several soon followed in each trajectory en route to their assigned targets. The first sixty-seven rounds exploded simultaneously, with unbelievable accuracy.

"With each ship concentrating all of its firepower on one designated target area, this process was repeated one hundred times. Airfields, fuel storage, and ammunition dumps were the targets of this raid. As we departed at flank speed secondary explosions and fires verified our successful mission."

In spite of problems inside of two mounts, we fired 497 rounds and our bombardment went smoothly. One man was injured on the 59th salvo in mount 3, when a pin sheered on the hydraulic ram.

In Bill Ferguson's mount 1 they were feverishly feeding the heavy powder casings and projectiles onto the tray, when a mishap occurred. Dan Wann describes it: "With the dimly-lit, smoke-filled, interior highlighted by the glow of firing instrument panels, the atmosphere inside our gun mount during bombardments felt scary. The tight enclosure housed Bill Ferguson, gun captain, who looked out of the hatch on top of our mount; Poppe set the sights, Richard Dugan was pointer, we had a range finder, powder-man, projectile-man, and I was hot shell-man.

"We spent many hours practicing our speed and rhythm on the simulator, available for that purpose. Our crew achieved twenty-two rounds per minute, which came in handy at Okinawa. After a firing sequence, near the end of our hundredth round -- suddenly there was no response. It was deadly quite inside our mount. We had a hang fire! This created a dangerous situation! The barrel was very hot and the round could explode. If we opened the breech, it could explode in our faces.

"They passed the word of our problem, so the gunner's mate came running over. Quick action taken by him and Bill, to cool the barrel and get everyone out, possibly prevented disaster. They placed a hose in the muzzle and flushed cold water inside."

*First Class Gunner's Mate Joe Reinders*

The gunner's mate who came running over was Gunner's Mate First Class Joe Reinders. He picks up the story at that point.

"I came aboard *Wren* as a second class gunner's mate. At that time I was in charge of mount one. After getting word about the hang fire, with Bill Ferguson's help, I cleared the mount and started cooling the barrel. After twenty or thirty minutes we decided to open the breech. I took the powder casing and quickly handed it to Bill. He threw it overboard! To remove the projectile, I put a short shot in the breach and fired it. A sigh of relief was given by all hands!

"After advancement to first class, I was placed in charge of all main batteries, on the *Wren*."

Although it seemed like routine at the time, this was a dangerous thing to have to do. Instead of telling their stories to me, every man involved could be dead! Acts of heroism were commonplace in those trying, dangerous days

There was a lot of anxiety before each raid and we were becoming confident about the successful outcome. It seemed like we were invincible. Very little news reached us about the new Japanese Kamikaze weapon. Had we forgotten what would happen if we were sunk? With no air support, this could be likely if we received a heavy counterattack.

The weather was relatively clear and the seas calm, for north Pacific waters, as we made good our high-speed departure. Task Force 94 set a zigzag course, on a 090 heading, and varied speed from 27 to 30 knots. Once again we hit our enemy where it hurt most -- at home.

*Wren* returned to Attu at 1659 on March 17th, where we moored to the starboard side of the middle pier. We took on ammunition to replace what had been fired, plus eight hundred forty extra rounds of 40 and 20mm shells. Did they know something we did not? That is a lot of extra antiaircraft ammunition. Word came down we were going back to bombard Japan, again. At 0843 the next morning we left the pier and moored to buoy 4 in Massacre Bay.

On the 18th and 19th, liberty was granted to both the port and starboard watches. By now we knew every rock and tree that did not exist on that tiny island. But, we still went over just to stop the rolling.

Dan Wann went fishing in small streams running through the soft, boggy ground of the flat land. "I took a three barbed hook on a string and snagged the most beautiful salmon you have ever seen," Dan recalls.

*Wren's* officers, including Captain Mac, also took advantage of those times to relieve anxiety ashore. Pat Olson, widow of First Lieutenant Frank Olson, recalls one such liberty.

"I've heard that story so often I feel as though I was there. Captain Mac, my husband, the Admiral, and a few other officers had spent the evening together, sampling the wares of the officers' club.

"On the way to their ship, in the dark, they dropped the Admiral off at the USS *Richmond*. The bay was a little choppy so the Admiral had to negotiate the very precarious sea ladder. The others being in a talkative, jovial, mood forgot about the Admiral for a few seconds after he stepped off the captain's gig, onto the ladder.

*First Lt Frank Olson*

"Eventually, someone did look up and panic quickly suppressed their mood. The Admiral was gone! My husband Frank, joined others reaching into the icy sea trying to locate the Admiral. He was not to be found!

"In the meantime Mac felt the call of 'nature', so he went back to the stern to relieve himself. The others frantically reached over the side, to try and find the Admiral. Suddenly, one of the men felt him and struggled to get him aboard.

"During the confusion and anxiety, the Admiral surfaced where Captain Mac was about -- 'mid-stream'. That's right, he caught it right in the face! The Admiral was so happy about *Wren's* officers heroically saving his life, that he did not even realize what happened.

"Next day the Admiral called Captain Mac, saying: 'I'm putting you in for a medal for saving my life.' Mac -- graciously declined his generous offer."

As usual, Reno and I were looking for some sort of devilment to get into. On this occasion, I had just left the liberty boat and walked down the boardwalk in a crowd of people when along came Reno, running toward the liberty boats. I thought he was looking for me so I yelled, "Reno, I'm over here." He looked over his shoulder as he continued running, with his usual big silly grin, and yelled: 'I can't stop now. I'll see you later on the ship.'

Well, in a few minutes it all made sense, here came two shore patrolmen running in the same direction. Later, back on board, he told a story about getting some guff from a doctor at the hospital. He had been over after medical supplies and had a slight misunderstanding. But that was our Reno. We had a lot of good times together on the *Wren*. About all we could do while on shore, anyway, was drink a little 3.2 beer, eat some ice cream, or occasionally take in a movie.

Weather permitting, Captain Mac continued his liberal policy of movies in the mess hall, every night. John Thedford, second class electrician, replaced our movies each time we got back. He was very popular on the ship.

On the 19th, rumors spread throughout *Wren* that we were going back to take another shot at the Japanese. We had hit them four times, once in the light of day. Would they get angry one of these times? We all felt like we were pushing our luck; so far away in the Japs back yard. What if they were waiting for us? A lot of concern about the suicide attacks began to spread throughout the crew.

During our few days at Attu the war clouds continued to build over Okinawa. March 15th, eleven minesweepers, including several high speed DMS's, (destroyer mine-sweepers) showed up and started to sweep the sea channels. Only one of eleven ships in Mine Division 20 survived those first days, unscratched. U.S. fast carrier task forces had paid the enemy several visits, leaving little doubt about our next major move in the Pacific.

Task Force 94 had also been getting more bold with attacks, the last two occurred in near-daylight with good weather conditions. We wondered what surprises might await us on one of those brazen attacks. What if they decided to get us with several hundred Kamikazes?

On March 20, 1945 at 0752, *Wren* got underway for her eighth trip across the mouth of the Bering Sea. Our target, once again, was Suribachi Wan, Paramushiro. On this trip we encountered the worst icing conditions while we were in the Aleutians. *Wren* looked like one big iceberg. Everything forward was covered with about three inches, and her heavy life nets were a solid wall of ice.

The morning of the second day, only a few hours from our target area, I had to make some electrical repairs in mount 1. Approaching the bow, the icy decks along with the heavy bounce made my footing very treacherous.

Getting into the mount also turned out to be a chore. Entrance through a hatch had about six levered closures, dogged tight. To get in I had to negotiate two steps while holding on to grab-bars, but space between the steps was a solid maze of ice. The grab-bars and hatch dogs with ice them, were several inches in diameter. Before doing anything, I went back to the electric shop for a hammer to chop ice. As far as we could see in the bright, clear sunlight, icebergs were floating on the ocean. It seemed like a small lake, surrounded by land.

*Typical Aleutian icing. View from bow looking aft, mount 1 to left.*

At 1741, operations were canceled. Heavy enemy air activity picked up by radar and reduced maneuverability because of icebergs, made this decision seem wise. We left for Attu at our usual high rate of speed. Considering the thousands of suicide aircraft expected to be deployed against the U.S. at Okinawa, this raid would not have been worth the risk. Every destroyer would be needed. Our Task Force sped away at 25 knots.

On destroyers, each group of people, skilled or unskilled, had their own little domain. The deck crew had the boatswain's locker, radio and sonar the radio shack, gun crews the handling rooms, carpenters, pipe fitters and metal workers had the carpenter shop, electricians and machinists mates the electric shop, and so on. Outsiders invading someone else's turf were usually less than welcome. I guess this came about because of the crowded condition we lived under.

*Mount one in a white out.*

While steaming back through the icebergs to Attu, Danny Wann, Al Copson, and Barney Pullen were among the usual gang of seamen hanging out in and around the forward boatswain's locker. They always had their pot of coffee and a lot of 'scuttlebutt' (rumors) to exchange.

Danny recalls an incident on that return trip: "We were on a break enjoying a cup of coffee as best we could, while trying to maintain our footing. Our locker was all the way in the bow of the ship so the bounce, even in relatively calm seas, was difficult to handle. We've actually had the coffee jump out of our cup. The bow dropped over a big swell and all of a sudden we were knocked off of our feet. *Wren* must have hit something! We ran topside to see what happened and found the entire bow covered with blubber and guts. We hit a whale. By the time we got to where we could attempt a cleanup, the mess had frozen, and we had to chip and scrub."

We arrived safely back at Attu at 0803, March 23rd. Because bad weather moved in, *Wren* got underway again; it was always safer riding out a storm at sea. Our Task Force headed for Adak arriving at 1303, On March 25.

For the next five days *Wren* moored alongside the *Bearss* at buoy 1, Sweepers Cove. We were on vacation again, in the garden spot of the Pacific. Many poems

*Close up of frozen life lines.*

have been written about the desolation and loneliness of the treeless Aleutian Islands. The only buildings that could stand against the wind were Quonset huts. They had roofs that started at ground level, formed a large half circle and returned to the ground, they came in

116

a variety of sizes for different purposes. (They were all built in this fashion.) But, we always enjoyed the break from shipboard routine and the view of civilization, ashore.

Medic, Reno Pellegrini had access to hypodermic needles, so we got the bright idea of making a squirt gun. I cut the small point off from a very large syringe, filled it with water and the fine stream would shoot thirty feet. It was amazing. By putting the tip of the needle between our fingers and flexing our wrists against the plunger, it became a very subtle instrument of pleasure or aggravation, depending on which end you were on.

Occasionally, I accompanied John Thedford in the wardroom when he ran movies, for the officers. On that particular evening, Reno also joined us with our new found toy. We selected an officer we were not particularly fond of, then gave him just a few drops. He would slap at his face and look up to see where the water had fallen from. Allowing a little time lapse for him to pass it off, we gave him a second zinger and so on. We carried a small vial of replacement water, to provide equal opportunity for other officer targets. They were all fair game!

Those targets were selected by both of us and the subtle treatment continued throughout most of the movie. But, being subtle was not enough for my Italian buddy. He selected an officer who had been giving him a particularly hard time and with both hands gave him a full broadside, emptying the entire vial. Well that did it... He jumped up yelling, "Turn on the lights." Both Reno and I sat there looking like two innocent little kids, we asked, "Who, me?". To this day they probably don't know exactly what happened.

Between March 30th and April 18th, *Wren* took part in extensive battle practice. We went out to sea every morning and back into the harbor at night, as if we were starting all over again.

During my first five months on *Wren*, life had improved very little. The mess cooks were still mixing my gravy and dessert together, and the 'deck apes' still hurried to get the deck roped off before I got there. They continually painted or chipped paint, usually on the dry leeward side, and quickly roped the deck off to force me back around to the wet windward side.

My electrical knowledge about destroyers earned some respect from electricians, but I also experienced a lot of hostility within our electrical crew.

The coffee pot was nearly always brewing, but friction about who would make it, became pretty bad. Because we were all good for a cup anytime, most everyone put a pot on when they came into the shop; however a few expected servitude from subordinates. We had to get our water topside in the head, so it was a little inconvenient. Schriner and Schwalen, were two who expected someone else to make their coffee and that simply did not set well with me.

One day, during our time at Adak, Shermer, Fullen, O'Neil, Howard, and I were sitting on the work benches, writing letters, reading or otherwise occupied, when Schriner walked in.

"Shriley make a pot of coffee." He ordered Richard Shermer.

"Oh Schriner, have someone else do it, I'm in the middle of writing a letter," he responded.

"Sholin, you make a pot." He directed his attention towards me for the first time, in that regard.

"Shriner, why don't you just make your own damn coffee like all the rest of us?  I didn't hire in this man's Navy as your personal servant."

Schriner got off from his seat and came to the center of the room shouting, "I've been waiting for you to smart off to me.  Do you want to go see the 'man'?  I'll take you to the 'man', right now!"

I angrily jumped down off the counter and went nose to nose with him in the center of the room.  "Schriner, you aren't gonna take me anywhere.  If you -ever- go to the 'man', you had better not advertise it!  Furthermore, shut your damn mouth or you'll pick your ass off the deck -- right now!"  Well, that ended my first little conflict in the electrical gang as Schriner stormed out of the shop.

My second run in came with Schwalen.  They always tried to run movies in the mess hall so they would not overlap watch times; however, occasionally if a movie ran a little longer, they did overlap the 8 to 12 watch.  Electricians had it worked out with one another to stand by a little longer, until the end of the movie.  We always made up the time in good measure.

One time near the end of a movie which had run a little over the 2000 watch, Schwalen came in and shouted; "Sholin, get out here."  He was hot, "Damn it, when you're supposed to relieve that watch, you do it.  Jerry O'Neil is looking for you."  As we walked aft I tried to explain what he already knew full well, this was a standard agreement.  He kept shouting at me as we walked aft toward the crew's quarters and entrance to the after engine room.  I was totally pissed!

"God-damn-it Schwalen, you've been riding my ass since I came onboard this ship.  I'm sick of it!  Why the hell don't we just go out on the fantail and have it out?"  I asked.  He stormed off through the hatch and back down to the electric shop.

As I relieved Jerry, I asked why that happened.  He responded; "I just called the shop to have someone see if you were sleeping, not to cause a big fury.  I don't mind standing by till the end of the movie."

As I sat there on the switchboard watch, my anger was building. I called the electric shop and had it out, some more, with Schwalen.

Next day, Chief Electricians Mate Joe Cannon, came to the electric shop. "Wild Bill, we've got to talk," he said. I followed him up to the quarter deck. Joe was a mild-mannered gentleman, who seldom came to the electric shop. "Bill, what's going on," he asked. Fifty years later Joe ordered one of my books, in his note he said, "Wild Bill we've got to talk."

I reiterated what I had been saying to the others. "My electrical knowledge is unique within this crew. I have supervised electricians building these very destroyers, and I damn sure didn't hire in this man's Navy as someone's mess cook."

"But Bill, you can't do that in the Navy."

"Bull-shit," I responded, "I won't knuckle under to those guys."

Well, after that my tensions continued to build on Wren, till I didn't even care if they put me in jail. I would not continue like that!

A few days later, I walked up the deck on the lee side, 'deck apes' noticed me coming and quickly roped off the deck before I got there. I just scowled at them, but went back around to the windward side. About halfway up, near the "Y" guns and depth charge racks the deck is very narrow. Two more deck apes were fighting over a high pressure hose that sucked water out of the icy bay. I patiently waited for them to quit their horseplay, so I could get by. After some time they raked the high pressure hose, like a firehose, right across my mid-section. It nearly knocked me down. I still would have accepted their apology. But they looked up to see who it was, then went right back to fighting over possession of the hose. That did it! I threw one guy in one direction, the second in another and took the hose away from them. They ran for the quarter-deck. I gunned them with icy water all the way.

I stood there unable to turn the hose off or put it down. When the seamen returned with the OD, I gave the hose back to them.

The OD said: "What's going on here?"

I told him what happened, as my anger continued to build. By the time I told the story of both incidents, my hostility was showing and I exploded.

"Sir, since I've been on this pig iron son-of-a-bitch, these guys have been dealing me a ration of shit. They slam food on my tray and mix it together with a scowl and rope the decks off ahead of me. They do that all the time. I'm serving notice!" By this time I'm shouting at First Lieutenant Frank Olson, the OD.

"I'm serving notice on this ship! The next guy who mixes my food up, I will drag his ass over those steam tables and kick the living shit out of him."

*Electricians -- Bill Sholin, Clayton Schwalen Frenchey Lammer, and Aaron Howard*

Frank Olson responded with the coy little grin that would become familiar to me, in later months. As rescue swimmer, I worked directly with Frank and we shared a couple of small bottles of ship's brandy, after each "recovery". He had us shake hands and the incident was closed.

All of my troubles on *Wren* stopped on that day. Both Schriner and Schwalen happened to get transferred off the ship at the same time, restoring peace to the electrical gang. We had a close-knit group with much mutual respect. In no way am I blaming anyone else for my trouble on *Wren*. I was hot-headed. Schriner and Schwalen were regular Navy USN, but most of the rest of us were USNR. They were more experienced, but their ways were difficult for a young guy, like me, to accept.

The purpose of telling this story has been to show what life was really like on destroyers. We were very young, our quarters crowded and we lived under the constant threat of death. Some conflict was inevitable.

At 1603 April 18th, we took on fuel and ammunition, then along with *Rowe, Watts, Smalley*, and *Stoddard, Wren* headed south. We were dispatched under a secret mailgram from ComNorPac. This signaled the end of our miserable cold and rough water duty. We had steamed across the north Pacific eight times to bombard the Kurile islands, with four successful raids. We had kept our enemy guessing as to where the main attack might come from. And yes, we had become a confident and deadly force to be reckoned with. But what would lie ahead?

# SIXTEEN
# PRELUDE TO OKINAWA

During the month of March the fast carrier task forces turned their attention towards the final stepping stone on the way to complete victory against Japan. While preparations for the April 1st invasion of Okinawa were underway, *Wren* wound down her Aleutian duty.

One major obstacle remained a thorn in the U.S. Navy's side. U.S. Admirals pondered: "What can we do to protect our fleet from massive Kamikaze attacks?" From Okinawa to Formosa, Indo-China, Japan, and all island bases between, the full might of United States Naval Air power was brought to bear on Japanese airfields. Still, U.S. Admirals knew we could not stop all of them!

During mid-March, advance units of the fleet were collecting at Ulithi for the invasion of Okinawa. This group of small islands is strategically located to provide a unique, sheltered lagoon, large enough to assemble a major U.S. fleet.

Frank Bohn, who told the story of the spilled soup in the Aleutians, was there onboard the USS *Williamson*, he recalls: "On March 11, 1945, we had been at Ulithi for a couple of weeks, it seemed like a vacation. The lagoon, eight miles wide and twenty miles long, looked like a big, beautiful, swimming pool, with a white bottom. As far we could see, ships of every size and shape were at anchor around us. This was the scene of massing the mightiest armada of ships ever assembled at one place. With calm winds, smooth water and the sky interrupted only by a few far flung white clouds, we felt safe in numbers and far from the war. We basked on the fo'c'sle in the late afternoon sun and waited for dark so we could see a movie.

*Machinist Mate First Class Frank Bohn*

"All of a sudden the big guns around us started shooting. We wondered, what the hell is going on. Are they practicing in here? Why aren't we at general quarters? Without warning, three suicide planes appeared, one broke from the others and veered off, straight at *"Willie."*

"Many of my shipmates gathered on the fo'c'sle to check on all the commotion, but that guy came looking for bigger fish. He made his run toward the USS *Kenneth Whiting*, a seaplane tender for PBY's, anchored near the carrier USS *Randolph*. The Kamikaze came under heavy fire from the two ships, so he finally chose a third, larger and more docile target, one not so hostile towards him. A shout and applause went up from *Willie* and echoed over the lagoon," Bohn continues. "The Kamikaze Pilot dove fearlessly -- into Sorlen Island. I guess the small three-story building with a palm tree next to it, looked like a carrier to him. Damage to the sand was minimal."

## USS RANDOLPH, CV15, MARCH 11, 1945:

However, the other two suicide pilots were not so dumb. One, a twin-engine bomber called "Francis," dove for the carrier *Randolph*. In spite of heavy antiaircraft fire the pilot made good his vendetta and crashed the starboard after side of the carrier, below her flight deck. Twenty-five crewmen were cremated and 106 wounded. Repairs were made at Ulithi and *Randolph* stayed with the fleet. The third Kamikaze was shot down by gunfire.

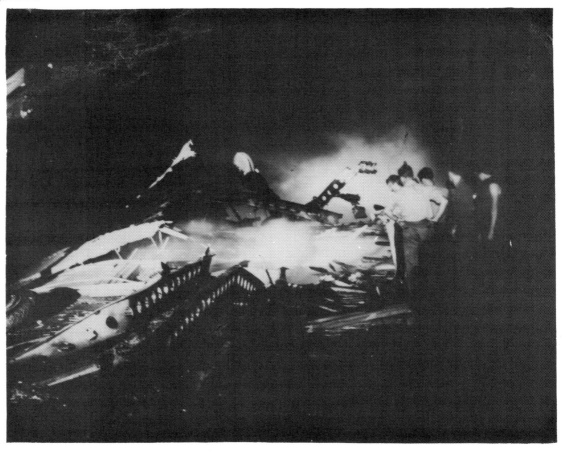

*USS Randolph, CV15, March 11, 1945, her crew fight fires on the hangar deck.*

*Williamson* got underway with Task Force 58 to participate in the bombardment and invasion of Okinawa. Following is a day to day account of events, prior to the invasion.

*USS Randolph, a hole is blown in her flight deck.*

**USS HANCOCK, CV19, and USS HALSEY POWELL DD686, March 20, 1945:**
While fueling the *Halsey Powell* during air strikes off Kyushu, both ships came under suicide attack. One aircraft dove for the ships and was disintegrated by gunfire about 700 feet overhead. Fragments hit *Hancock,* but the engine and bomb hit the fantail of *Halsey Powell.* This was the second of three Kamikaze hits on *Hancock*, still they shot down a second plane moments later.

*USS Halsey Powell, DD686, and USS Hancock, CV19, March 20, 1945*

Coming under attack is the worst scenario for a fueling destroyer. The aircraft ricocheted off *Hancock*, hit *Halsey Powell* and jammed the destroyer's steering. Fuel lines were cut to keep from colliding. The bridge watch skillfully controlled the destroyer and they broke free from *Hancock*. On fire, with nine dead and 30 wounded, *Halsey Powell's* damage control parties had a desperate situation. Finally, after getting fires under control, the destroyer managed to steam to Ulithi, safely. Temporary repairs were made and the ship left to San Pedro, California for a permanent overhaul, she arrived May 8.

*USS Hornet CV12, March 18, 1945, taken from the USS Wasp.*

## USS HORNET, CV12, and USS WASP, CV18, MARCH 18, 1945

March 17 to 23, reported to be one of the busiest times for Fleet Carriers in their history, turned out to be a fateful time for both ships. While under almost continuous air attacks, they were on the offense. *Hornet* was hit by a Kamikaze and *Wasp* took bomb hits, but they both inflicted heavy damage on the enemy. April 13, *Wasp* returned to the Puget Sound Navy Yard for repairs, then proceeded to Bayonne N.J. where she received the bow of the decommissioned *Hornet*.

## USS FRANKLIN, CV13, MARCH 19, 1945

*Franklin* had been hit by a suicide plane on October 13, 1944, with heavy loss of life. This time it apparently was not a suicide hit, but we cannot tell this story without including CV13.

While operating in the same vicinity as the *Halsey Powell* and *Hancock*, *Franklin* was hit by two bombs, that caused catastrophic damage and heavy loss of life. As the ship lay dead in the water, with no radio communication, a 13 degree starboard list, and only 50 miles from Japan, with 724 men killed and 265 wounded, *Franklin* seemed doomed. But, they performed in the highest naval tradition. Her crew saved their ship and she was taken in tow by the cruiser, USS *Pittsburgh*. The carrier later succeeded in steaming under her own power at 14 knots, but *Franklin's* war was over and she returned to the U.S. for repairs.

### USS GILMER, (DD233), APD11, MARCH 26, 1945

As flagship for the UDT's (Under Water Demolition Teams), the converted WWI four stacker destroyer arrived at Okinawa the 25th. Next day APD11 lost her galley deckhouse to a Kamikaze. The aircraft took it clean off. With one killed and three wounded, *Gilmer* sailed for Pearl Harbor to be repaired on April 9 and returned to Okinawa, July 4.

### USS KIMBERLY, DD521, MARCH 26, 1945

The destroyer left San Pedro Bay, Philippines on the 21st and had just arrived in the Ryukyus for picket duty, when she was crashed into by a Kamikaze. They were attacked by two "Vals" but her gunfire had scored many hits. Trailing fire and smoke, one of the persistent pilots got through and crashed into her after gun mount. Four were killed and 57 wounded. *Kimberly* left for Mare Island April 1, arriving for repairs on the 25th.

### USS HALLIGAN, DD584, MARCH 26, 1945

Sunk by a moored mine, she lost half of her crew of 300.

March 27, the nearby Kerama Retto Islands were invaded by the United States forces. These islands provided an advance base of operations.

### USS O'BRIEN, DD725, MARCH 27, 1945

While providing gunfire support for the Kerama Retto invasion forces she was hit for the second time, by a Val. After splashing one aircraft, the second crashed into the destroyer's port side and exploded a magazine. With heavy damage, 50 killed or missing and 76 wounded, *O'Brien* got underway to Mare Island Navy Yard for permanent repairs. She returned to the Third Fleet near the end of the war.

### USS DORSEY, DD117, MARCH 27, 1945

The veteran destroyer was struck a glancing blow from a suicide plane, killing 3 and wounding 2 of her crew. The ship remained in the area until April 4, when *Dorsey* sailed to Pearl Harbor for repairs.

### USS BILOXI, CL80, MARCH 27, 1945

Slightly damaged by a suicide plane, the cruiser remained on station until April 27. At that time she returned to the west coast for complete repairs.

### USS NEVADA, BB36, MARCH 27, 1945

This battleship, a part of the massive invasion force that supported the Okinawa operations, arrived March 24 and took part in the pre-invasion bombardment when a Kamikaze crashed into her. A main battery turret was damaged and 11 men killed. April

5, *Nevada* was hit by fire from shore batteries, killing two additional men, but this veteran battleship stayed in action.

## USS INDIANAPOLIS, CA35, MARCH 31, 1945

A diving suicide plane crashed onto her main deck. The bomb went all the way through to the bottom before it exploded and left two gaping holes. After heavy flooding was under control and temporary repairs made, CA35, returned to the United States for major rebuilding.

An interesting sidelight: After being repaired, *Indianapolis* transported crucial Atomic Bomb components from San Francisco to Tinian. At Tinian they were guarded by PFC Lloyd Clark of Las Vegas. Lloyd says: "The cage containing the bomb was very insignificant. It looked like an old chicken coup." Ultimately, this the first Atomic Bomb was dropped on Hiroshima!

Because of a shortage of escort destroyers, *Indianapolis* traveled unescorted. On July 28, she was hit by two torpedoes from a Japanese sub and sank rapidly. On August 2, 316 survivors were picked up from a crew of 1,199. Many horror stories have been told by those survivors about being attacked by sharks, and no one knows how many died from shark attacks.

*USS Louisville, CA28, damage to the forward stack caused by a Kamikaze in January.*

# SEVENTEEN
# BLOODY OKINAWA APRIL 1 TO 6

In preparing for Okinawa, U.S. Admirals faced a challenge. Since Admiral Ohnishi launched his first Kamikazes, Japan's entire defense centered around suicide attacks. Censorship prevented the press from writing about the disaster, and the Navy did not talk about it. But, it was like concealing a -- roaring lion...

The Japanese managed to cripple the U.S. Navy, with only a few hundred Kamikaze pilots. What defense could there be against such insanity if thousands were used? Those thoughts haunted U.S. Admirals. How could we continue to sacrifice our men and ships? What price victory?

Okinawa is only about 350 miles from the Japanese home islands, so suicide pilots could fly from their home bases directly to the target area. Could they in fact wipe out our entire invading fleet? With over 1200 ships, there would be no shortage of targets. How could we ever defend against such an onslaught? Advance warning of approaching enemy aircraft would be essential. But -- how? That's enemy territory. U.S. Admirals had serious questions that shouted for answers!

Radar picket destroyers were given the task of early detection. Located in the East China Sea to the north and northwest of Okinawa, in a half circle about 40 to 70 miles from shore, their radar could detect aircraft up to 150 miles from the northern tip of Okinawa. U.S. fighters could then be vectored directly to the enemy.

A good idea, but what would happen to those destroyers? How many aircraft would get through? More questions without answers. The U.S. had no choice; this was the only defense. Captain Moosebrugger was put in charge of the destroyer squadrons.

On March 25th, the last time *Wren* entered Adak, all hell broke loose at Okinawa. This was it! The big one had started. Heavy ships bombarded, while the carriers launched air strikes.

Never in the history of Naval warfare had so many ships gathered in one place; code name for the operation was "Iceberg." The battleships -- USS *Tennessee, Idaho, Colorado, Maryland, Arkansas, West Virginia, Texas, New Mexico* and *New York* -- led the offensive. Ten cruisers and 25 destroyers completed the bombarding force.

The Japanese, although heavily fortified, decided not to retaliate against the bombarding fleet; choosing instead to keep their heavy guns concealed until U.S. troops started landings. They felt this gave them a chance to slow down our invasion, until the "Divine Wind" could destroy our invading fleet.

On the 27th, the Kerama Islands were invaded and quickly taken by the 77th division. Kerama Retto became the main base of operations for the United States fleet.

A history book entitled "Battle Reports" featured the USS *Laffey*, DD724, in one of a few references to the Okinawa Picket Line. We feel the first three pages of that chapter, written at the time, will set up our story. The following is an exact reproduction.

## SEVENTY-NINE MINUTES ON THE PICKET LINE

*IN TELLING WHAT HAPPENED on the destroyer picket line on April 6, April 12, April 16th, or any other day; what happened aboard the ABELE, BUSH, BENNETT, NEWCOMB, or the LCS57 when all the suiciders crashed, something more than a blow-by-blow description of actual battle is needed if for no other reason than to record how a man feels who has been to hell and back again. One of this volume's authors, Lieutenant Commander Frank A. Manson, who was communications officer of USS LAFFEY, here tells of his brief, bloody vigil of Roger Peter One. (Radar Picket)*

*"Let's begin with the end, for invariably in retrospect victory in battle is thought of in terms of the price paid to win. Especially so, if the price includes a son, father, or shipmate.*

*It was 2:00 P.M., April 17, 1945. A topless dusty brown Army truck bounced down a red-clay Okinawan lane. In the ditches on either side of the road, tiny, wrinkled, dirty, half-clothed natives trudged along looking for food or a hole in which to crawl should shells start falling again. This particular lane's roadbed, winding around to the 6th Marine Division Cemetery, located on the western side of Okinawa overlooking the transport anchorage, was well hardened and seemingly more traveled than many others. This Army truck, like the dozens of others that passed each day, was taking more of the fallen to a place of rest, carrying sufficient dead to tie up all the funeral homes in a city the size of Boston.*

*"In the truck's front seat sat the driver, an Army corporal, and two naval officers, a lieutenant from the destroyer whose dead lay in the truck, and the other a chaplain, Lieutenant Curt W. Junker, from Admiral Turner's flagship Eldorado.*

*"In the rear of the truck, wrapped in dark-green flashproof mattress covers, lay the dead. All of them from one destroyer that had been knocked off the radar picket line by the Kamikaze.*

" 'Can't figure where all these stiffs are comin' from,' said the corporal, obviously trying to break the uncomfortable silence. No one had spoken since the bodies had been transferred to the truck from an LCVP at Yellow Beach.

" 'But ya know I've been on this island almost three weeks and ain't even seen a Nip plane. Beats me -- all these stiffs comin' in from our boats at sea, and no planes. Somebody said our boats wuz catchin' hell out sight of land, way up north some place.' Nodding understandingly, Chaplain Junker continued to look at the little Okinawans walking and crawling alongside the road. The Lieutenant made no reply. He hadn't heard the driver, hadn't seen the Okinawans--he was trying to forget. Trying to forget about the radar picket line and the destroyer Navy, the loss of thousands of shipmates and dozens of ships. Why not send the cruisers to the picket line; they could take more punishment. Why not the battleship; she could never be sunk. Or even better, why not unload the supply ships quickly and clear the area? Why pick on the destroyer? How about a dummy ship, a concrete barge? Anything for a change, anything but destroyers. He hoped the United States Navy had more destroyers than the Japanese had Kamikazes.

" 'Yes, yes, those "boats" are having quite a struggle, Mr.--er--ah.'

" 'Just call me soldier,' broke in the driver.

"The big Army truck slid to a stop at the 6th Marine Division Cemetery.

"'Did you ever see so many stiffs?" marveled the soldier. 'Just look. Don't even have time to cover 'em up.'

A haggard, bone-weary officer approached and introduced himself as Chaplain, Lieutenant Commander Paul L. Redmond.

"'More Navy,' he said, in statement rather than question. 'At Guadal, Saipan, Peleliu, and Iwo it was mostly Marines, but here it's Marines and the Navy too.

" 'Driver, lay them alongside the fourth column.' The padre pointed toward four long columns of the shrouded dead. Hundreds of them. The toiling burial detail, instructed to keep 100 graves ahead, was more than that number behind.

"The 6th Marine Cemetery seemed quiet and peaceful except for an occasional sharp crack of artillery or the dry snap of a sniper's rifle.

" 'Could you help me with a few prayers, Chaplain Junker?' asked tired Padre Redmond, as the work on the graves was resumed. The bulldozer operator, in his converted gravedigger, pushed slowly ahead with his massive steel blade, audibly hating his job more and more--more than if he were on the front being shot at, he declared to nobody in particular.

"Suddenly, 'Flash Red!' and all hands scattered for foxholes, not so much to escape the Japanese planes, which probably weren't coming near them anyhow, but to dodge the murderous shell fragments soon from the ship in the harbor.

"'Flash White!' The shooting ended almost as abruptly as it had begun and hardly before the truck driver had found a pit to ditch himself.

"'Why didn't you jump in one of the graves with me,' asked Redmond upon the driver's return from his foxhole. 'You know you could have been hit before you reached that ditch.'

"'Grave? Ugh, I'd ruther be killed than use one of them graves,' returned the driver, shuddering.

"It was time to bury the dead. Empty sake bottles containing each man's identification tucked inside his battle dress, the shrouded bodies were gently placed side by side in soldierly pattern.

"It was now late afternoon and the sea breeze had quickened, making audible only scattered phrases of the Chaplain's message to grieved comrades standing uncovered nearby. 'God is our refuge and strength...though the earth be removed and though the mountains be carried into the midst of the sea earth to earth, ashes to ashes, dust to dust.'

"Then sunset, and a few evening stars brightened the night which could not conceal the freshly covered graves and the unburied. This April 17, 1945, was just another day at the 6th Marine Division Cemetery."

On April 1, 1945, at 0406 Admiral Turner unleashed the powerful U.S. forces against Hagushi, Okinawa and our heavy guns pierced the darkness in the pre-dawn bombardment of the invasion beaches. Simultaneously, on the opposite side of the island, a second decoy invasion force had assembled at Minatoga. This is where the Japanese expected the invasion, and here the 2nd Marine Division started the mock landings. That's where the first American blood was spilled. Daybreak replaced the darkness, exposing a balmy day. A few far flung clouds whipped by a gentle breeze graced the landscape. This was Easter Sunday morning.

At about 0630 the 1st and 6th Marine Divisions, along with the Army's 7th and 96th infantry, stormed the beaches at Hagushi. Maximum effort was used to capture the Yontan and Kadena Airfields. The third airfield on Oriku Peninsula, near Naha, would be the last to fall.

### USS LST, 884, APRIL 1, 1945:

They prepared to unload troops at Minatoga when the first suicide plane crashed, destroying the landing craft. Eight marines were killed, 8 missing and 37 wounded in this first suicide attack. Ironically, those troops were not even scheduled to land at that time and place.

### USS HINSDALE, APA120, APRIL 1, 1945:

While approaching the transport area, her lookouts spotted an enemy plane skimming low over the water. Her marines were poised on deck, ready to go, as the suicide bound pilot headed straight at *Hinsdale*. With little time to retaliate, he crashed into her port side, just above the waterline. Three explosions occurred as he ripped into her engine room. Scalding steam released from exploding boilers, killed all but one sailor! Power and communications failed immediately, and Hinsdale stopped -- dead in the water. Marines massed on her main deck jammed against the starboard rail, to help counteract the heavy port list. Three gaping holes in her side -- put *Hinsdale* in immediate danger of sinking.

Below decks her damage control parties groped through the smoke filled darkness, trying to extinguish fires and shore up against flooding. With 15 men dead and 40 missing or wounded, *Hinsdale* made good her task of unloading marines. After they corrected her 13 degree port list and restored limited power from an emergency generator, *Hinsdale* was taken in tow by the tug, USS ATR80. The 20 miles to Kerama Retto took them over four hours. After transferring her cargo to the USS *Pitt*, APA 223, *Hinsdale* was used to house other Kamikaze victims. April 14th the transport started her long voyage home, under tow by the USS *Leo*, AKA6.

### USS WEST VIRGINIA, BB48, APRIL 1, 1945:

As they prepared to lend close support to landing troops, she moved near the assault beaches. But before she opened fire, a plane was spotted off her port quarter. The battleship fired her 5-inch 40 and 20mm antiaircraft guns and splashed the Kamikaze 200 yards away. Before her guns cooled, the battleship engaged four more Kamikazes, shooting down one.

At 0630, *West Virginia* opened fire with her main batteries. The sea soon became alive with landing craft. Only 900 yards off shore her crew had a panoramic view. They watched as hundreds of small landing craft moved; each had its own rendezvous with destiny. At 0842, her lookouts reported seeing the first troops hit shore. The land battle for Okinawa began. Throughout the day the battleship continued her bombardment against what appeared to be little resistance on shore.

At 1903, while off shore awaiting further orders, *West Virginia* came under suicide attack again. Three enemy planes picked up by radar soon closed her formation; however despite heavy flack, one crossed over the port side of BB48, looped and crashed into her superstructure. Four men were killed instantly and seven wounded in a nearby 20mm gun gallery. The bomb penetrated to the second deck, but fortunately failed to explode. They disarmed it and temporary repairs kept *West Virginia* in service. After burying her dead at sea, the battleship continued supporting ground troops.

### USS HOWORTH, DD592, APRIL 1, 1945:

The destroyer gained experience with the Divine Wind when she was hit at Mangarin Bay, Mindoro. At Okinawa, *Howorth* with the cruiser USS *St Louis*, en route to their assigned station, came under attack by at least eight suicide planes. Their combined firepower splashed Kamikazes from all directions, when suddenly *Howorth* was crashed into! After the suicider crashed into the destroyer's bridge, fires raged throughout. Nine men were killed and 14 wounded. *Howorth* shot down one last plane, then returned to Mare Island for repairs, arriving May 2nd.

*Howorth*, was *Wren's* XO LT Commander Robert Pauli's last ship. A few days after Pauli transferred to the *Wren*, his replacement was killed in another suicide attack, on December 12, 1944.

### HMS INDIFATIGABLE, APRIL 1, 1945:

Task Force 58 gathered near Sakishima Gunto, an island chain south of Okinawa, when just prior to April 1, a strange looking fleet of ships joined them. Not only were they different in appearance, but they had funny names, *Indomitable, Illustrious*, and *Indifatigable*. Unlike U.S. wooden flight decks, theirs were steel. Probably slippery and more difficult to land on; however they were more impervious to suicide planes. Some people thought, these must be super carriers. But, the U.S. Command was not impressed. They did not appreciate their presence, at first. Commanded by Admiral Philip L. Vivan, Royal Navy -- their actions soon spoke louder than their names.

Not only did those ships show their worth in combat, but they paid the price of membership. All three suffered severe damage from Kamikazes. *Indifatigable* was the first carrier crashed into during the Okinawa invasion.

### USS ALPINE, APA92, APRIL 1, 1945:

Off Leyte, on November 18th and again before her troops disembarked April 1, Kamikazes hit this transport, before she was a year old.. The plane crashed forward, setting fires in number 2, 3 and 4 holds. Eight crewmen and 21 passengers were killed and another 18 wounded, before they could get into the ground war. Her repair parties took charge, they put out fires and cleaned up debris, then after temporary repairs *Alpine* got underway to Seattle for battle repairs, she arrived May 30, 1945.

April 2 arrived with a vengeance for U.S. transports. Five became landing fields for Admiral Ohnishi's suicide pilots. Troop laden transports were prime targets for Kamikaze attacks. The Japanese had a field day.

### USS ACHERNAR, AKA53, APRIL 2, 1945, 1945:

AT 0043, the first fell victim; she was crashed into off Hagushi, shortly after midnight. With 6 crewmen killed and 41 wounded, her damage control parties remained in charge.  They extinguished fires, controlled flooding, cared for the wounded and kept *Achernar* on station until April 19.  Then AKA53 left, under their own power, for the long trip home to San Francisco.

### USS TYRELL, AKA80, APRIL 2, 1945:

A twin-engine bomber dove through a heavy barrage of AA fire and attempted to crash on the transport.  The pilot sheared off the ship's main radio antenna and hit the lower yardarm, as he tried for the bridge and missed.  His momentum carried him to the 5-ton cargo boom at number 5 hatch and the explosion showered debris everywhere.  April 4, the cruiser USS *Minneapolis*, CA36, off loaded 600 rounds of 8-inch projectiles and 1,200 cans of powder from the transport.  Then *Tyrell* sailed to San Francisco for repairs.

The other three transports to feel the suicidal stings were part of Task Group 51.1, which had provided troops for the Kerama Retto invasion a few days earlier.  Still in the area, they provided materials and retrieved 77th division troops.  The transports, escorted by USS *Dickerson*, APD21; *Bunch*, APD79; and USS *Herbert*, APD22; retired southwest of the islands for the night.  They felt safe, then suddenly; ten suicide planes swarmed in on them.

### USS DICKERSON, APD 21, APRIL 2, 1945:

While screening transports the ships came under heavy attack.  One suicider in a low glide, headed for APD21, he cut off her two stacks and crashed into the bridge.  Almost simultaneously, a second Kamikaze scored a direct hit on her fo'c'sle.  That one started intense fires which threatened her forward magazine.  The ship was almost sliced in two by the blasts!  Despite heroic efforts to save *Dickerson*, her officers had to give the "Abandon ship" order.

As they fought *Dickerson's* fires, the USS *Bunch* and *Herbert* took survivors on board and extinguished fires -- leaving a burned out hulk.  Still smoldering, they towed the ship to Kerama Retto on April 4.  Then they towed her back to sea and sank her.  Fifty-four officers and crewmen, including her commanding officer, died.

### USS HENRICO, APA45, APRIL 2, 1945:

A fast suicide bomber flew out of cloud cover, straight for *Henrico*.  Despite AA fire, the Kamikaze crashed into the starboard side of her bridge, causing heavy damage.  The bombs exploded below decks and caused immediate loss of all power.  Forty-nine men, including her Captain -- died!  After temporary repairs at Kerama Retto, *Henrico* sailed for San Francisco, under her own power, for battle repairs.

### USS TELFAIR, APA210, APRIL 2, 1945:

At 1830 while close by her sister ship, *Goodhue*, the ships were attacked by three planes in quick succession.  The combined firepower exploded one in mid-air, but the second crashed into *Telfair's* bullwork, then bounced overboard.  APA210, remained on station until April 26, then got underway for Seattle, by way of Ulithi, for repairs.

## USS GOODHUE, APA 107, APRIL 2, 1945

In the furious action taking place around her the transport witnessed hits on *Henrico* and *Dickerson*. The loaded ships fought for their lives. After *Goodhue* splashed one plane on her starboard quarter, another took aim at the bow. The aircraft dove from dead ahead, but unable to effect an adequate defense the Kamikaze hit the mainmast, then crashed astern. The bomb exploded causing fires and heavy casualties; however surprisingly minimal structural damage occurred. Despite 27 killed and 117 wounded, *Goodhue* stayed in action and rejoined her transport squadron April 10. After temporary repairs at Kerama Retto the transport unloaded her troops on Ie Shima, April 20.

## USS ZELLARS, DD777, APRIL 12, 1945

The Allen M. Sumner class destroyer with 10 5-inch guns had completed her shakedown training by March 1945, in time for the April 1st invasion. During the afternoon, while screening the battleship USS *Tennessee*, BB43, three "Jills" attacked the destroyer. They came at her port-quarter, about 15 feet above the water, in a coordinated approach. DD777 rang up 25 knots, maneuvered to bring her guns to bear and opened fire. *Zellars* splashed the lead attacker at 1,800 yards, caught the second at 3,000, then turned her attention on the last Jill.

However, *Zellars* duty was cut very short. The last Jill crashed into her port side, forward of the bridge. After going through the number 2 handling room the bomb exploded on the starboard side, in the scullery. With all power temporarily lost and the forward fireroom secured, the destroyer limped to Kerama Retto for temporary repairs, then to Terminal Island, California, arriving June 1. *Zellars* -- war ended.

*USS Zellars and the USS Tennessee*

## USS TENNESSEE, BB43, APRIL 2, 1945:

April 2 or 12?: Studying the histories of both *Tennessee* and *Zellars*, we found a discrepancy in the date of these events. *Zellars* history indicates they were hit on April 2, while *Tennessee* says the 12th. However, they both agree on the details.

*Zellars* was crashed by a Kamikaze while screening *Tennessee*. Five aircraft picked *Tennessee* as their targets. They flew through flack and heavy smoke from the stricken *Zellars* and closed on *Tennessee*. Four were shot down, the last three close aboard. The fifth Kamikaze, on fire while diving for the battleship, crashed in the sea. At the same time a Val dive bomber, flying low off the starboard bow -- headed directly for *Tennessee's* bridge. All guns that could be brought to bear opened fire. They shot off one wheel and set the engine on fire, but the Kamikaze got through to crash the signal bridge. Burning wreckage skidded over the superstructure and crashed among antiaircraft guns and their crews. The 250 pound bomb went through the wooden deck and exploded below. Twenty-two were killed and 107 wounded.

*Tennessee's* wounded transferred to the USS *Pinkney*, APH2 and her dead were buried at sea, but the battleship stayed in action. May 1, Admiral Deyo shifted his flag to a cruiser, and *Tennessee* returned to Ulithi for repairs. USS *Ajax*, AR6, installed new guns and patched her up by June 3.

## USS PRICHETT, DD561, APRIL 3, 1945:

The destroyer arrived off Okinawa on March 25, as part of Task Force 54. They supported the pre-invasion minesweeping, UDT operations, and provided fire support for the Kerama Retto invasion. DD561, then took part in the decoy invasion at Minatoga. Their missions completed, *Prichett* swung around the south end of the island and joined the invasion forces at Hagushi.

At 0100, as her group came under suicide attack, a long day started for the destroyer. After beating off several other attackers, two bogies closed DD561. The first veered off and left, but the second pressed home his attack. He dropped a 500 pound bomb on her fantail. The bomb blew a hole beneath the waterline and started fires in the 20mm clipping room. The ship maintained a speed of 28 knots to minimize flooding and extinguish fires. After temporary repairs at Kerama Retto, *Prichett* remained on station. A second suicide crash caused extensive damage, on July 29th.

Later the same day, the USS *Hambleton*, (DD455) DMS2, suffered slight damage by a near miss, and the USS *Foreman*, DE633, was hit by a bomb.

## USS WAKE ISLAND, CVE65, APRIL 3, 1945:

The escort carrier operated southeast of Okinawa, landing her fifth reconnaissance mission, when GQ sounded. At 1742, while they spotted the next flight, a violent wave hit the ship. Two FM-2's were thrown over the side, two fighters flipped over on their backs and two others were damaged severely by the wave.

Two minutes later the suicide planes attacked. A single-engine aircraft dove at a steep angle, narrowly missed the forward corner of her flight deck and exploded in the water. Thirty seconds later, a second plane roared down her starboard side at tremendous speed. He nearly hit her bridge, as he crashed in the water within 10 feet from the hull, and exploded. A hole 45 feet long was blown in the side, below her waterline. Exploded parts of the plane covered the ship, but miraculously there were no casualties.

*Wake Island* suffered heavy structural damage and flooding, her shell plating buckled, cracked main condensers were flooded and 70,000 gallons of fuel oil were contaminated with salt water. With her forward engine secured, they got under way with only one propeller. Four hours later her repair parties managed to restore power and they steamed with both propellers again. At 2140, *Wake Island* escorted by USS *Dennis*, DE405, and USS *Gross*, DE444, left for Kerama Retto.

For two days the escort carrier underwent inspection by the fleet salvage officers, then left for Guam April 6th, to be repaired.

### USS HALLIGAN, DD584, MARCH 26, 1945:

The destroyer hit a mine, her magazines blew up and she sank. Fifteen men were killed on the first destroyer casualty at Okinawa. This clearly indicated the dangerous, but important task of mine division 20. Unfortunately, they were unable to guarantee that all mines had been removed.

Admiral Ohnishi's fanatics made their presence known on the third day of the bombardment, with Kamikaze hits scored on the cruiser USS *Biloxi*, CL80, and the destroyer USS *Dorsey*, DD117. Only slight damage was inflicted on the *Biloxi*. *Dorsey* suffered sufficient damage from a glancing hit to require repairs at Pearl Harbor. She returned, just to be grounded and sank in a typhoon, October 9, 1945.

# Eighteen

## Lambs, Who Fought Like Lions, Led To Slaughter April 6 to May 15, 1945

This is a story about -- destroyers!  Up to this time 30 destroyers and four DE's were crashed into in the Philippines and eight were sunk or scrapped.  Those destroyers were hit while carrying out their normal routine duties -- sweeping mines, landing troops, bombarding, protecting larger fleet units, escorting landing craft and patrolling against submarines.  But now they became expendable!  Thus enters -- "The Sacrificial Lambs."

April 6, the dreaded "What if" day everyone wondered about, was the day that started the trend for U.S. Destroyers at Okinawa.  The Japanese launched their massive suicide attacks called "Ten Go".  They came over in mass flights like swarms of yellow jackets, after someone who had destroyed their nest.  They came from all angles and altitudes, usually in a high speed dive.  Destroyers caught alone -- were virtually doomed.  Run, shoot and dodge fast or die!  This was the order of the day.  In spite of their ability to do all three, many died anyway.  The sheer horror of a single small ship facing a swarm of aircraft, all determined to die, would tax anyone's sanity.

They drank their saki, said their good-byes and received their last rites.  Given only enough fuel for a one-way trip, family and friends sent them on their way -- to a hero's sayanara.

*Sayanara*

What about the men who would die fighting them? We had no such resolve. Most of us had been gone from home for months and many for years. Our hearts and thoughts were full of remorse and loneliness. We just wanted to get the war over with and go home, to see our mothers, fathers, wives and sweethearts once again. We had forgotten what they looked like.

But we fought, every man for survival. Almost 50 years later, during memorial services at ships reunions, grown men cry like babies. Survivors of ships like USS *Newcomb, Leutz, Rodman, Emmons, Bush, Calhoun, Morris, Drexler* and *Kidd,* remember those events and the loss of friends, closer than brothers. Each of us will take our memory to our grave. Never allow anyone to minimize or rewrite this Pacific history!

Airfields on Okinawa and Ie Shima, still in Japanese hands, were prime targets of U.S. air attacks. Although it was possible for one-way suicidal aircraft to take off after quickly repairing bomb holes, the probability was that most mass attacks came from Formosa or Kyushu. Flights coming up from Formosa would most likely approach the south end of Okinawa; or fly west of Kerama Retto, they could then approach Hagushi from the west.

The exact locations and number of radar picket stations did not seem to be clearly established at that time. Radar Picket 1 (RP1) 40 to 70 miles northwest of the northern tip of Okinawa, was occupied. With the possibility of aircraft reaching the transport areas from so many different locations, U.S. defending destroyers appeared to have been pulled in, to form a tight circle of defense. Through stopgap means, 16 clearly defined radar picket stations were eventually established.

The destroyers USS *Newcomb, Leutze, Hyman, Beale* and the minesweepers USS *Robin* and *Defense* operated in the area of Ie Shima. The minesweepers finished sweeping operations at Keise Shima and Ie Shima in preparation for landings on those islands. Destroyers protected that operation while patrolling as picket ships in the area of RP 14 and 15. Thirty-five aircraft were detected approaching the minesweepers in late morning.

## USS ROBIN, YMS311, APRIL 6, 1945:
Three Vals closed the minesweeper while two others attacked a second nearby ship, she took the five aircraft under fire. Their combined efforts shot down three, while another crashed into *Robin's* fo'c'sle, skidded over the deck and plunged off the port side into the sea. With one man killed and two wounded, *Robin* returned to Kerama Retto, then on to Saipan for repairs.

## USS DEFENSE, AM317, APRIL 6, 1945:
The minesweeper took four suicide planes under fire. She shot one down, drove another off, but the other two Kamikazes crashed into her. Despite her own heavy damage and casualties, later in the afternoon, *Defense* picked up 50 survivors from USS *Newcomb* and towed the crippled USS *Leutze* to Kerama Retto.

## USS HYMAN, DD732, APRIL 6, 1945:

As the Japanese desperately attacked her formation, the destroyer shot at planes on all sides, splashing several before a damaged aircraft got through to crash near her torpedo tubes. While fighting fires and flooding, *Hyman* helped down two additional aircraft. With 10 killed and 40 wounded, the destroyer limped back to Kerama Retto. After emergency repairs, *Hyman* left for San Francisco for battle damage overhaul, arriving May 16th.

## USS NEWCOMB, DD586, APRIL 6, 1945:

Over 40 aircraft had been noted in the area during the day, but at 1600 with low ceilings and limited visibility, the ships came under heavy attack. During a furious hour and a half, *Newcomb* shot down several Kamikazes -- but five crashed into her decks. As she maneuvered to avoid further crashes, *Newcomb* fought back.

The USS *Leutze* came to *Newcomb's* rescue. While alongside rendering assistance, a fifth Kamikaze skipped across *Newcomb* and the USS *Beale* and crashed into *Leutze*.

Miraculously, still afloat with 18 killed, 25 missing and 64 wounded, *Newcomb* was towed to Kerama Retto by the tug USS *Tekesta*, ATF93. Temporary repairs were sufficient to allow the destroyer to proceed, under tow, to Mare Island Navy Yard, where she ultimately succumbed to the cutters torch.

Her crew received the Navy Unit Commendation for their heroic fighting effort to save their ship.

## USS LEUTZE, DD481, APRIL 6, 1945:

Assisting her 2 sister ships, *Leutze* was crashed into by a ricocheting Kamikaze. The suicider nearly severed the fantail, when he hit her port quarter. With 1 man killed, 7 missing and 30 wounded, the destroyer recalled her fire fighters from *Newcomb* to extinguish their own fires. USS *Defense*, AM317, herself crippled by two suicide crashes earlier that day, towed *Leutze* to Kerama Retto. *Leutz*, eventually made it back to Hunter's Point -- where she was scrapped.

## USS RODMAN, (DD456) DM21, APRIL 6, 1945:

At 1532, the destroyer minelayer, assigned to picket duty early on the 6th and later transferred to cover minesweepers, took up station with *Emmons*, between Iheva Retto and Okinawa. By mid-afternoon another swarm of Kamikazes flew in. At 1532, the first dove out of clouds and crashed into *Rodman's* port bow. His bomb went under the ship before it exploded, killing 6 and wounding 20 men. *Emmons* circled the stricken destroyer, protecting her from other attackers.

Marine Corps Corsairs arrived on the scene and shot down a total of 20 aircraft. During the three and a half-hour battle, two more Kamikazes crashed into *Rodman*. *Emmons* splashed six -- but was demolished, herself. After nearly a month of temporary repairs at Kerama Retto, *Rodman* started her long journey back to Charleston for rebuilding.  Her war ended there.

### USS EMMONS, (DD457) DMA22, APRIL 6, 1945:

While circling the stricken *Rodman*, *Emmons* was crashed into by a total of five aircraft, almost simultaneously.  They shot down many, but the destroyers were overwhelmed!  One crashed her fantail, another number 3 gun mount, one at the waterline aft, and another to the port side of her CIC room.

*Emmons* was ablaze, ammunition exploded everywhere and her damage control parties fought a hopeless battle.  With 60 killed and 77 wounded, the others were forced to abandon ship.  Next day, her smoldering hulk was sunk!  *Emmons* received the Navy Unit Commendation.

How can we describe or even understand this nightmare?  Can we empathize the feelings of those who had to leave the mangled bodies of their friends, in that tangled wreckage?  This was -- war at its very worst!

### USS BUSH, DD529, APRIL 6, 1945:

On November 1, 1944, at 1515, the destroyer suffered slight damage in an encounter with Admiral Ohnishi's suicide pilots.  Then on the sixth, *Bush* came under heavy Kamikaze attack on radar picket duty.  Just before 1515, she splashed at least one plane, then a Kamikaze hit the starboard side at deck level, between number 1 and 2 stacks.  The bomb exploded in the forward engine room!  Believing the ship could be salvaged, tugs were called.  As she raced to assist the stricken Bush, USS *Colhoun* was hit by a suicide plane.

At 1725, a second Kamikaze crashed into *Bush.*  He hit the main deck on the port side, between her stacks.  It nearly cut the ship in two.  While they fought ferocious fires, plane number three crashed into her port side.  Ammunition caught fire and exploded. *Bush* was doomed!  As they pondered if both halves were salvageable, a huge wave settled the question.  *Bush* caved in amidships and 225 surviving crewmen abandoned ship just before the destroyer folded and sank!  Stories from *Bush's* crewmen about what happened in the water, are unbelievable!

Jack Day, recalls: "I think I was the last man off the *Bush.*  I stepped into the water just as she broke in two.  I was the carpenter and had been all over the ship trying to get weight off, to keep her afloat.  I ended up in the water with 15 to 20 men hanging onto a raft type float.  Before it got dark, we lost some of this group to strafing by Jap planes. After dark we lost more; because they just stopped hanging on.  We were picked up just before dawn.  It was a very long night!"

### USS COLHOUN, DD801, APRIL 6, 1945:

At 1530, as they sped to the aid the stricken *Bush, Colhoun* started to fire in her own defense.  Under fanatical attack, the destroyer shot down three planes before another crashed into one of her 40mm mounts. The bomb exploded in the after fireroom and flaming wreckage spread over her main deck. Under emergency power, but with no power to her helm, the destroyer came under attack by three additional suicide planes. After splashing the first two, the third crashed into her starboard side. The bomb broke her keel, pierced two boilers, ripped a 20x4 foot hole below the waterline, started uncontrollable oil and electrical fires and her remaining guns had to be controlled manually. *Colhoun* gamely faced another wave of three attackers, splashed one and damaged a second. She took the third attacker aboard, aft. The bomb bounced overboard before it exploded, and blew another three foot hole in her side.

As the crew continued the fight, still another suicider in a mass of flames -- crashed into her bridge! At 1800, USS LCS48, removed all but a skeleton crew and a tug tried to tow the hulk to Okinawa. Flooded and out of control, fires rendered this endeavor impossible. *Colhoun* was sunk by gunfire from the *Cassin Young*. She lost 34 killed and 23 men wounded.

### USS MULLANY, DD528, APRIL 6, 1945:
At 1745, she patrolled the transport area near the Hagushi invasion sight, and they came under low level strafing attack. Trailing smoke from several hits, the suicide plane aimed for the bridge, then veered right to crash between mount 3 and 4. While three additional Kamikazes attacked, damage control parties removed wounded from twisted wreckage. Amidst flames and exploding ammunition, her forward guns shot down two aircraft and drove off the third. It seemed imminent that her magazines would explode. Some depth charges exploded and Captain Albert O. Momm gave the order to abandon ship. USS *Gherarda*, DMS30, stood by to receive survivors and USS *Purdy*, DD734, came alongside with fire fighting assistance.

They reduced the fear of further explosions by flooding crucial compartments. At 2300 Commander Momm led a skeleton crew back aboard. With one engine in operation, the destroyer limped to San Francisco, by way of Pearl Harbor. *Mullany* lost 30 men killed and 36 wounded.

The destroyers USS *Witter, Morris, Richard P. Leary, Gregory* and USS *Arikara*, ATF98, were patrolling southeast of Okinawa when they came under attack.

### USS WITTER, DE636, APRIL 6, 1945:
At 1611, when two aircraft were sighted closing from the southwest, the DE increased speed to 23 knots and opened fire. Trailing smoke, one crashed into the sea, but the other found his mark. The Kamikaze crashed into the starboard side at the waterline, and his bomb exploded in number 1 fireroom. Momentarily out of control, with massive flooding in several compartments, her damage control parties came to the rescue. *Witter* soon turned up 10 knots, on her own. Escorted by the other three destroyers, *Witter* returned to Kerama Retto, arriving a little more than five hours after she was hit. After temporary repairs, the DE returned to the Philadelphia Navy Yard for damage repairs. *Whitter*, like many others, failed to divulge their casualty figures.

## USS MORRIS, DD417, APRIL 6, 1945:

At 1745, before entering Kerama Retto, *Morris* left the *Witter* to continue patroling. About an hour later, she was crashed into by a flaming Kamikaze. The Kate carried either a heavy bomb or torpedo and hit the port side between number 1 and 2 mounts. For the next two hours her repair party worked to save their ship. With her bow demolished, *Morris* limped back into Kerama Retto. After extensive cutting to eliminate protruding steel, *Morris* left for Hunters Point Drydock. They considered her neither seaworthy nor habitable. *Morris* was scrapped.

## USS HAYNSWORTH, DD700, APRIL 6:

The destroyer was hit by a suicide plane and heavily damaged. They returned to Mare Island, via Ulithi, for repairs.

## USS FIBERLING, DE640, APRIL 6:

The destroyer was damaged by a near miss.

*USS Morris, DD417, April 6, 1945*

*Side view USS Morris, DD417*

**SS HOBBS VICTORY AND SS LOGAN VICTORY, APRIL 6, 1945:**
Even merchant ships were sunk on this awful day at Okinawa.

Among the 16 ships hit by Kamikaze aircraft this day, ten were destroyers. Of those, six were either sunk outright, later, by U.S. ships -- or scrapped.

As the land battle gained momentum, U.S. ships continued fighting for their lives.

On April 7, in the pre-dawn darkness, Task Force 54 headed north from Okinawa. This array of battleships, cruisers, destroyers, and aircraft carriers headed out to intercept the largest suicide weapon of all -- the remaining Japanese fleet.

Fortunately, while heading directly for Okinawa, this fleet had been discovered by U.S. submarines. The Japanese fleet of ten ships included the mighty battleship *Yamato*, one cruiser and 8 destroyers, had orders to attack the U.S. fleet -- and fight to their death. The worlds largest battleship, *Yamato*, with her 18-inch guns, presented a formidable challenge to the U.S. invasion forces.

Before U.S. ships were close enough to engage the Japanese, our carrier based aircraft attacked. As the seven Japanese destroyers fled north, *Yamato*, the cruiser, and one destroyer were sunk! Three additional fleeing Japanese ships were later sunk, and the remaining four, heavily damaged destroyers limped back to Sasibo, ending that threat.

## USS MARYLAND, BB46, APRIL 7, 1945:
The battleship sailed at dusk with Task Force 54, but as they left Okinawa, she fell victim to a Kamikaze. The suicide plane managed to sneak in on the battleship's starboard side and crashed into her number 3 turret. The explosion destroyed all 20mm mounts in the area and killed 53 men.

*Maryland* stayed in service until April 14, when they left for the Puget Sound Navy Yard at Bremerton, for repairs. This was the third time the battleship had been hit by Kamikazes. June 22, 1944, *Maryland* fell victim to an airborne torpedo and November 29, 1944, to a Kamikaze.

## USS BENNETT, DD473, APRIL 7, 1945:
*Bennett*, a Fletcher class destroyer, was attacked by a suicide plane as she supported the invasion ships. At 0850 with every gun firing, the Kamikaze struck home. The explosion damaged her forward engine room and knocked out all electrical power. With 3 killed and 18 wounded, escorted by her companion ship USS *Sterett*, DD407, *Bennett* limped to Kerama Retto. The following day, under tow by USS *Yuma*, ATF94, she left for Saipan and temporary repairs, then on to Puget Sound Navy Yard.

## USS HANCOCK, CV19, APRIL 7, 1945:
The carrier operated off shore providing close air support for ground troops when she suffered her third devastating Kamikaze crash. *Hancock* sustained her first damage

November 25, 1944, her second March 20, 1945, and now they would be forced back for repairs again. The suicide plane cart-wheeled over the flight deck, then crashed into a group of aircraft, causing a tremendous explosion.

With 62 killed and 71 wounded, they had to bury their dead at sea. *Hancock* then left for Pearl Harbor. The carrier rejoined the Third Fleet off Japan on July 10, 1945.

*USS Hancock, CV19, April 7, 1945 -- her 62 dead are buried at sea.*

### USS GREGORY, DD802, APRIL 8, 1945:
The Fletcher class destroyer came under attack by three aircraft that approached from the setting sun. The first Kamikaze blown apart and spinning, crashed into *Gregory*. The destroyer shuddered and slowed down when the aircraft crashed amidships above the waterline. The Kamikaze flooded her forward fireroom. Without power, in a blaze of gunfire, the destroyer shot down the other two Kamikazes. After limping to Kerama Retto for temporary repairs, *Gregory* sailed to San Diego for rebuilding. Her war ended.

### USS CHARLES J. BADGER, DD657, APRIL 9, 1945:
When she returned to Okinawa with Task Force 54, *Badger* resumed her fire support mission for ground troops. While on station during the half light of dawn, a Japanese suicide boat suddenly appeared, dropped a depth charge close aboard -- then sped away. Her engine rooms flooded almost immediately and *Badger* lay dead in the water. A tug towed her to Kerama Retto. After temporary repairs the destroyer left for Bremerton. *Charles J. Badger's* war also ended.

**USS STERETT, DD407, APRIL 10, 1945:**

Three days earlier the destroyer led her companion ship, *Bennett*, to relative safety. As they patrolled station four, northeast of Okinawa, five enemy aircraft attacked *Sterett* and her charges, the USS LCS36, and LCS24. The first plane was driven off and later splashed. The destroyer knocked the second aircraft from the sky. However, the third Kamikaze struck *Sterett* and exploded on impact! He hit her starboard side at the waterline, causing loss of power, communications, and steering failure. With her forward fuel tanks ruptured, she still fought back with her 40 and 20mm guns. *Sterett* shot down the fourth aircraft.

USS *Jeffers*, DMS27, assisted the stricken destroyer to Kerama Retto. (Three days later, *Jeffers* was hit.) After temporary repairs, *Sterett* left for Bremerton by way of Ulithi and Pearl Harbor. Her war ended.

April 11th and 12th were especially dangerous days in the waters around Okinawa. Twenty ships were crashed into by Kamikazes.

**USS KIDD, DD661, APRIL 11, 1945:**

With the help of the USS *Bullard*, DD660; *Black*, DD666; *Chanucy*, DD667, and their CAP, *Kidd* and her division mates fought off three air raids during the morning. But that afternoon -- luck ran out for *Kidd*!

Thirty-eight men were killed and 55 wounded when *Kidd* was crashed into by a single engine plane. As other determined Kamikazes tried to finish her, *Kidd* fought them off and headed south for the protection of other ships. After patchwork repairs at Ulithi, *Kidd* headed for Hunters Point Naval Shipyard at San Francisco. Her war was over.

*USS Kidd, DD661, April 11, 1945, seconds later this Kamikaze crashed into her decks.*

## USS WESSON, DE184, APRIL 7, 1945:

The DE relieved *Sterett* north of Ie Shima joining USS LCI's 452 and 558 on picket duty. *Wesson* opened fire on three Kamikaze attackers crossing her bow, but a fourth, in a dive out of the sun, crashed into her torpedo tubes. Eight men died and 25 were wounded. They went to San Francisco for repairs.

## USS ENTERPRISE, CV6, APRIL 11, 1945:

After damage caused by a bomb was repaired at Ulithi, they returned to action on April 5, only to be hit again six days later. The *Big "E"*, forced back to Ulithi for repairs again, would be hit still another time on May 14.

## USS BULLARD, DD660, APRIL 11, 1945:

In the same action with *Kidd, Bullard* suffered slight damage from a Kamikaze. After repairing damages at Okinawa, she joined the Third Fleet, gathering at Leyte Gulf.

## USS MISSOURI, BB63, APRIL 11, 1945:

The battleship opened fire on a low flying suicide plane; however, the determined pilot managed to penetrate her incredible firepower and crashed just below her main deck. Gasoline fires ignited at number three 5-inch gun mount, but damage was minimal and *Missouri* stayed in action until May 5. May 27th, the *"Mighty Moe"* returned to Okinawa where she wreaked havoc on Japanese defenses, until the end of that campaign.

## USS HANK, DD702; USS SAMUEL S. MILES, DE186 AND USS MANLOVE, DE 36, APRIL 11, 1945:

The destroyer and three destroyer escorts, were slightly damaged by the Kamikaze suicide pilots.

## USS IDAHO, BB42, APRIL 12, 1945:

After shooting down five Kamikazes, a sixth got through to cause slight damage with a near miss. After temporary repairs, she sailed to Guam arriving April 20.

*Wren* escorted *Idaho* back to Okinawa after she was repaired.

## USS CASSIN YOUNG, DD793, APRIL 12, 1945:

The destroyer operated northwest of Okinawa, near the hot spot, with the USS *Stanly*, DD478, and *Purdy*, DD734, when at about noon six aircraft attacked. She shot down five, but the sixth crashed high up in her foremast and exploded in midair, only 50 feet above the deck. Miraculously, only one man was killed, but 59 were wounded.

*Stanly* took up *Cassin Young's* fighter director duty, guiding CAP to the attack. After temporary repairs at Kerama Retto, DD793 went to Ulithi for further rebuilding; then the destroyer returned to the bloody island in time to be crashed into again, July 29.

## USS PURDY, DD734, APRIL 12, 1945:

Six days earlier the destroyer picked up survivors from the stricken USS *Mullany*, returning them to Kerama Retto. On the 12th, she did likewise for *Cassin Young*. Some

30 aircraft attacked the destroyers, most were shot down by CAP, but two crashed into *Cassin Young* and a third closed *Purdy*. Although hit and disintegrating, its momentum carried the Kamikaze to *Purdy*. The explosion caused extensive damage, killed 15 and seriously wounded 25 men. After temporary repairs at Kerama Retto, *Purdy* returned to San Francisco. Her war was over.

## USS STANLY, DD478, APRIL 12, 1945:
### (BAKA BOMB)

By the time *Stanly* established herself as fighter director, the Kamikazes were swarming around her, like bees. With her effective control, CAP aircraft shot down six Vals in rapid succession.

U.S. fighters and Kamikazes were fully engaged overhead, as the desperate struggle continued. Suddenly, without warning a manned, flying torpedo called Baka Bomb was released from an aircraft and closed *Stanly* at 500 knots. With no possible chance of retaliation, he crashed into the starboard side, five feet above the waterline. Fortunately, the warhead passed through *Stanly* and exploded in the water, close aboard. Within minutes a second baka whizzed over the ship -- and sucked an ensign along with it. The guided torpedo skipped over the water and disintegrated. *Stanly* was ordered back to Hagushi and experienced another near miss by a Zeke. In all the hair-raising action, they had only three men wounded. After repairs at Kerama Retto, they stayed in action at Okinawa.

**This war steadily became total devastation!**

## USS MANNERT L. ABELE, DD733, APRIL 12, 1945:
### (BAKA BOMB)

At 1345, while patrolling RP 14 the hot spot, three Vals attacked, gunfire drove off two, and the third crashed while trying to dive on one of her two LSMR's, (pallbearer). By 1400, 15 to 25 additional Kamikazes had them surrounded. At about 1440 three broke ranks and dove for *Abele*. She drove off one, splashed the second, but spewing flames and smoke the third Kamikaze crashed the starboard side and exploded in her after engine room. The explosion broke her keel just aft of number two stack, and the bridge and all gun directors, lost power.

One minute later *Mannert L. Abele* took a second fatal hit. A manned, 2,600 pound Baka bomb, crashed into her starboard side. He hit the forward fireroom at the waterline and *Abele* broke in two almost immediately! Her bow and stern sections -- sank rapidly. As survivors clung to floating debris in the churning water, the enemy bombed and strafed them. "The two pallbearers, USS LSMR189 and LSMR190, were worth their weight in gold," according to *Abele's* Captain Commander Parker. They splashed two of the remaining attackers, repulsed further attacks and rescued *Mannert L. Abele's* survivors.

**Quoting Mannert L. Abele's historian from the last paragraph of her history:**

*"Mannert L. Abele the only ship sunk by the Baka bomb during the Okinawa campaign, was the first of three radar pickets hit by it. Despite the enemy's desperate efforts, the radar pickets successfully and proudly completed their mission, thus insuring the success of the campaign. Those on picket line forged new shining traditions of heroic devotion to duty. Captain Frederick C. Moosbrugger, overall commander of the radar pickets, acclaimed their hazardous duty ... 'A symbol of supreme achievement in our naval traditions.' And paraphrasing Sir Winston Churchill, he wrote: 'Never in the annals of our glorious naval history have naval forces done so much with so little against such odds for so long a period.'"*

### USS JEFFERS, DD621-DMS27, APRIL 12, 1945:

While on RP duty near *Abele*, she repulsed heavy air raids, shooting down at least one of the attackers. In the encounter, *Jeffers* suffered a near miss by still another deadly Baka bomb. This was at least the fifth manned Baka released this day. Before returning to Kerama Retto for repairs, *Jeffers* assisted survivors of the sunken *Mannert L. Abele*.

### USS LINDSEY, DM32, APRIL 12, 1945:

In the afternoon the destroyer came under mass Kamikaze attacks. *Lindsey* scored hits on seven dive bombers, but two damaged and out of control Vals, crashed and blew 60 feet off her bow. Commander Chambers ordered, "All back full," which prevented pressure of in-rushing water from collapsing the fireroom bulkhead and sinking the ship. Fifty-seven men were killed and 57 wounded. The same night, they towed *Lindsey* to Kerama Retto for temporary repairs; then on to Guam for a temporary bow. The destroyer minesweeper, steamed under her own power to Norfolk Navy Shipyard, for overhaul.

*USS Lindsey, DM32, April 12, 1945*

### USS WHITEHURST, DE634, APRIL 12, 1945:

In mid-afternoon, while operating off the southwest coast of Okinawa, a low flying Kamikaze was driven off by her gunfire; then at 1430, four Val dive bombers approached the area from the south. Three started an attack on *Whitehurst*, first a Val already in a steep dive, the second, low on the water, came in on the starboard beam, then the third approached from the stern. The latter two aircraft spun down in flames from antiaircraft fire, but despite 20mm hits, the first diving Kamikaze crashed into her forward port side superstructure. The plane entered the pilot house, engulfed the entire bridge in flames and the bomb continued on through the ship and exploded 50 feet off her starboard bow. Assisted by the USS *Vigilance*, AM324, *Whitehurst* circled out of control. The DE's repair party extinguished her fires and got the ship back under control. The minesweeper saved many lives with her quick first-aid response. After temporary patchwork at Kerama Retto, *Whitehurst* went to Pearl Harbor for repairs.

### USS RALL, DE304, APRIL 12, 1945:

While screening on station about 10 miles southeast of Ie Shima, a number of enemy aircraft forced the destroyer escort to GQ, as five Kamikazes pressed the attack. The DE shot down three, and a cruiser got the fourth, but the fifth suicider crashed into *Rall*. A 500 pound bomb tore through the ships port side, exploding in the air about 15 feet away. *Rall's* 38 wounded were transferred to the hospital ship, USS *Pinkney*, APH2 and her 21 dead were buried in the Sixth Marine Cemetery on Okinawa. The DE went to Puget Sound Navy Yard for repairs. *Rall's* war was over.

### USS RIDDLE, DE185, APRIL 12, 1945:
### USS BENNION, DD662, APRIL 12, 1945:

The ships had only slight damage; however *Riddle* lost 1 killed and 9 wounded and *Bennion* lost 1 killed and 6 wounded. Kamikazes scored big on the terrible day of April 12th.

### USS BRYANT, DD665, APRIL 13, 1945:

While patrolling on her assigned RP station, the Fletcher class destroyer was attacked by six enemy planes. One Kamikaze crashed into the port side of the *Bryant's* bridge -- exploding on impact. The Kamikaze caused extreme damage. Thirty-four men were killed or missing and 33 wounded. *Bryant* went to Alameda, California for repairs. Her war ended.

### USS SIGSBEE, DD502, APRIL 14, 1945:

*Sigsbee*, a Fletcher class destroyer, on RP duty off Okinawa, was struck aft of mount 5 by a suicide plane, knocking out her port engine. Her starboard engine could only be run at five knots, with no steering control, and much of her main deck awash -- *Sigsbee* was in big trouble. With only 3 killed but 75 wounded, they were still lucky.

They towed *Sigsbee* to Guam for temporary repairs, then she steamed to Pearl Harbor where a new 60 foot stern was installed. Her war was over.

*USS Sigsbee, DD502, April 14, 1945*

## USS NEW YORK, BB34, AND USS HUNT, DD674, APRIL 14, 1945:
These ships received slight damage by Kamikazes.

*USS Laffey, DD724,  explodes, April 15, 1945*

## USS LAFFEY, DD724, APRIL 15, 1945:
A large number of enemy aircraft broke the screens of U.S. destroyers to attack the *Laffey*.  The game destroyer shot down nine and U.S. aircraft destroyed many others,

but when the attack was over, the ship was badly damaged by four bombs and the impact of five suicide planes.

Lloyd Megee, probably one of the luckiest sailors in the U.S. Navy, who told his story in chapter nine about the sinking of *Abner Read*, recalls his experience on *Laffey*, for our book:

"I went aboard *Laffey*, January 28, 1945, at Lingayen Gulf and was still onboard at Okinawa. During *Laffey's* epic battle April 15th, I was at GQ in the forward repair party, inside the midships deck house. The first attack came from our stern, about 7:30am, but missed us. Then, about 45 minutes later all hell hit us in quick succession. The first plane crashed into number 3, 5-inch gun, and two more followed on his tail to crash on our stern.

"Our repair party jumped into action; we stretched hoses and started pumps to fight fires that were consuming our ship. Many men in our repair party were killed during those few minutes.

"Then still another plane dove for our port bow. His bomb exploded close aboard, and a big piece of shrapnel went through the mount 2 handling room door into the fire control panel. With the gun disabled, I was given the job of fixing it. We got the mount working manually, but by that time the battle was over. We then fought fires that continued to ravage our ship and transferred wounded to the LCT that pulled alongside.

"Eventually we were towed into Kerama Retto by a tug. I stayed aboard *Laffey* until she made it back to Todd Shipyard, in Puget Sound."

**Lloyd Megee had a charmed life.** *Laffey* had 32 killed and 71 wounded.

### USS PRINGLE, DD477, AND USS HOBSON, DD464, APRIL 16, 1945:
After being repaired from her first encounter with Kamikazes on December 30, 1944, at Mindoro, the destroyer returned to action in time for the Okinawa invasion. Assigned to picket duty April 15, she joined the USS *Hobson*, already on the station where *Mannert L. Abele* had been sunk, three days earlier.

At about 0900 on the 16th, at least four Kamikazes approached the destroyer. They shot the first two down, but the third crashed directly into *Pringle's* bridge. After going through the bridge, the aircraft plowed on through the after superstructure and came to rest at the base of number one stack. The 1000 pound bomb exploded at that point and broke her keel. *Pringle* was blown in two! Almost immediately a fourth Kamikaze crashed just off *Hobson's* starboard side; then the bomb wound up on *Hobson's* main deck and exploded. Raging fires engulfed the ship.

*Pringle* sank in six minutes. Two hundred fifty-eight survivors had to watch their ship disappear -- to her watery grave!

While still fighting off Kamikazes, *Hobson* extinguished her fires and picked 100 of *Pringle's* crewmen from the sea.

*Hobson* then anchored at Kerama Retto to prepare for her long, slow voyage home. They arrived at the Norfolk Naval Shipyard June 16, 1945. Her war was over.

### USS HARDING, (DD625) DMS28, APRIL 16:

After sweeping mines around Okinawa for seven days before the invasion, *Harding* protected the invading fleet in the outer screening position on April 1, 1945. Having survived the savage air attacks of April 6, she took part in a shore bombardment on the 8th and came under heavy air attack en route to RP14 on April 16.

Thanks to *Harding's* historian, Robert G. Hiskey, we have the following stories of what happened. Following is Captain Ramage's own account of *Harding's* last days, the Captain died shortly after making this tape:

*"April 6. enemy bombers and Kamikazes were in the area most of the day and night, inflicting damage to several ships. Our division operated off the southeast corner of Okinawa, later named Buckner Bay. Our mission was to be on call to provide gunfire support ashore and to protect the small minesweepers, still sweeping.*

*"Harding was stoogin around, and about 1820 commenced playing 'ring around the rosie' with a "Judy" 33 dive bomber that was trying to get astern of us for a no deflection dive. With lots of rudder and speed we kept them on our starboard side. The Judy was doing a lot of jinks at an estimated 5,000 to 8,000 yards. Finally, at about 1830, he gave up and made his run on our beam. He dropped a bomb that exploded just astern in our wake. He lifted the stern of our ship a little bit, but the pilot was not much of a duck hunter and did not lead his target enough to score a hit. Part of the steering gear was lost for a brief time. The rest of the evening was quiet.*

*"April 16 was a fateful day. While still on a screening station north of the island, we were ordered to proceed to RP14, about 72 miles north of point Bolo. We were to take over picket duty from ships that were sunk or damaged earlier that morning. We never made it!*

*"Aircraft reports started coming in about five minutes after we left our screening station. One aircraft to port in raid one and four to starboard in raid two, were identified as enemy and they started making threatening faints towards us. Raid one was hit, and dove, on fire into the sea. We then turned hard to starboard. The high speed and sharp turn caused our gyro repeater amplifiers to cut out and we lost gyro input to the computers and 5-inch director.*

*"An aircraft in raid two, which had been making faints, continued on in. Our 40mm and 20mm guns did a fine job. The plane, on fire, at 1700 yards kept coming on*

*in and crashed just short of the starboard bow, but the bomb came on in and exploded next to the keel. The remaining planes of raid two, departed.*

*"At the time of the hit, about 0959, the ship was traveling at all-out speed, with full right rudder. The forecastle settled down from the flooding, until the bullnose was just above the water. The sea was smooth as glass, otherwise Harding would surely have taken a dive! We also had an enormous port list.*

*"The aircraft's engine had landed on the starboard bridge wing. Engine room communications were lost, so I leaned over the flag bags and shouted to the men on deck below. 'Tell the engine room -- back full' By 1005 most of the water we had scooped up was gone, so we stopped to check the damage. Most of the damage was contained forward of the forward bulkhead.*

*"After damage control efforts and care for the dead and wounded, an attempt was made to steam ahead, but the ship simply scooped up the water again and down went the bow.*

*"We suffered 14 dead, 10 wounded, and 8 missing. The USS Shea DM30, took our wounded. So we backed the ship towards Kerama Retto where a tug towed us on into the harbor. Next morning the tug placed the ship port side to, APA214. By good luck the beer stored forward of number-1 fireroom came through unscathed.*

*"A memorial service was held on 26 April for those crewmen killed and missing"*

Walter Volrath, Jr. had just been replaced as gunnery officer and was at GQ. He recalls: *"During the first attack on April 6, I happened to be on the port wing at the time, although my battle station was on the starboard wing. I was told about the plane coming in on the starboard side, so I ran back over, arriving about the time the bomb hit the water. It was close but caused little damage.*

*" On the 16th, I saw the plane come on in, and still think I could see the pilot's helmet and goggles. We had a young man on the starboard 50 caliber machine gun, (can't remember his name.) He emptied his magazine at the Kamikaze.*

*"I said to Lt Mel Cairns, in plot, 'Target angle zero, Mel, speed 100 to 120 knots.'*

*"Mel said, 'He is closing very fast."*

*"Those were probably Mel's last words; because then it hit about in number 2 magazine. I dove into the pilot house as it hit, but still got wet from the spray"* **Walt** concluded.

Ship's cook, **Mike Mevorah**: *"My battle station was as a 20mm gunner, forward under the bridge, on the starboard side. About 10:30am, all hell broke loose. We were* cruising north because the sun was on the starboard side. Then suddenly, in line with the sun, two suicide planes started to dive toward the bridge of our ship. The glare of the sun made it very difficult for me, and the other gunners, to get a good aim at the targets.

"I remember our 5-inch guns firing, but could not hit the targets. Then the 40mm guns began to fire and still they did not hit the planes. When they came within range of our 20mm guns, I began to fire. I saw my tracer bullets hitting the plane's motor. I then saw fire flashes and thought the Jap pilot was shooting back at us. The plane was so close and on a collision course for our bridge. I said my prayers and was prepared to die! The next moment I saw the plane explode.

"He must have been about 50 feet away. He scattered debris all over our ship. A piece of the plane's motor hit the deck about six inches away from my foot. A split second before the plane exploded he dropped his 500 pound bomb. It hit our ship below the water level and exploded number 1 and 2 magazines. With a gaping hole in the bow, the ship was submerged like a sub. We would have sunk if it wasn't for the quick thinking of Captain Ramage. He put all engines in emergency reverse, and the watertight integrity, back aft, kept our ship afloat.

"We were a sitting duck for further attacks. I remember the destroyer, USS Hadley, DD774, came to our aid, shooting down three planes in a matter of minutes.

"I saw an officer coming top side from where our mess hall had been; his helmet was bashed in and blood was streaming down his face. We ran slowly in reverse to the nearest island and tied up to a PA transport for aid. To this very day, I give thanks to God for giving us our courageous Captain Ramage. I truly believe he saved my life and the rest of our crew." Mike Mevorah concluded.

LT jg. William Carter recalls: "As we steamed northward, in the darkness, towards RP14 at flank speed, we had to negotiate our way through and around many large and small ships, a navigational nightmare.

"We knew our chances to survive on that station were nil, to none. We had been monitoring the radio for days and had listened to one account after another about the fate of our predecessors . They were faster, more heavily armed destroyers that were getting knocked off as fast as they got on station, now we were speeding to replace them.

"I was on the flying bridge directing the starboard machine-gun fire at the time the aircraft crashed and the bomb hit. The starboard side flying bridge, about 40 feet above the water, was awash as the bow nosed under the sea. I thought we were going over! My large, talker, bell helmet, over ear phones, had a very strong chin strap, and I could not get it to release. By the time I decided we might not rollover, I had cut the chin strap and felt much relieved.

"For over 40 years now I have lived with the regret that our guns proved unequal to keep safe the 23 brave soles that died that day and the others that were wounded. If we had known the Kamikazes would not be shooting back, we might have shot better. A known suicide plane attack is psychologically difficult for individuals to deal with."

Chief Engineer Lt Frank Stratman: "My GQ station was in the forward engine room. When we were hit by the Kamikaze we were running at flank speed and taking radical evasive action. When we, in the engine and firerooms, felt the blast of the Kamikaze hit, a number of things happened, simultaneously. Our gyroscope had failed and our Chief Electricians Mate Jerome W. Maxwell had been dispatched to fire control, where he lost his life. All communication with the bridge was lost. We could feel a substantial list by the bow, and a member of the repair party shouted down the hatch to stop all main engines. We maintained good communications between engineering spaces throughout this ordeal.

"Number-2 boilers showed the low water alarm, a very serious problem, but the firemen responded flawlessly. The number-1 generator shorted out; however quick action got it restarted. I went up the ladder to observe the damage, then went back down to reverse the engines.

"Repair party-1 was decimated, so engineering personnel were pressed into service to limit damage and begin the evacuation of wounded and deceased personnel.

"The forward bulkhead of the mess hall required shoring and welding before we could start pumping. This was necessary to gain access to the fire control room where we knew about eight people were dead, since we had obviously lost the keel at about frame 32. We knew that we might lose our bow section if we pumped too much water out of it. The forecastle deck was the only thing holding the bow to the rest of the ship. We continued backing the ship towards Kerama Retto. All engineering personnel reacted flawlessly"

Jack Singer, Fire control division: "As 5-inch gun director, I was approaching my GQ station and called to James Beck, standing director watch, he responded, 'I'm glad you are here so I can go down to the fire control room where it is safe.'

"After the hit I left my director which was of little use and learned all in the fire control room were dead. I thought of Jim, how he had just been married and wondered how we could tell his wife, who I had just met. Our crew stood tall that morning and we are proud of our place in history."

Machinist Mate Robert Hiskey: "My GQ station was on the lower level in the forward engine room. The hit put us in total darkness, and the shock and severe port list threw me against the port side. After re-gathering my orientation lights came back on, so I started pumping the bilges which were taking water fast. The strainer kept filling up with a strange orange substance and I had to keep switching from one to the other, as *they filled and became plugged. There was a tremendous amount of that substance scattered all over the deck plates on the lower level. They turned out to be dried apricots from a storage room up forward and I'll probably never know exactly how they got there."*

*Harding* finally went to Norfolk where she was sadly scrapped.
Thanks to all of you guys for your exciting stories.

### USS WILSON DD408, APRIL 16, 1945:

While escorting a convoy entering Wiseman's Cove, *Wilson* came under attack by two Kamikazes. They took the lead aircraft under fire and failed to knock him down, but the second suicider did a wing-over and dove for the destroyer. *Wilson* shot him down about 75 yards off the starboard quarter. The aircraft bounced off the sea and flew between 5-inch mounts three and four and crashed in the sea, near the port side. His propeller wound up in the 40mm gun tub, and his unexploded 250 kilogram bomb wound up in the after living compartment. Five men in the group three magazine were killed by drowning and three others were blown overboard. *Wilson* remained operational.

### USS TALUGA, A062, APRIL 16, 1945:

While fueling ships at Kerama Retto, shortly before dawn, the tanker came under attack. The intruder strafed her deck, then headed for the bridge and exploded through her forward well deck, near 300,000 gallons of aviation fuel. Twelve men were wounded, but the oiler was soon back in business.

### USS INTREPID, CV11, APRIL 16,1945:

The carrier had been hit by Kamikazes on three different occasions and on this date she took her fourth Kamikaze aboard. As usual, he went through her flight deck, killing 8 men and wounding 21. The plucky carrier stayed in action until the following day, then sailed to San Francisco for repairs. *Intrepid's* long war was finally over.

*USS Intrepid, CV11, April 16, 1945 A Fletcher class destroyer speeds to protect the stricken carrier.*

## USS BOWERS, DE637, APRIL 17, 1945:

Two Kamikazes had just been splashed when a third scored a direct hit on her bridge. *Bowers* suffered extensive damage, heavy loss of life, with 48 killed and 59 wounded, many fatally. After temporary repairs at Kerama Retto they sailed to the Philadelphia Navy Yard. *Bower* was converted to a high speed transport and reclassified APD40, but her war was over.

*USS Bowers, DE637, April 17, 1945*

## USS AMMEN, DD527, APRIL 21,1945:

The destroyer had her second brush with disaster when a near miss wounded 8 men. Her first encounter November 1, 1944 killed five and wounded 21.

## USS HUDSON, DD475, APRIL 22, 1945:

How close can a Kamikaze come to a destroyer? On this day a chief petty officer got clipped on the head with a wing tip! The aircraft missed the ship.

## USS ISHERWOOD, DD520, APRIL 22, 1945:

On April 16, the destroyer sped to rescue the *Pringle* and *Laffey*. They went to RP14, where *Mannert L. Abele* was sunk April 12, *Laffey* was greatly damaged April 15, and *Pringle* sank April 16.

After fighting off many heavy air attacks at dusk on the 22nd, a Kamikaze crashed into number 3, 5-inch mount. *Isherwood's* firefighters quickly extinguished all fires, but one, which burned among depth charges on the fantail. At least one charge exploded and inflicted great damage to the after part of the ship, including the after engine room. Eighty men were killed, missing or wounded.

*Isherwood* arrived at San Francisco June 3, for repairs. Her war was over.

## USS SWALLOW, AM65, APRIL 22,1945:

After sweeping the invasion beaches for seven days before April 1, *Swallow* patrolled the outer harbor for submarines. At 1858 on the 22nd, a Kamikaze diving out of clouds crashed into the minesweeper's starboard side, amidships at the waterline. With both engine rooms flooded, *Swallow* took on a 45 degree starboard list. The order to abandon ship was given at 1901. Three minutes later she capsized and sank. Her sunken hulk was donated to the government of the Ryukyu Islands.

## USS RALPH TALBOT, DD390, APRIL 27, 1945:

The veteran destroyer arrived at Okinawa on the 26th where they were put into service screening Task Group 51.5. At 2200 on the 27th, while patrolling off their anchorage, she was closed by two Kamikazes. The first crashed *Talbot's* starboard side aft and the second crashed off her port quarter, close aboard. PCE852 pulled alongside providing a doctor and seven corpsmen. Repairs were made at Kerama Retto and *Talbot* returned to service May 20.

## USS RATHBURNE, DD113, APRIL 27, 1945:

On April 18, the old four stack destroyer was also pressed into service. While screening Hagushi in the evening of the 27th, a Kamikaze crashed into her port bow. As *Rathburne* slowly returned to Kerama Retto for repairs, fires and flooding were soon controlled.

## USS HUTCHINS, DD476, APRIL 27, 1945:

While on close support operations off Nakagushku Wan, (Buckner Bay) a small, fast suicide boat slipped through the entire formation to deliver his deadly package, personally. Radioman First Class John Tucker describes *Hutchins'* silent rendezvous with destruction, for our book:

*"I had served aboard Hutchins since she was commissioned at Boston in 1942, until that fateful night that ended her life. We were on condition watch at the time (not at GQ) with my watch being off duty, I was asleep in my top bunk.*

*"Fully loaded, Fletcher class destroyers weigh about 3,000 tons, but at about 0230 we went sky-high! I was rudely awakened and wedged between two bunks, so I broke loose and went topside. During the confusion we were taking on vast amounts of water. As leading petty officer I went to the CIC room to see what had happened and they announced over the PA 'all hands abandon ship.'*

*"We never did learn the full story. There were stories that the boat actually hit us head-on, while other stories said it came close aboard and dropped its charges. I tend to the latter version. However, the repair parties did an outstanding job, with the assistance of "billie pumps" we were able to pump out as much water as was coming in, enabling us to stay afloat and proceed to Kerama Retto.*

*"We waited for over a month to get patched up so we could take the ship back to the states, for a determination whether or not it could be salvaged. The verdict was that it should be scrapped. The trip back was quite interesting, at a steady 5 knots, with the rudder hard to starboard to compensate for only one screw turning, we thought we would never get there. About 500 miles from Pearl Harbor, the port shaft let go and we sat there like a cold duck waiting for an enemy sub to show up. The Army sent out a bomber which circled us until a liberty ship showed up to haul us into Pearl. We were glad for the tow, but weren't very happy for the "distinguished" tow. We stayed in Pearl for repairs and then more limping across to Oregon, then up to Bremerton where she was decommissioned."*

*Hutchins* war ended and she was ultimately sold for scrap, but fortunately they did not sustain a single casualty.

## USS TWIGGS, DD591; AND USS DALY, DD519, APRIL 28, 1945:

On this day of heavy air attacks a Kamikaze splashed close aboard the *Twiggs*. The bomb blew in the hull plating between her main and first platform deck, caused structural damage and bent the starboard propeller. *Nestor*, ARB6, repaired the damage. *Twiggs* returned to service May 17. One month later she was sunk!

*Daly*, slightly damaged by a near miss that killed three and injured 16 crewmen, was repaired at Kerama Retto.

## USS WADSWORTH, DD516, APRIL 22 AND 28, 1945:

Even though her damages on two separate occasions were slight, we must tell her story.

On the 22nd, *Wadsworth* shot down a Kamikaze that landed 20 feet from the ship, showering it with debris. Fortunately, only slight damage was inflicted and only one sailor wounded.

On April 28, *Wadsworth* had a very hectic day! They repelled six determined attacks by 12 enemy aircraft. One torpedo plane dropped a fish from 1200 yards, then came on in to crash on her deck. His wing struck the forward port 40mm gun, then the body of the aircraft spun into the gig, carried away a life raft, smashed into a whaleboat, then crashed in the sea. The destroyer turned hard left rudder and the fish passed harmlessly down her starboard side. Showered with debris and gasoline, that's about as close as a ship can get to disaster. *Wadsworth* earned the Presidential Unit Citation.

## USS PINKNEY, APH2, APRIL 28, 1945:
### (HOSPITAL SHIP)

*Pinkney* and Comfort were hospital ships. At least one had white paint and a large red cross, visible for many miles, and could not be miss identified. Still they became targets of that Japanese Kamikaze madness!

From April 10 to the 28th, *Pinkney* took on casualties from the land action, as well as from destroyed or damaged ships. In Hagushi anchorage, the "Safe Haven," they cared for an over supply of badly injured patients and transferred many to the USS *Samaritan,* AH-10. At 1730 on the 28th, they spotted a low flying Kamikaze closing the hospital ship. Seconds later *Pinkney* was rocked by an explosion! The after end of the superstructure was walled by a sheet of flame. Ammunition exploded and waterlines, electrical conduits, and steam pipes ruptured. The crew immediately formed rescue and damage control parties.

All but the 16 patients killed in the initial explosion had been transferred to safety. A hole 30 feet in diameter extended from the bridge deck to the bulkhead deck. All wards in the amidships hospital area were burned out.

Tugs and landing craft assisted fighting *Pinkney's* fires, but they persisted for another three hours. Eighteen crewmen were killed, in addition to the 16 patients. After 8 days of clean up and repairs, *Pinkney* went to San Francisco, for further repairs.

## USS COMFORT AH-6, APRIL 29, 1945:
### (HOSPITAL SHIP)

On April 29, six days after the hospital ship arrived, they were also crashed into by a Japanese suicide plane. Twenty-eight persons, including six nurses, were killed and 48 wounded. The hospital ship received considerable damage and they had to go to Los Angeles for repairs.

What more can I say, but to simply tell this story as it happened. Even though we suspected the Japanese were using their hospital ships to evacuate healthy troops to fight again, *Wren* allowed one ship safe passage. This was U.S. policy. I believe all Japanese hospital ships had free uninterrupted passage.

On April 21st, USS LST15 was sunk, April 22, USS *Ransom*, AN283 received slight damage, April 27, SS *Canada Victory* sank, and on April 30, SS *Hall Young* was hit. All ships hit were by Kamikazes during April, 1945.

## USS HAZELWOOD, DD531, APRIL 29, 1945:

As they operated with a carrier group off Okinawa, the fleet came under Kamikaze attack. While the destroyers guns were fully engaged with two Zeros, a third aircraft came screaming out of nearby clouds, from astern, and dove straight at *Hazelwood*. Although her gunners managed to get on the third most threatening target with several hits scored, the determined Kamikaze struck home at number two stack. He crashed and exploded on the bridge!

The mast toppled, all forward guns were out of action and the destroyer suffered severe damage. *Hazelwood* had heavy casualties with 102 killed, including her Commanding Officer V. P. Douw.

*USS Hazelwood, DD531, April 29, 1945*

The Engineering Officer Ltjg C. M. Locke, took command. They extinguished fires, cared for wounded, then were taken in tow to Ulithi. The badly damaged ship eventually got back to Mare Island, California, for rebuilding. *Hazelwood's* war ended!

### USS HAGGARD, DD 555, APRIL 29, 1945:

On her way out to radar picket duty the destroyer came under attack. *Haggard's* guns blew the aircraft in a shallow dive, nearly apart, but he crashed aboard, penetrating the hull near the waterline. The bomb exploded in the engine room! *Haggard* quickly started to sink from massive flooding, but the badly crippled ship had to fight off another attacker. He was quickly shot down. Miraculously, her crew saved their ship and the destroyer USS *Walker* towed them to Kerama Retto. *Haggard* eventually made it back to Norfolk, just to fall victim again, to the cutters torch!

Like the month of April 1945, May entered with a large explosion, as Kamikazes continued their reign of terror. Nineteen U.S. ships fell victim during the first five days.

### USS TERROR, CM 5, MAY 1, 1945:

The 455 foot, sleekly built minelayer was the only ship of its type built during WWII. *Terror* spent the entire month of April at Kerama Retto, providing logistic support and received casualties from ships hit by Kamikazes. On April 6, she took casualties from LST447 and SS *Logan Victory*, hit while in the harbor.

On April 28, she was anchored near the hospital ship *Pinkney,* when they were hit by a suicide plane. *Terror* sent boats to *Pinkney's* aid and treated many of her casualties. Three days later, *Terror* herself fell victim to the dreaded Kamikazes.

At about 0400, May 1, while anchored in the harbor, a Kamikaze darted through a hole in the smoke screen and dove towards *Terror*. The suicide plane came in on the port beam, then banked sharply around her stern and came in from the starboard quarter so fast that only one stern gun could fire. He crashed into the ship's communication platform! One bomb exploded on contact, the other penetrated the main deck before exploding. The aircraft's engine tore through the ship's bulkheads, like they were butter, and landed in the wardroom. Fires and flooding followed, but quick flooding of the ship's magazines prevented further explosions. Her engineering spaces were spared. The attack cost *Terror* 41 dead, 7 missing, and 123 wounded.

The following day the battered ship was moored to USS *Natrona,* APA214, for emergency repairs, then they sailed for San Francisco. Her war ended.

### USS AARON WARD, (DD773) DM34, MAY 3, 1945:

On the 28th the destroyer minelayer also came to the aid of the hospital ship *Pinkney,* rescued 12 survivors and helped bring fires under control.

On May 3, while on picket duty with the *Little*, DD803, a suicide plane crashed into *Aaron Ward's* port side, exploding a bomb in the forward fireroom, causing the ship to come dead in the water. Then two more suicide planes crashed her decks, in quick succession, and a bomb landed near number one stack!

Badly damaged, they were assisted by USS LCSL's 14 and 83, then taken under tow by the USS *Shannon*, DM25, into Kerama Retto. *Aaron Ward* limped back to the states, through the Panama Canal, and all the way up to the New York Navy Yard -- just to be scrapped! *Aaron Ward* received the Presidential Unit Citation.

*USS Aaron Ward, DM34, May 5, 1945*

## USS LITTLE, DD803, MAY 3, 1945:

While on RP10, which was 73.5 miles from point Zampa Masaki (due west) with *Aaron Ward*, USS LSM195, LCS14, 25 and 83, (pall bearers) the group came under heavy air attack.

Thanks to *Little's* crewman, Gunners Mate Second Class Frank Whall, we have the war diaries, and Frank's personal experience, as reference.

*Little* had been on station for four days, when the fateful events took place. At about 1415 enemy aircraft were observed in the vicinity and the ensuing action lasted into the darkness.

Four enemy raids were observed by CIC, all of which apparently took part in the attacks on our RP stations. Coordinated suicide tactics were utilized by attacking planes.

Fighter (CAP) consisted of four planes which were sent out to intercept. The Japanese planes slipped through cloud cover, as a result of inaccurate altitude information. Lookouts reported, "Six enemy planes came down through the same hole in the clouds our aircraft entered." The two destroyers were swarmed with Kamikazes!

Quoting from Commander Madison Hall Jr, *Little's* Captain's action reports and her ship's reunion paper: *"At 1843 they struck at the picket destroyers. One in a vertical dive, one low on the sea, and one gliding in. That such coordination could be achieved is almost unbelievable, but such was the case.*

*"Little's gunners got two of them. But four others got Little. Like a chain of thunderbolts they smashed into the destroyer, shattering her superstructure, crashing her hull and wrecked her vital machinery. It was all over between 1843 and 1845! The dead were vanishing in flood water and flame. The living were going overboard.*

*"The pall bearers closed in! At 1855 Little sank into an Okinawa grave. Down with her, she took 30 of her crew. Some 280 survivors, 52 of them wounded, were quickly picked up by the rescuers. Seldom had a ship been subjected to such punishment -- and seldom so many survivors lived to fight again!"*

Gunner's Mate Frank Whall was on duty, standing by the two forward 40mm guns #41 and 42. Following is his direct quotation for our book: *"Having been in the Pacific for four years and earned six battle stars before those Kamikaze attacks, I was so scared I couldn't speak. When one of our ammunition passers was standing, blank faced, and doing nothing, I had to kick him in the ass and point to the ammunition. No matter what you had seen or been through before, Kamikaze attacks were the ultimate terror!"*

## USS MACOMB, (DD458) DMS23, MAY 3, 1945:
After surviving the rigor of Mine Division 20, where only one ship out of 11 survived, *Macomb's* charmed life expired, during the twilight hours of May 3. She downed the first intruder, but a second, running fast on the tail of the first, crashed into her causing extensive damage.

She went to Saipan for repairs and rejoined the 3rd fleet in Tokyo Bay. *Macomb* earned the Navy Unit Commendation for her outstanding services at Okinawa. Not enough praise can ever be given about all eleven ships of Mine Division 20.

## USS MORRISON, DD560, MAY 4, 1945:

Six days earlier the destroyer had replaced USS *Daly*, DD519, on RP station after the latter was hit and put out of service.

On April 30, *Morrison* transferred to one of the critical RP stations and three days of bad weather prevented attacks, then May 4 was bright and clear. At 0715, they called CAP to stop an approaching force of about 25 aircraft, but some got through.

The first aircraft, a Zeke broke through heavy flack to drop his bomb off *Morrison's* starboard beam, it exploded harmlessly; then another Zeke accompanied by a "Val" were shot down. About 0825 the first suicide plane struck home! A Zeke came through intense AA fire to crash into her stack and bridge. *Morrison* lost most of her power and suffered heavy casualties. The next three aircraft, old biplanes, crashed into the damaged destroyer despite heavy AA fire. With the fourth hit, *Morrison* began to list sharply to starboard.

They still had enough working communications to issue the abandon ship order. Two explosions occurred almost simultaneously, the bow lifted into the air -- and *Morrison* quickly sank. So quickly, most men below decks were trapped! At 0840, 153 men went down with their ship.

## USS LUCE, DD522, MAY 4, 1945:

While on RP station north of Kerama Retto, at 0740, Japanese suicide aircraft were picked up by combat air patrol. The area north of Kerama Retto and west of Hagushi was getting a lot of attention on this morning; many stations were under attack, early. Enemy planes slipped through CAP and attacked *Luce* from the port side.

Fireman Second Class Dwaine Erstad gives his personal account for our book: *"Having just completed my watch in the after fireroom, about 0650, I was in the chow line about to be served, when GQ sounded. I grabbed an orange and run to my battle station as port lookout, on the flying bridge.*

*"It was real eerie when I got there that morning; the sea was calm, the skies were clear, but full of suicide planes. There must have been 150 of them. They looked like swarms of bees and I knew what every man topside knew -- we were doomed!*

*"The first plane to attack us was a Zero. He came in low on the water and we couldn't even get our guns low enough to hit it. I remember the prop was hitting the water. He raised up and cut all our lanyards for signal flags and hit us amidships. He took the superstructure off all the way to the fantail. The explosion ruptured our fuel oil tanks and the sea was covered. I was blown up in the air and when I came down the orange was smashed, my watch and life jacket were blown off and I was in daze for awhile. I crawled in behind our fighter director for protection.*

*"The second plane hit between number one and two stacks, knocking out our 40mm. I think they were number 43 and 44. Most of those guys were killed. One guy, a friend of mine, did survive. I saw him hanging there, full of blood, and thought he was dead, but found out afterward he had survived.*

*"The third plane knocked out number five 5-inch gun. All power was out, we had no steering and number 1, 2, and 3 mounts were firing manually. It was just a turkey shoot! The pilots were very deliberate, they knew what they wanted to do -- and they did it."*

At 0814 *Luce* took a heavy list to starboard and the order to abandon ship was passed. Moments later, with a violent explosion, *Luce* slipped beneath the sea -- carrying with her 126 men!

*Dwaine concludes: "Two shipmates and I shared a floating mattress for three hours, in the oily sea, while sharks swam around the perimeter. The pall bearers were a welcome sight."*

### USS SHEA, DM30, MAY 4, 1945:
### ("BAKA BOMB")

Like *Shea*, most DM's (destroyer minelayers) we have been writing about were *Allan M. Sumner*, or *John H. Smith* class, 2200 ton, destroyers.

On RP station only about 20 miles northeast of Zampa Misaki Point, *Shea* was running in smoke that had blown over from Hagushi anchorage and limited visibility to a maximum of 5,000 yards.

After shooting down one of two attackers on her way out, *Shea* arrived on RP station about 0600. Receiving information about approaching formations of Japanese aircraft, they went to GQ. A "Betty" was sighted at 0854 about six miles away, so *Shea* directed CAP to intercept and shoot it down. Five minutes later a "Baka bomb," traveling at 450 knots, was sighted closing *Shea's* starboard side. Almost instantly the piloted suicide bomb struck *Shea's* starboard bridge! The bomb entered the sonar room, then the chart house, through the passageway and hatch, and exploded on the surface of the water, close aboard. *Shea* was in shambles and on fire.

She lost 5-inch gun mounts 1 and 2, all communications, main director, gyro and computer. With 27 men killed and 91 wounded, the ship was basically out of service. While repair parties surveyed the damage and attended the wounded, *Shea* took on a five degree port list, so they limped towards Hagushi for help. After arriving at 1052 they transferred wounded to the USS *Crescent City*, APA27, and her dead were transferred for burial at Okinawa.

After temporary repairs at Kerama Retto, *Shea* set sail for the Philadelphia Navy Yard, arriving June 9, 1945. *Shea's* war was over.

### USS GWIN, DM33, MAY 4, 1945:

On RP station off Okinawa the destroyer minelayer came under attack by two groups of enemy aircraft. While firing on group one to port, group two suddenly swept from the setting sun to starboard. *Gwin* swung her guns to the more threatening latter attack, splashing two; then back to port where three additional aircraft were splashed. But the last attacks struck *Gwin* in a 40mm platform. Two men were killed, 2 missing and 11 wounded. After brief repairs at Mansei Shoto, the destroyer minelayer returned to service. *Gwin* earned the Navy Unit Commendation for her outstanding service.

### USS INGRAHAM, DD444, MAY 4, 1945:

While on RP station the destroyer came under attack by five enemy suicide planes. After shooting down the first four, the fifth crashed the ship above the waterline, on the port side. The bomb exploded in the generator room! With only one gun operative and 51 casualties the 2200 ton Sumner class destroyer retired. They returned to Hunter's Point, California for repairs. Her war ended.

### USS CARINA, AK74, MAY 4, 1945:
### (SUICIDE BOAT)

She arrived in Okinawa waters April 26 and on May 4 the Cargo ship was crashed into by a suicide boat. The violent explosion on her port side knocked out her boilers and flooded one compartment. Six crewmen were wounded and her war was over. They sailed to Suisun Bay, California.

*USS Sangamon, CVE26, May 5, 1945 -- badly damaged flight deck*

### USS SANGAMON, (AO28) CVE26, MAY 5, 1945:

Commissioned as a fleet oiler in October 1940, the oiler became destined for greater things. In 1942 they converted her into an auxiliary aircraft carrier and reclassified AVG26, eventually to be reclassified again as CVE26.

At 1830 the carrier left Kerama Retto, at 1933 a Kamikaze dropped his bomb and crashed the center of her flight deck. The carrier and her escorts had shot down one aircraft which crashed 25 feet off her starboard beam, but the second ducked into clouds and came out in a high speed dive to strike home.

The bomb and aircraft parts went through the flight deck to explode below -- hurling flames and shrapnel in all directions. Damage was extensive! Fires engulfed the flight, hangar, and fuel decks.

*USS Sangamon, CVE26, hangar deck*

### USS DOUGLAS H. FOX, DD779, MAY 5, 1945:

On the same day *Fox* arrived at Okinawa for picket duty, her duty was over. But, the new 2200 ton destroyer left her calling card. Attacked by 11 aircraft they shot down 7; however one of her victims got her. The Kamikaze and it's bomb exploded on her decks, killing 7 and wounding 35. After damage control efforts, *Fox* sailed to Kerama Retto for temporary repairs then on to San Francisco. That ended her war.

### USS OBERRENDER, DE344, MAY 9, 1945:

While carrying out her escort and patrol duties at Okinawa the DE fell victim to a sneak Kamikaze. He crashed into her starboard side and his bomb exploded in the forward fireroom. Twenty-four sailors were killed or wounded and the DE was beyond repair. *Oberrender* was stripped of all useful gear and equipment, then sunk by U.S. gunfire.

### USS ENGLAND, DE635, MAY 9, 1945:

On station north of Kerama Retto the DE came under attack by three dive bombers. On fire, the first suicide plane crashed into her starboard side, just below the bridge. With the bomb exploding just after the crash, her repair parties had to deal with the dangerous job of trying to save their ship, as CAP shot down the other two aircraft. *England* had 37 men killed or missing and 25 wounded.

The DE arrived at Philadelphia July 26. Her war was over.

### USS EVANS, DD552, MAY 11, 1945:

The destroyer delivered her charges of escort carriers to Okinawa to provide pre-invasion air strikes, and screened for them until May 2. She then put in to Kerama Retto and eight days later *Evans* got underway for her first picket duty.

On station 15, she was joined by the USS *Hugh W. Hadley* and four pall bearers. This would prove to be one of the most incredible days on any RP station.

During the first night, enemy planes were constantly lighting up their radar, estimated to be 150 by *Hadley*, the Fighter Director Ship (FIDO). *Hadley* did a good job vectoring CAP to the aircraft, and CAP did an excellent job of shooting down suicide planes. But they were absolutely overwhelmed!

Both *Evans* and *Hadley* fought like Lions, during those few minutes. Coming at them from all directions, they knocked down one aircraft after another. But the Kamikaze ultimately got to the gallant destroyers! In quick succession, four bomb laden suicide planes struck *Evans*. Her after engineering spaces flooded and she lost power. The battle ended as fast as it started.!

With 32 killed and 27 wounded, her crew now struggled to save their ship. Miraculously, fires and flooding were controlled, then they towed the ship to Kerama Retto. After temporary repairs, *Evans* was towed to San Francisco where she was decommissioned and sold. *Evans* earned the Presidential Unit Citation.

### USS HUGH W HADLEY, DD774, MAY 11, 1945:

In the afternoon of May 10, the 2200 ton destroyer went on picket duty for her first time. She joined the *Evans*, DD552, and four pall bearers already on RP15, the hot spot.

Early the following morning, *Hadley*, with her FIDO team, started vectoring U.S. aircraft towards incoming Japanese suicide planes. For nearly two hours *Hadley* and *Evans* came under severe attack from some 150 Kamikazes. Both ships ran all-out, at flank speed, maneuvering constantly to provide maximum firepower on the most threatening targets.

After *Evans* took several serious hits and went dead in the water, about 0900, *Hugh W. Hadley* fought alone. At 0920 she was attacked by 10 planes, simultaneously, from both ahead and astern. The ship destroyed all 10, but not without damage to herself. A "Baka" bomb and two Kamikazes crashed into the gallant ship and a bomb hit her stern. When the attack ended all but 50 men were ordered overboard, into life rafts. Badly holed, with flooded engineering spaces, the determined repair parties kept their ship afloat.

They were eventually towed to Ie Shima, then to Kerama Retto, for temporary repairs, after which they were towed to Hunter's Point, California by the tug USS *Undaunted* AT58. *Hugh W. Hadley* arrived on Sept. 20, 1945, just to fall victim, once again -- this time to the cutters torch.

During this remarkable battle *Hugh W. Hadley* shot down 23 aircraft, earning her the Presidential Unit Citation.

### USS BUNKER HILL, CV17, MAY 11, 1945:

Hit by two Kamikazes, the fleet carrier immediately became engulfed in fire and smoke. Gasoline fires and several secondary explosions wreaked havoc among her crew, and 389 were killed and 264 wounded. After overcoming the horrible terror of violent death and devastation, her heroic surviving crewmen saved their ship. They eventually managed to get her back home to Bremerton, Washington on her own power. The war ended on this day for the valiant, veteran carrier.

*Bunker Hill* received the Presidential Unit Citation for their heroic effort.

*Bunker Hill, as a Sumner class destroyer moves in to assist.*

*Above--Bunker Hill, during her time of disaster -- lookouts and gunners watch for Kamikazes.*
*Below--The Battleship USS New Mexico, BB40, pictured at night, taken at the moment of impact.*

### USS NEW MEXICO, BB40, MAY 12, 1945:

Thanks to the terrible price being paid by picket destroyers, remarkably few Kamikazes found their way to the invasion beaches, but when they did, even mighty battleships fell victim.

While she provided fire support for the invading troops on May 11, *New Mexico* destroyed 8 suicide boats. Then as she returned to her berth in Hagushi, on May 12, the battleship came under attack by two Kamikazes. The first suicide plane crashed on *New Mexico's* decks. In the confusion, the second hit her with his bomb. Fifty-four men were killed and 119 wounded in *New Mexico's* second encounter with the Japanese suicidal madness. She lost Captain R. W. Fleming and 28 others killed and 87 wounded on January 6, 1945. May 28 she departed for repairs at Leyte, followed by rehearsals for the planned invasion of the Japanese home islands. The Atomic bomb rendered that invasion unnecessary -- saving many thousands of American lives! But *New Mexico's* long war proved to be over.

### USS BACHE, DD470, MAY 13, 1945:

The destroyer sustained slight damage 10 days earlier from the near miss of a Kamikaze. Later the same day she went to the aid of USS LSMR195 and rescued the surviving crew of 74 men.

On May 13, several enemy dive bombers attacked the RP stations and one crashed on the deck of *Bache*. The Kamikaze's bomb exploded about seven feet above the main deck. The aircraft bounced off number two stack catapulting over the main deck amidships, among her crewmen. Forty-one were killed and 32 wounded. After temporary repairs at Kerama Retto, *Bache* left for the New York Navy Yard. Her war was over.

*USS Enterprise, CV6, at the moment of impact, as she suffered her second direct Kamikaze hit.*

## USS ENTERPRISE, CV6, MAY 14, 1945:

Slightly damaged by a suicide plane, April 11, she had gone to Ulithi for repairs, returning May 6. The *Big "E"*, flying 24 hour missions against the Kamikaze menace, became a victim again on the 14th. A suicide plane destroyed her forward elevator, killing 14 and wounding 34 men. *Enterprise* sailed for repairs at Puget Sound Navy Yard. Her war was over.

*Bunker Hill heads into the wind to keep her smoke trailing aft, away from firefighting crewmen.*

## OTHER SLIGHTLY DAMAGED OR MISCELLANEOUS SHIPS:

USS LSMR195, sank May 3; USS *Birmingham*, CL 62, slightly damaged May 4; USS *Pathfinder*, AGS1, slightly damaged May 6; USS *St George*, AV16, slightly damaged May 6; USS *Sims*, DE145, May 18; USS *Chase*, DE158, heavy damage sold for scrap May 20; *John C. Butler*, DE339, slight damage May 20;

# NINETEEN
# WREN HEADS SOUTH

*Wren* shed her dingy, solid, battleship-gray color, for a lighter, two tone "East Coast Camouflage" paint-job; then at 1727, April 18, the five colorful destroyers of squadron 57, left Adak for Pearl Harbor. Even though we knew we were heading into a bigger mess, our crew seemed happy. I think everyone was ready to leave that deep freeze.

About the fourth day, steaming south straight down the center of the Pacific, we started to shed clothing, and by day five we surveyed (discarded) all extra cold-weather gear. Case after case of new, sheep-lined jackets were dumped overboard; cramped quarters on destroyers made this necessary. One must wonder why they could not have been transferred. Items to be surveyed in the electric shop included a few cases of single-cell flashlights, to be clipped on life jackets. I don't know where so many came from, but the Navy has a saying, "Take anything that's issued to your unit; otherwise you might not get it when you want or need it." I held a few lights back, lit them and threw them overboard at dusk. Running aft we yelled, "Look at the sea monsters" and pointed at the water, as the lights tumbled causing an eerie, pulsating effect.

We entered the engine rooms by means of a vertical ladder. It must have been a couple of stories to the bottom and the rails were very hot and we could not hold on, so we grabbed and let go, fast. By day six, those of us standing engine and fireroom watches, thought we were going to die from the heat. Coming off night watch we stripped our shirts and gathered on the fantail.

Each day as we traveled south, Captain Mac ordered GQ drills, antiaircraft practice and rehearsal with our fighter director teams, "Fidos." We knew where we were going and no time was wasted, but drills, continually, bored everyone. Captain Mac, a real stickler for preparedness, gave his crew little rest in that regard.

Electricians kept busy chasing shorts and grounds in electrical circuits; they showed up at the main switchboards, when we tested for them. After exposure to Aleutian seas, there is no such thing as a weatherproof junction box. When we left the Aleutians, all sound powered telephone jacks and weather deck circuits were checked. This proved a considerable task, as each circuit was traced to its end and grounds removed.

On April 24, *Wren* put into berth X-20, at Pearl Harbor, for five day's tender-availability, by the USS *Alcore*. This meant liberty for all hands. Even though we remained at Pearl Harbor for 11 days, our liberty time was limited to the five days *Wren* spent dock-side. We had many preparations before heading to the nightmare at Okinawa.

While alongside the *Alcore*, I lost my best buddy on the *Wren*. Reno Pellegrini transferred to that ship for surgical room training; then he went to the hospital ship USS *Relief*, AH1, where he stayed for the rest of the war.

For some reason still not clear to me I remained on good behavior during Honolulu liberties. Having work to finish, I left by myself after everyone else had gone ashore. As I walked through the destroyer base I noticed a sailor lying in the gutter, between parked cars. I picked him up and he was obviously thoroughly inebriated, so I leaned him against a car and asked, "What ship are you from, mate?"

"*Wren*" -- he responded incoherently.

He was a third class machinist's mate and I thought I knew all of them. After taking a closer look at this thoroughly messed up shipmate, I asked "McCabe?"

He faintly responded, "Yeah."

I could not believe my eyes, this "clean-cut kid" so messed up, and alone. Dickey was one of my best friends, still I didn't even recognize him. I'd never known him to drink. I managed to get him over my shoulder and back to the *Wren*. Unable to salute the colors, or the OD, I simply said, "Sir, we've got a sick one here."

The OD shook his head, then assigned someone to help, saying "Just take him down and put him in his bunk."

"Aye, aye sir" I cheerfully responded, happy to get him aboard without a hassle.

Having done my good deed for the day, I went to Honolulu and soon located some buddies. The bars were expensive, the women hated sailors, so what's to do? The sidewalks were filled from curbs to the buildings with mostly drunk, obnoxious, sailors. A drunken sailor was a terrible ambassador of good will. No wonder the beautiful, olive-skinned ladies, "Wahines," hated sailors so much.

We spent the rest of our liberty enjoying the many sidewalk milk bars and watched the fiasco around us. Horror stories about the Honolulu brig made this liberty seem prudent. Marine SPs threw drunk sailors into small open cells and blasted them with high pressure fire hoses.

Each liberty section was given a beer and steak party on an isolated side of Oahu. There were garbage cans full of iced beer, steak sandwiches, and a lot of sunshine. We played "king of the mountain," in the surf, with a rubber raft made available to us. The bottom dropped off near shore, so there was practically no wading space and the big breakers really rolled in. We pushed the raft out beyond the breakers, then fought to see who could occupy it. In a few minutes we drifted back into the breakers and the sea settled the conflict. The raft and all its occupants were thrown -- ass-over-teakettle -- and we all wound up beached.

As the day progressed, Bud Brennan and I swam out into the shipping lanes, probably a mile from shore. We were scared shitless when we saw a tidal wave rolling in, directly at us! It was far enough away so that we had time to decide what to do. As the angry wave got closer it looked like a wall of water, capping on top. Just before it hit us, I yelled to Bud, "Dive deep and swim as hard as you can." We came up safely on the other side.

"Wow" Bud said, looking like he had seen a ghost. We swam back to shore, now over the horizon, without delay. It was a frightening experience both of us would remember. This was one of my best liberties, sunburn and all.

Ensign L. D. "Cris" Criswell, a slightly built, mild-mannered, gentleman came aboard at Pearl Harbor. A former school teacher and Texas highway patrolman, Cris was going to sea for his first time.

May 1, Squadron 57 was complete again, when the USS *Bearss*, *John Hood*, and *Jarvis*, rejoined us. Operating in a restricted area south of Oahu, on order number OP-0140, *Wren's* crew trained intensely for the next three days. The destroyers USS *Knapp* and *Burns* joined squadron 57. For six days our ships operated around the clock.

We practiced day and night shore bombardments off Kahoolawe Island, antiaircraft gunnery, night anti-torpedo-boat drills and worked with our "Fido" teams. This was our final rehearsal before the "big one". Our crew received a scoring of "superior," for gunnery. Fido practice continued until we arrived back at Pearl Harbor.

At 0755 May 5, after replenishing ammunition, *Wren* got underway with *Rowe* and *Watts* for Ulithi, by way of Eniwetok. On the 9th, *Wren* investigated a floating life raft, but found it had been abandoned. We destroyed it with 40mm gunfire.

As *Wren* headed south, Ensign Criswell recalls a side trip we made: "We were sent to investigate one of the islands bypassed by our troops. It was reported the Japanese had a sizable number of aircraft stashed there. While searching with our radar, we circled the island, and stared at the shore line for signs of life. My heart pounded! How did I ever get here?

"Thoughts wandered back to my boyhood, to the share-croppers existence we lived, and how we children were moved to four different schools, in one year. My father tried to scratch a living from the hard south Texas soil. How, at 18 years of age, I had to take over the family responsibility when my father died. Yet somehow here I stood, high above the water, on the bridge of *Wren* -- an officer. *Wren* continued to circle the island, but we found nothing." Criswell concluded.

The engine and fireroom heat became unbearable. We dodged icebergs and chipped ice a couple of weeks ago, but now our engineering people passed out from the heat, which kept sick bay busy. We drank water by the gallon and used salt pills from dispensers placed around the ship.

*Ensign L. D. "Cris" Criswell*

We stood switchboard watch eight hours a day. The humidity was high and perspiration dripped from our faces, like a stubborn faucet. If we stayed in front of the fresh air vent too long, we got sick. Staying out of the airflow our clothing soon became soaked, so Wally Rupe and I took turns in front of our vent.

Coming off engine room watch was great! Lying on the tip of *Wren's* bow, I looked down at the cool blue water. As *Wren* rose to the gentle swells and pushed the water away to make room for her hull, the force created a phosphorescent turbulence that was fascinating at night.

Hap Rogers and his forward fireroom gang were still as popular as ever. After finishing off the 20 gallons of diluted 180 proof alcohol, they had to learn a new trade -- Bootlegging! Raisin Jack was the product. They only needed raisins and some glass jugs. With their ability to trade, this became a simple matter. Electricians had five gallon jugs that held distilled battery water and the cooks had raisins. They didn't even have to barter for those, just turn the steam pressure down. Given the regulation amount of pressure, extra duty time was required to cook the food. However, with Hap's cooperation the steam valve could be opened a little more. The raisins and containers -- put them in business.

Hap tells how they did it: "We put raisins in the glass jugs and filled them with water. We needed a way to vent the jugs and a place to hide them while they fermented. A small rubber hose was inserted into a hole drilled in the caps and the other end went into a jar of water. Well, things were going along fine so I sent Jimmy Webb up to get a sample, but we decided it needed more fermentation time.

"One day Captain Mac shouted over the PA system to the fireroom."

'Rogers, get up here.'

"What now, I wondered? While walking from the fireroom to the bridge I pondered the situation. When I got up there, Captain Mac was waiting for me. He stared me in the eyes like a cat ready to pounce on a mouse.

'Rogers, do you smell anything here?' he asked.

"No sir, I don't smell anything."

'Come on over here Rogers. Now put your nose down there.'

"He pointed to the vent, I thought oh, oh, but did as he asked."

'Do you smell it now -- Rogers?'

"Yes sir, I smell something."

'What do you think that smell is -- Rogers?'

"I'm not sure, sir."

'Doesn't it seem to have a -- wine -- smell, Rogers?'

"Well...yes sir ... maybe..."

'Do you know where that smell could be coming from -- Rogers?'

"No sir..."

'Well Rogers, why don't you just go back down to the fireroom, check it out and come back up and report to me.'

"Yes sir," I responded and headed out the hatch and down the ladder.

"The first thing I did was check out our stash. I got the ladder, crawled up into the vent shaft, and wow! The fumes could have intoxicated the entire crew. Our jugs had exploded. We hadn't compensated for the extra heat. We quickly cleaned up the mess.

"Returning to the bridge, I tried to find a convincing excuse about where the smell came from. I assured Captain Mac we had -- skillfully corrected -- the problem.

"Captain Mac gave me that distorted smile he was famous for and said, 'OK...Rogers.'

"I had the distinct feeling I hadn't fooled anyone."

At 0656 May 12, we anchored in berth S-4 Eniwetok. After refueling, *Wren* and *Watts* got underway, leaving the *Rowe* behind. At 0721 May 16, we moored alongside the USS *Cossotot*, at Ulithi, where *Wren* fueled and our  officers reported to the Fifth Fleet Commander, for duty.

LT jg Lowell Clark, recalls his first trip with our captain: "I joined Captain Mac, to see the Fifth Fleet Commander, my first trip in the Gig. During our trip ashore, the size of that place and the number of ships in the massive, sheltered harbor, impressed me. This elaborate, modern, base was huge.

"We arrived on shore, and walked down the boardwalk toward command headquarters, when we were startled! Right in the middle of that Naval base, coming directly towards us, was a sight I will never forget! A large group of natives in full colorful dress, walked by. It looked like a Hollywood set.

"We proceeded to our appointment with the Commander and picked up our orders to Okinawa! We were to be the sole escort for the battleship USS *Idaho*."

Captain Mac published the following message in the *Wren's* Nest on the occasion of *Wren's* first anniversary.

## A MESSAGE FROM THE CAPTAIN

*It is always fitting that the Commanding Officer state his sentiments during any special occasion that occurs on a ship. Previously in the pages of the WREN'S NEST, my writing has mostly taken a humorous trend. The latter may be open to some question, but at least I, myself, have derived a great deal of pleasure in having the outlet for my writing quirks. This, I promise you, will not be an attempt at humor.*

*A year ago the ship was commissioned at the Seattle Tacoma Shipbuilding Company in Seattle. On that day, if you will remember, I made a short speech concerning the intensive training that was before us, and how it was necessary for everyone to work as a team. That was a year ago.*

*Everyone aboard must admit that we have come a long way since then. Then, the fellow standing beside you was only an individual. Now he has developed into a definite personality. You see him in a different light altogether. He is your friend. Yes, you have a lot of friends aboard the USS WREN ... over three hundred of them. You are immediately aware of this if a group of you hear a man from another ship say something disparagingly about the WREN. It's all right for you to criticize it. But for the stranger it is a different story.*

*This isn't the only way we have changed. Ships are like homes and villages in certain respects. They have a certain air or personality about them. When the ship is neat, the watch well run and alert, orders carried out smartly, and men are cheerful and willing, that ship has a pleasing "air." When a ship shoots well, does well in other forms of competition, and the men take pride in their accomplishments, the ship has a fully developed and attractive personality. The WREN has it.*

*Some time in the future each and every one of you will brag about the time when you were aboard. Those "reminiscence" will mean something to you. Gone and forgotten will be the tedious routine events of shipboard watches. Bright and clear will be the excitement of some event that happened aboard ship. I, as commanding officer, fondly reply that I have a fine and wonderful ship.*

**Edwin A. MacDonald, Commander of WREN**

At 1210 the following day, *Wren* and *Idaho* got underway to Okinawa. As we traveled south, our days were filled with new and different spectacles. The ocean was often alive with flying fish springing from the sea for a short flight, occasionally they landed on our deck. Porpoise lazily played around our bow, as if guiding our way.

As we looked out over the vast, calm ocean, where blue sky and sea were one, *Wren* seemed alone in this peaceful surrounding. But, behind us steamed the mighty *Idaho*. A grim reminder that we were headed into a new kind of war. Periodically, *Wren* ran circles around the *Idaho*, searching for subs, like a puppy running around its mother; then we returned to our station, 3,000 yards ahead. We felt insignificant and full of apprehension in that vastness.

Danny Wann, Barney Pullen, Al Copson, and the other flying bridge crewmen thought they had died and gone to heaven. Life was beautiful for them. Scanning the horizon with powerful binoculars, they remembered what life was like just a few weeks ago. They went from the worst duty on *Wren* -- to the best.

As *Wren* neared Okinawa, sailors continued to die by Admiral Ohnishi's hand. Slaughter of "THE SACRIFICIAL LAMBS," continued.

**USS LONGSHAW, DD559, MAY 18, 1945**

After four days of providing close fire support, the destroyer ran aground. While being assisted by the tug, USS *Arikara*, ATF98, she was pulverized by shore batteries. Hits in the forward magazine exploded her ammunition, and blew the bow completely off. Eventually U.S. ships had to sink the sitting duck. Eighty-six men, including her Captain, Commander C. W. Becker, were killed. A mishap can soon become a tragedy in war.

**USS THATCHER, DD514, MAY 20, 1945**

The destroyer had just arrived at Okinawa. Approaching the transport anchorage a large number of enemy aircraft came in, so all ships opened fire. *Thatcher* turned broadside and increased speed to 25 knots. An Oscar passed down her port side, climbed sharply, did a wing-over and crashed just aft of *Thatcher's* bridge. USS *Boyd*, DD544, and USS *Pavlic*, APD7, came alongside to help extinguish fires and evacuate wounded.

With a 6 x 9 foot hole under the waterline, no steering, gyro, radar or external communication, the destroyer limped towards Kerama Retto. *Thatcher* lost 14 men killed and 53 wounded.

After drydocking for temporary repairs July 1, she moved to Buckner Bay where they rode out the typhoon. On the 19th, another Kamikaze snuck in the bay and dove at the destroyer. Damage was slight, but two additional men were wounded. They left for Bremerton, August 20, -- where she was scrapped. *Thatcher* had a long, successful combat record, but her luck ran out immediately at Okinawa.

### USS CHASE, DE158, MAY 20, 1945

Smaller ships also felt the Kamikaze sting. *Chase* was crashed into and destroyed, with heavy loss of life. The DE -- was scrapped.

### USS JOHN C. BUTLER, DE339, MAY 20, 1945
### USS REGISTER, APD92, MAY 20, 1945

These ships were also crashed into; however they eventually repaired and returned them to service.

At 1908 May 20, the USS *Abercrombie*, DE343, joined our formation. The DE would later be featured in the book <u>Little Ship, Big War</u>. At 0926, the following morning, *Wren* fueled at sea. *Abercrombie* delivered the *Idaho* to her berthing. After fueling from the USS *Pecos*, *Wren* proceeded to berth H-136, Hagushi, Okinawa, for assignment to picket duty. *Wren* had arrived at that man-made hell!

*Seaman First Class Jim Pridmore had rough duty on Wren He stood watch with Danny, Barney and Al on the flying bridge, but now they had the best duty on the Wren. Jim passed powder in a magazine during GQ and that job was about to become a living nightmare.*

*Seaman Adolph Rossman, did Wren's laundry.*

# Twenty
# Wren at Okinawa
# First Picket Duty -- Suicide Boats

The Navy hurried to complete two long-range, land-based radar towers on Hedo Saki and Ie Shima, this gave the United States better information on Japanese aircraft. With higher more effective radar for advance warning, U.S. picket stations could be reduced from nine active stations to five. By increasing the number of destroyers from one or two, to three on each RP station, firepower would be increased.

CAP was hard pressed to provide aircraft to protect the picket stations; consequently they established TAF (Tactical Air Force,) to provide exclusive air cover for destroyers. Initially, two aircraft provided cover for each of three RP stations, then eventually three aircraft each for all five.

They completed the radar towers May 16; then two aircraft in direct voice communication with our destroyers, covered the three RP stations. This was the plan; however, continuous coverage could not be provided. RP15 and 16, located on the north end of the island, where RP 1 had been, were on a direct route between southern Honshu and Hagushi. The hot spot!

May 22, they assigned *Wren* to CTG 51.5. We moved to the western edge of the transport area at Hagushi and patrolled station 2, at 10 knots until 2105, then anchored on the outer edge for the night.

During our first 48 hours at Okinawa, under the threat of constant suicidal attacks, we learned how fast we could move to GQ. We got lots of practice, both day and night. Each time it was like someone had yelled fire in a crowded building, then turned out the lights. In the narrow passageways, between bunks, if we fumbled putting on our pants, stopped to get cotton for our ears, or were slow getting out for any reason, we could be trampled. Every man ran through the compartments at breakneck speed; yelling and pushing at near panic levels. We scrambled out of hatches leaving them open, so it remained pitch dark inside. We were groggy from lack of sleep, but still fully aware a Kamikaze could be on his final dive, for *Wren!*

Ensign L. D. Criswell recalls: "I had been monitoring and timing our boys as they went to GQ. Prior to Okinawa, we had achieved a minimum time of three minutes. Under the threat of suicide attacks, all of our boys reported combat-ready in an amazing thirty seconds."

*Wren's 20mm gun in action, note the bell shaped helmet on the "Talker" standing next to the gunner.*

I often slept on the 20mm ready box at my GQ station on the port side amidships. As clip-handler I almost always arrived first when the GQ alarm sounded, and had the technique of getting our gun combat ready, down pat. With my right arm I stripped the barrel sleeve and threw it into the corner of the gun tub; then with both arms I jerked the main gun cover upward, flinging it off with one sweep. To cock the gun, a fixed piece of heavy flat iron with a slot in the end slipped over the cocking bolt. I then grabbed the two shoulder brackets, threw my legs straight ahead, and rode the gun to the ground. That cocked it. By that time a second member of our crew arrived to take a clip of ammunition out of the ready-box, and loaded the gun.

The 20s were the only guns on *Wren* totally fired by the gunner. Strapped in from behind, the shoulder brackets stayed in place as the gunner leaned back on the strap. Two hand holds were provided on either side, with the trigger mechanism on the right. The lead computing sight was at eye level on the stationary part of the gun. As they fired, the barrel moved in and back out with each firing cycle; thus by holding the trigger down, the action became automatic.

At our station we had two guns with a three-man crew on each. We also had a man connected to CIC with a headset, (talker). He relayed audio orders such as the firing condition, range and relative position of each target. A gunner's mate, also assigned to our station, kept the guns operating. Frequently, as those guns fired rapidly the barrels became hot, so he stood by with heavy asbestos gloves and a replacement barrel. As the barrels were removed, they dropped them into water-filled containers.

Kamikaze pilots were taught the fine points of approach and final crashing techniques on Formosa. A high-altitude, long-range approach had some advantages for the inexperienced pilots. At eighteen to twenty thousand feet they were sure to be picked up by U.S. radar, but the Japanese had the distinct advantage at that point. They increased speed by decreasing altitude. American pilots not pre-positioned at high altitude, were forced to climb at a slower intercept speed. The chance of interceptors attacking the Kamikaze prior to its final dive, could be lost.

Their second alternative, to come in low just over the tops of waves, caused great difficulty for U.S. radar, and the Kamikazes were almost invisible to our pilots flying overhead. This often allowed the Japanese to get within a few thousand yards of U.S. ships before being detected.

The success of suicide pilots depended upon their final approach and glide path, which could be taught, but not practiced. They only had one shot. Coming in low they increased altitude to about 1,000 feet, then established a final dive path of about 45 degrees or less. This created a fast moving target, but still left the pilot with good final maneuverability. Crashing into an evasive high-speed ship while being shot at, was difficult to teach and the outcome could never be assured.

### USS SPECTACLE, AM305, MAY 22, 1945:

While *Wren* patrolled the entrance to Hagushi transport area, *Spectacle* fell victim a few miles away, near Ie Shima. After splashing a Betty early that morning, she was hit at 0805. Badly damaged, on fire, with a jammed rudder and many people blown overboard, they dropped anchor to keep from running over their own men. The USS LSM135, picked up the minesweeper's survivors. Fifteen minutes later the medium sized landing ship also fell victim. USS *Takesta*, ATF93, towed *Spectacle* to Kerama Retto for temporary repairs, but she was ultimately scrapped at Puget Sound Navy Yard. Twenty-nine men were killed or missing and six wounded. On May 13, *Spectacle* had also been attacked by five suicide boats.

At 1421 on May 23rd, *Wren* got underway for her first picket duty on RP16, "The hot spot," fifty miles northwest of Zampa Misaki Point, Okinawa. At 1705 we joined the USS *Van Valkenburgh*, DD656; USS *Dyson*, DD572; and USS *Cowell*, DD547; and the USS LCS14, 17, 18, and 90, on station. Although the LCSs did a fine job against aircraft with what they had to fight with, we called them "pallbearers," for their primary task seemed to be picking up survivors of sunk or damaged destroyers. The destroyers usually ran in tandem a (straight line) with the LCSs several thousand yards behind. The problem was to keep them out of the destroyer's line of fire when things got hectic.

We now joined " **THE SACRIFICIAL LAMBS**" who were led to slaughter before us. Lambs only in reference to the almost certainty of death. But, they fought like Lions, often against impossible odds. We can never give them enough praise.

U.S. destroyers were probably the best in the world and our equipment state of the art. But our odds were terrible! We followed a long line of destroyers that faced those odds and lost. How much more -- **'SACRIFICIAL BLOOD'** -- would be required to bring this terrible suicidal conflict to an end?

With foggy and misty weather Admiral Ohnishi's Kamikazes were still there. At 1950 the first alarm sounded, 'ping,ping,ping....,' "All hands man your battle stations." This chilling sound always caused anxiety among *Wren's* crew, but now it took on new significance.

*Wren* stayed at GQ for fifteen minutes, then a group of enemy aircraft closed to within ten miles of our position, before they changed direction.

At 2020 the second alarm sounded. Once again the mad scramble as we went to our stations. This time three groups of enemy aircraft closed to within fifteen miles. Communications Officer LT jg Bill Johnessee had his hands full keeping track of bogies that lit up their radar screen. The Japanese had launched another -- "Kikushi" raid -- (all out effort.)

Each time we arrived at GQ it became fingernail-biting time. Our crew of about three hundred fifty men, each on his assigned station, watched and waited. Plotting analyzed information coming in from radar and relayed it to CIC, who notified the bridge and all combat stations. Lookouts scanned the darkness for movement or sound, as *Wren* slipped slowly and silently through the East China Sea.

Our radar rotated high on top of the mast, searching the blackness for the enemy. We were there to track him and notify Captain Moosbrugger's Command of the enemy's position and how many aircraft they had.

To make our job difficult, the suicide pilots stayed low on the water at night and came in from the sun, or out of clouds, during the day. The Japanese searched the darkness for any sign of telltale phosphorescence, or gunfire. The last thing we needed was to expose our position, and they did not want to get shot down by U.S. fighters. The

*Above-Wren's radar searched the sky off Okinawa.*
*Below-a Japanese Kamikaze receives his orders.*
*The two bars on his sleeve indicate he is a Lieutenant.*

Japanese suicide pilots would die a certain and violent death, but the worst thing that could happen would be to do so in vain. Could anything be worse than becoming an unsuccessful suicide pilot?

We secured from our second GQ after forty minutes to be recalled at 2345. This time we remained at GQ under threat of nearby enemy aircraft until 0150 May 24th. Fifteen minutes later GQ called again and we continued our little game of "Hide and seek, or Gotcha" with Admiral Ohnishi's suicide pilots.

At 0330, *Van Valkenburgh* and *Dyson* returned to base, leaving us alone with the *Cowell*. *Wren* remained at GQ for the rest of the night and next day until 1310. At 1600 we were joined by the USS *Ingersoll*, DD652, then at 1840 GQ sounded again. With suicide aircraft all around us, we cruised at slower speed and were not detected.

At 1905 we secured from GQ again, just to be called back at 1920, but CAP knocked down two aircraft before we could get to our station. U.S. Navy and Marine pilots shot down six additional aircraft within five miles of our position, between 1920 and 1955. Aircraft shot down in flames could be seen for many miles at night. Five could be seen in the distance, before the first extinguished in the sea. The -- F4U, Corsair -- was the Navy and Marines number one fighter and U.S. pilots -- were the best.

At 2025 we ran in a column 1,000 yards apart, with *Cowell* on the point and *Ingersoll* in the rear.

*The F4U Corsair, our number one defender*

*Seaman First Class Roger Jones, a 20mm gunner. He did his job well, but will always remember that night.*

While sitting through a quiet time at GQ, Seaman First Class Roger Jones, the gunner on the 20mm adjacent to ours, confided in me.

"Bill, I'm so scared my guts are churning and I just don't know if I'm going to be able to even shoot my gun!"

Being a little older than most, I did my best to console him. "Jonesie" I responded, "You're no different than any of us. There are no heroes here. We're all scared! You'll do your job -- and do it damn well." I assured him.

In a few minutes he proved me right. Roger became one of *Wren's* best 20mm gunners.

LT James Evans, assistant communication officer, was in charge of the SG (surface) radar.

His operator Joseph Snyder, glared at the screen, suddenly he could not believe his eyes! Surface blips started to appear briefly, then disappeared. Joe wondered: "What's going on? Am I seeing things?"

For 21 minutes we headed northeast, then gradually turned southeast, trying to determine what we were dealing with. It was whisper quiet in the dead of night, then without warning -- *Cowell* opened fire off her port-bow!

Lowell Clark, bridge, picks up the action: "Captain Mac called for everything *Wren* had. Willard Smith, responded by slamming the engine order telegraph from 1/3 ahead to flank speed, then 397 turns were rung up on the enunciators in the engine rooms. First Class Machinist's Mate Clay, "Catfish," Harris, responded in the forward engine room by spinning the throttle wheel to open the steam valve. Both powerful turbine engines whined in unison.

"Hap Rogers reacted quickly in the forward fireroom to feed the four hungry boilers the increased fuel required to provide the surging steam. Moments later the bell clanked on our bridge, indicating all engines were spinning to achieve maximum speed. Bob Moon, helmsman, cranked the wheel hard to starboard in response to Captain Mac's command. *Wren* went on the attack!"

From our gun station, *Wren* seemed to rumble and shake from stem to stern! A streak of fire followed by a belch of smoke from our stacks, temporarily lit up our gun tub. It felt like an earthquake! In the turn, water came over our port side -- and we were suddenly in the middle of raging rapids! *Wren* dipped under the sea at over 40 knots and the water became airborne. It flew by our heads at nearly 50 miles an hour. It tried to tear fixed items from their welds in its rush to the stern, in the blink of an eye. We stayed behind our heavy steel-walled gun tub, but it still was downright scary, as the raging water found its way behind us. Getting hit by even a bucket-full, could be devastating.

The ship took a shocking jolt in the turn. Our gunner's mate was nearly washed overboard! During his moment of panic he thought I had pushed him. He came at me like a madman.

He yelled: 'You son-of-a-bitch, you pushed me. If you do that again I'll cut your fucking throat!'

"God-damn-it, I didn't push you. You were six feet away from me!" I responded. When I realized he was panic stricken, I dropped the issue.

In the radar shack, Joe Snyder still wondered about the elusive surface blips. Then there they were again, distinct and clear, at a true bearing of 138 degrees. Joe quickly relayed the information to Francis Stephenson in plotting. He determined the relative bearing, speed, and heading, then notified CIC. James Atkinson, CIC talker, then relayed the information to the bridge and all gun locations.

All target bearings were given relative to the ship, so the bow point was always 00. This allowed every man to locate the targets, relative to his station. From our gun station we covered a field of fire from about 220 to 305 degrees.

Our combat information talker shouted in a very excited voice, "Stand by for destroyer attack. Target bearing 290 degrees at 2600 yards." Five-inch mount 3 let go right over our heads. I yelled as loud as I could at Jonesie, "Get them Jonesie, we've got a full scale war on our hands." When they started firing I continued to shout them 'up,' as best I could.

Almost immediately the talker shouted again: "Stand by for torpedo attack, they're PT boats." Then, "They're trying to ram us!" All of *Wren's* guns fired, as we twisted and squirmed our way through the East China Sea. The bridge tried to keep us from being rammed! The attackers turned out to be -- suicide boats.

Never before had *Wren* fought so desperately for her life! Everything was on the line. Our 5-inch guns, pointed down against the stops, lower than they had ever been fired before. With *Wren's* gunfire being directed so close, our radical turns often put the suicide boats right alongside of our ship. We fought against being rammed and blown up! While firing at those elusive targets, concussion from mounts 3, 4 and the 40mm on the catwalk, seemed almost unbearable. The end of mount 3 barrel, directly over my head, felt dangerously close. Each time they fired, about every three seconds, my helmet cracked me on the nose and hair on the back of my head was singed. Concussion from mount 3 buckled the heavy steel screened air intake to the engine room, burned paint off the inside of our gun tub, damaged the nearby life raft, and permanently damaged my inner-ears. Roger Jones told me, 'My ears were also damaged, I still must keep cotton in them at all times.'

Our 20mm gunners removed their straps so they could shoot low enough to spray the area in the direction of our 5-inch tracers. They fired our big guns by radar, but we could see nothing.

Jim Evans kept busy identifying surface blips being reported and Francis Stephenson plotted our next target. Bill Johnessee kept busy, tracking "Bogies," (aircraft) that lit up the air-search radar. We continued to fire until the targets disappeared from Joe Snyder's SG radar.

Nine minutes after we opened fire on our first target, Joe's radar screen lit up with surface contacts all headed for our gun flashes. Targets, spread out to the northeast of our position, searched for our ships. Each target traveled on a different heading, at speeds ranging from 18 to 26 knots. The *Ingersol* reported tracking targets on a zigzag course, that accelerated to 38 knots.

LT Commander Robert Pauli, *Wren's* XO, CIC room: "We didn't know what was going on. One minute they stood still, then we clocked them up to 50 or 60 knots."

Each of our ships chose targets closest to their position and most threatening. The first suicide boat flared up and burned with an intense flame, for about one minute, then disappeared from radar.

At 2055 *Wren* opened fire on the second target, traveling at 20 knots, off our port-quarter at 6,400 yards. We continued to fire at that suicide boat until it disappeared from Joe's radar screen. Three minutes from the time we started firing on target number two, *Wren* took number three under fire. He aimed at our port side from 3,060 yards, traveling at 20 knots.

Lowell Clark, bridge: "All hell broke loose again, as *Wren* opened fire with all guns. We continued to maneuver and tried to keep our guns directed broadside, (unmasked) for maximum efficiency, and ran as fast as we could. During those high speed, close range, gun battles, our ships all had major problems staying out of each others' way.

"I soon realized this was a serious problem. Our ships had to maneuver independently to deal with their own threatening targets, whether they were low flying aircraft, or suicide boats. Planes or boats that attacked from zero bearing came at our bow, or from 180 degrees at our stern. Before we could shoot, all ships running in a column had to turn. This formation left only the nearest ship able to fire. We wove our way through and hoped to hit -- only the enemy."

Gun crews in Jim Hutzel's mount 4 and Bill Ferguson's mount 1, and all others, wound up to the max. That is what it was all about. The hours they trained on the simulator and the pride and competition, paid off. Some crews claimed their ability to fire all the way up to 22 rounds of 5-inch per minute, but each thought their crew to be best.

It was desperation time for all hands on the *Wren*. Men in the engine and fire-rooms, as well as those in magazines and handling rooms, had trouble keeping their footing, as our ship continued to maneuver, radically. Each time the 5-inch, then the 40 and finally the 20mm guns opened up, they knew something had tried to get our ship without knowing what. They had to listen without seeing. They knew the Japanese were dangerously close every time the short range 20mm guns fired. Like sitting ducks, we sat, waited, and expected to be blown to bits at any second.

Handling the heavy projectiles and powder casings at such a feverish pitch, while in tight quarters without ventilation, Wally Rupe, Jim Pridmore, and all others in the magazines thought they would melt.

Wally recalls: "Sweat rolled off from our bodies in that hot, stagnant magazine. As the ship maneuvered, puddles of perspiration rolled back and forth on the deck. We had big problems keeping our footing and no way to anticipate those turns, until we were off balance."

Lowell Clark, bridge: "Fire on target number three continued until it disappeared from radar. They came at us a scant three minutes apart. Target number four tried to ram us at 23 knots, from 2,850 yards. We turned to port while firing towards the stern, as all guns continued to fire until this target disappeared from radar. Target number five was taken under fire immediately. This one came at *Wren* from 270 degrees, at 2,630 yards, running at 23 knots. Each time we took another suicide boat under fire, the fury continued until it disappeared.

"During this time -- CAP kept busy shooting down aircraft all around us. Our CIC people didn't know where to direct their fire. Keeping track of the most threatening surface target was difficult, but our air-search radar also kept filling with Kamikazes.

"Radar operators on all three destroyers deserve immense credit for the way they worked with TAC and identified the most threatening air targets. They had to follow up on each initial aircraft contact to make sure it got shot down. If one did get through, our ship's fire had to be re-directed and left us vulnerable to attacking suicide boats. This appeared to be a coordinated air-sea attack against our ships. Fortunately, our corsair fighters showed up in force, and each -- "Angel of Okinawa" -- effectively handled a number of Kamikaze aircraft.

"As our gunfire stilled one suicide boat, they directed it at another. *Wren* took nine targets under fire during the first 29 minutes and they all disappeared from radar. Some were as close as -- 900 yards. We used VT (variable time) projectiles, also called "proximity fuses," for the first time. Those exploded as they got near metal and most rounds exploded above the targets. The suicide boats simply filled with holes and slowly sank," Lowell concluded.

Jim Hutzel, describes the problems they had in mount 4: "About halfway through the first attacks, we had our gun depressed as low as it could go. With the breach elevated so high we had difficulty handling the rounds, and our hot-shell man, Johnson, had trouble handling the ejected casings. He dropped one which grazed his cheek, taking the skin along. I jumped down and offered to take over for him, but he refused. He was a real fighter and stayed with it to the end.

"Williams, my powderman, a tall, quiet guy whose first ship had been torpedoed and sank in the Atlantic, while in the 'Armed Guard,' -- went clear off his rocker! During those furious attacks -- he was like a madman! We had to enlist the help of Joe Martino's repair party to get him out of the mount. They later transferred him to the States for treatment, and he never returned to the *Wren*."

Danny Wann recalls problems he had during those attacks: "It was so hot in mount 1 we worked without shirts, and I got burns all over my body fumbling those hot shells. We threw out a lot of rounds, I don't know how many, but we were low on ammunition when it ended. Later, Doc Romig treated me by smearing salve all over my body and gave me a couple of APC pills. Duncan, our pointer, looked through his sight that night and said: 'I saw a lot of fires in the direction we were firing.'"

LT Jack Clemens, engineering officer, watched from his duty station as the battle developed. He alternated his watches between CIC, the bridge and main battery director, while not at GQ. He was relieved to get to the engine room when GQ sounded.

*Chief Carpenter's Mate Joe Martino, in charge of the after repair party forcibly removed Williams from mount-4.*

Jack recalls that desperate night: "My fears were probably much the same as everyone in the engineering spaces, during combat. Would our 600 degree, 600 pound per square inch steam lines, remain intact? Steam was the "life blood" of our ship and a major steam line rupture could kill many people. This thought -- still remains with me!"

*Wren's* destiny virtually rested on the shoulders of a few key people during those historically significant days. With Jack's experience and knowledge, our vital steaming capability was in good hands. He recalls his greatest fears during *Wren's* first time as a "SACRIFICIAL LAMB."

"When so much depended on our combined skill and teamwork, the -- what if -- syndrome often weighed heavily on my mind. What if -- one of our four crucial water-tenders, responsible for quickly and accurately opening and closing the valves to the boilers, would over or under react? Surges in steam use caused by the erratic speed requirements, due to the fight for survival topside, required quick and accurate reaction by our water-tenders. An under supply of water could quickly cause permanent boiler failure and loss or reduction of vital speed and electricity.

"What if -- we lost vacuum in the main condensers due to failure of steam ejectors that created it, or due to warm sea-water flowing through them? Losing vacuum would result in loss of engine and electrical power; the ship would lose speed or stop and the radar would go dead. The main battery pointing, training, and the hoisting of shells and powder, would have to be operated by hand. The *Wren* nor many of her crewmen would have survived any of those -- what if syndromes."

Jack's fears point out the value of all crucial, highly trained engineering people on the *Wren*: Clay "Catfish" Harris, Wally Rupe, Hap Rogers and Rufus Miller were just a few.

Chief Electrician's Mate Rufus Miller, wrote in his diary: "I was more scared than I have ever been in my life; they seemed to have us surrounded." This seems to pretty well sum up all of our feelings.

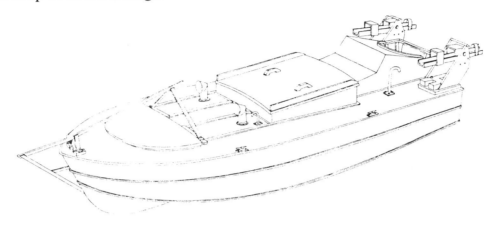

*A "Shinyo" suicide boat, the pilot sat in the small stern cockpit, aimed the boat at his target and tried to run directly into a US Ship. The improvised detonator on the bow, did the rest.*

Many suicide boats were reported momentarily dead in the water before they disappeared from radar. Some had two inboard engines in their 16-to-18-foot length and all carried either two 600 pound depth charges or a heavy load of HE in their nose. The combined weight caused them to ride very low, about 12-inches, above the water.

Why were they called "ghosts?" At best a wooden hull was difficult to pick up on radar, but being so low presented special problems. They ran the valleys between ground swells and remained undetected, until they had to go over the top. This caused the targets to become elusive. They appeared and disappeared. A good operator, if he were fully aware of our problem, could pop over swells change course and run the valleys.

At times the Japanese dropped foil from aircraft, in an effort to confuse our gunners. As this foil settled to the sea, it could be picked up by our more accurate SG surface radar; however all targets would have to approach from 330 degrees at 7 knots, the wind direction and speed. At times our radar played tricks on the operators, but not that time.

This is what Captain MacDonald said in his war diary and action report: "No targets were sighted, due to poor visibility (dark night) and the proximity of threatening air attack. However, all contacts were positive and could not have possibly been 'sido lobos' (false readings). We continued firing on each target until it disappeared from our radar screen."

*Wren* probably had the most accurate radar in the fleet; because our radar technicians were such a dedicated, "Gung Ho" group of people. First Class Radar Technician Bob Pierce recalls his group and how they burned a great deal of midnight oil keeping *Wren's* radar, the best.

"We found it necessary to develop and build our own individual tube tester, and continually check our equipment for accuracy. Each time *Wren* returned from a raid to a familiar port, we were up most of the night checking our equipment against known targets. By switching tubes and comparing our image, we always had the most accurate radar in the fleet."

I asked Bob about the suicide boats, whether they could have been fooled by foil dropped from aircraft and how he felt about my explanation of our dilemma: "They could not have fooled us like that. Your explanation seems to be the only answer. I know that night presented a real challenge for all of us."

At 2122 our guns were silent and Joe Snyder's SG radar was clear. Everyone on the *Wren* tried to relax and recount what had just happened, but our hearts pounded, as if trying to break out of our chests.

For the next couple of hours we remained at GQ. Every man topside stood in the still, quiet darkness -- staring and listening. The air spectacle continued around us. We could think of nothing -- but what had just happened.

Lowell Clark, bridge: "For two and a half hours, *Wren* patrolled the same area in uneasy silence. The talker occasionally broke our solitude with word on enemy aircraft in our vicinity and TAF continued their excellent job of shooting them down. We felt lucky --but apprehensive. Was this it? Had we seen the end of suicide boats? How many could we fight off if they kept coming? Captain MacDonald didn't seem to be worried, he appeared to be dozing.

"*Wren* moved slowly through the darkness, as if we tiptoed and occasionally corrected our course on orders from *Cowell*. Everyone remained quiet, except our talker. But, the shrill ping...ping...ping... of our sonar reminded us the enemy was there, in several forms. Each time we started to feel safe and complacent, gunfire from other picket ships appeared in the distant sky. Then there was a pop, as another plane crashed in flames. When aircraft exploded in the air, they fell so slowly it looked like they were hanging on parachutes. Each time this happened we were startled and scared. They were miles away, but looked very close. This was total madness!"

Lowell continues: "At 2338, while traveling north, our talker broke the silence again, in an excited voice -- 'Surface craft, surface craft, bearing 10 degrees, speed 26 knots, course 270.' It was action time again for *Wren*, so I relayed the order, flank speed, hard aport and the helmsman cranked *Wren's* wheel. The vibrating deck became alive under us. We held on to keep our footing in the turn and opened fire to starboard.

"In a couple of minutes, as quickly as the firing started, the cease firing order came down. The bridge became quiet again as we turned north to investigate. Four minutes from the time we started firing on the first target, our talker shouted out a second: 'Surface craft 002 degrees, 5,000 yards at 25 knots and a course of 276.' Again we turned hard to port and opened fire. But in a hail of fire from our ships, the target quickly disappeared from radar.

"We immediately directed our fire to the third target, in the same area. He traveled at 27 knots, from 4,700 yards away. With fifteen 5-inch guns firing at each target, it was like taking a sledge hammer to an ant, if we hit him, but if one suicide boat slipped through to hit *Wren* at the water line -- it would all be over. When the third target disappeared from radar the fourth appeared off our port side, immediately. This target traveled down our port side at 23 knots, only 1900 yards from *Wren*. We opened fire again.

"In a total of eight minutes, our three destroyers had apparently destroyed four additional suicide boats. This was about as desperate as things could get, but it wasn't over yet. At 2353, the fourteenth and last suicide boat appeared on radar. He was 3800 yards to the northwest and headed for our ships at 20 knots. We opened fire again over the starboard side and quickly closed the book on Japanese suicide boats."

Captain MacDonald who was modest and conservative, reported this night in his action reports: "One craft was seen burning on the surface for about one minute, then disappeared. One suicide boat was probably sunk and fourteen possibly destroyed."

Those small craft would normally not have been a real challenge to three destroyers; however they played for keeps and our gunfire exposed our position to nearby aircraft. The idea that the Japanese wanted our ships destroyed and us dead bad enough to crash their craft and kill themselves, made every encounter a nightmare. Whether in the engine rooms, firerooms, on the flying bridge, or the galley, we were vividly aware that we could die suddenly and violently!

Several suicide boats did get through to crash into U.S. ships. January 10, 1945, at Lingayen Gulf, the transport USS *War Hawk*, AP186, was hit and severely damaged. April 9, 1945, at Okinawa, the destroyer USS *Charles C. Badger*, DD657, was crashed into, and nearly sunk. April 27, the destroyer USS *Hutchins*, DD476, came under attack. The suicide boat made his way through their formation and dropped a large explosive charge, close aboard. The destroyer was towed to Puget Sound, and -- scrapped.

The Japanese had hundreds of boats available for use at Okinawa; however only a few were encountered up to this time. Several ships, including one battleship fired on them and destroyed one here and there. But to the best of my knowledge, this was the only coordinated mass attack.

At 0120 we secured from general quarters, just to be called back at 0130. Enemy aircraft were closing on us and Captain MacDonald ordered flank speed, immediately.

Seaman First Class LJ Adams, on the starboard mount 43 director, describes his first air action that night: "I was perched high above the main deck on my Mark 20, 40mm director, where I had spent the night. Mount 43 covered the starboard side and most of the night suicide boat action had been from our port side, so I went along for the ride.

"My director had a selector switch that provided three firing options. I was able to take control myself, visually, pass it down to the pointer on the gun below, or connect to the bridge where they fired automatically, with radar. My standing orders were to keep control unless otherwise specified. Because of darkness, we had been on remote control all night.

"Things had just quieted down from the suicide boat attacks. At 0122, the cease fire came down, and at 0130 we got the flash red, condition yellow, for another enemy air attack. This target headed south at 78 degrees, like he was after me, personally. When the aircraft reached 3,500 yards we opened fire and fired continuously until he crashed, 1,370 yards away. The plane nearly hit the *Cowell* causing some damage, but I thanked God, we got him.

"Sitting there on my open director, unable to see or control anything, I felt vulnerable. With hammering from concussion, the guns belching fire and smoke around us and me in the middle of it -- I was scared!"

Lowell Clark bridge: "We were still running in tandem with *Cowell* on point and *Ingersoll* in the rear, the situation became increasingly uneasy. During the past few hours, keeping track of other ships while trying not to hit them, had been our worst nightmare. The *Cowell* was damaged during the night when one of our five-inch rounds hit her anchor. Fortunately no one was hurt. Even as a junior officer I knew there had to be a better formation. Like a big, jigsaw puzzle, my brain would not let go.

"At 0145, before our guns cooled off, another Bogy was approaching. We picked him up at 25,000 yards and he closed to 10,000, then we opened fire again, to our starboard quarter. Once again, we faced live-or-die time on the *Wren*. If there is a hell on earth, it had to be in the darkness off Okinawa. All of our main batteries were firing when we kicked it back up to flank speed. We soon lost the LCSs, but we knew they would be there to pick up survivors, if we were sunk. Once again we were lucky, as he crashed at a safe distance."

We secured from GQ at 0210 until 0350, then GQ sounded again. He slipped around in the darkness, but decided not to attack. This was like a big game of Russian Roulette, if you had enough exposure, they had to get you. Even with all of our combined firepower the odds were still with the aircraft at this point. The Kamikaze pilot was on a one way trip and his ticket had been punched. They always headed straight at us.

Sometimes it seemed like a game. A deadly, vicious game. We were definitely playing for everything. This time we won!

When the suicide-bound aircraft flew in close over the water, they were difficult to pick up on radar; likewise, they had trouble finding us slipping around in the darkness. The Japanese tried to find death -- while we tried to avoid it. Each encounter became a contest to see who would prevail. Fortunately for *Wren*, we still beat the odds. Even though we had short periods of time between raids when GQ secured, we had no sleep. Most of us remained at our GQ stations.

LJ Adams, recalls his thoughts during that time: "As dawn started peeking over the East China Sea, my guts still churned from the passing night. The sultry night had me glued to the director's seat that overlooked *Wren*. The tiny crack of light allowed me to penetrate the darkness to see what ships were still with us. God -- answered my prayers. We got through that awful night. I wondered what the day would bring. Would we still have two destroyers and four LCSs with us? Could they all make it?

"I scanned the horizon and wondered how such a peaceful place could become so violent. Other than the LCSs far off on the horizon, our destroyers were alone. At least they all got through the night. Sitting there almost in a trance from lack of sleep, my thoughts wandered.

"What am I doing on this destroyer anyway? They chose me for submarine duty, safe under the ocean! Instead, I've had my brains beat out from surface seas, and now a bunch of guys are trying to annihilate us by committing suicide. I thought about the months of waiting for sub-school at the sub base near Kodiak, Alaska, and how they had me schooling on 40 and 20mms during that time. Was this a conspiracy? If that's what they wanted, that's what they got. Finally, they sent me to Treasure Island for more 20 and 40mm training, and ultimately I wound up in director school. And here I sit with my education. As daylight progressed, the bridge ordered the directors to take firing control on all 40mm guns."

LT Lowell Clark, Bridge: "We secured from GQ again, but the relentless Japanese simply would not have it that way. The alarm sounded at 0815, with approaching aircraft which had survived the night. Now they were able to visually seek targets. Our first contact was picked up off our port side crossing our bow, low on the water, at 12,000 yards. A moment later we sighted the aircraft running down our starboard side. This one, a twin engine bomber called "Betty," had *Wren* written all over it! After getting directly off our starboard quarter, he turned straight at us. All ships opened fire simultaneously, with 5-inch guns, as he reached 9,800 yards."

Ensign L. D. "Criss" Criswell recalls: "I was in charge of the repair party, standing directly under the starboard 40mm, when that Betty came at us. The two loaders on that twin 40 were about nine feet above the main deck, over my right shoulder and the gun director was back toward midships. Betty continued poking her nose through the flack and smoke, getting closer... and closer... when those 40's opened up on her. He was right on the water when a 5-inch round from our ship hit a swell just ahead of him and exploded. The waterspout from that exploding round looked very near our ship, and the eruption was about a hundred feet high.

*A loaded "Betty," is ready to take off. This one is carrying an "Ohka," manned "Baka Bomb!"*

"The suicide pilot swerved left to avoid the eruption, as our boys on that 40mm poured fire right into the nose and fuselage. All of a sudden it blew with a tremendous explosion -- right alongside of *Wren!*

Criswell continues: "As if in slow motion, I could see an object that appeared to be half of a wheel spinning out of that black cloud, directly at us. Still spinning it hit the water next to our ship. I believe it could have hit us, but I'm not sure about that.

"When that Betty came in I decided he was headed right for my battle station. It seemed prudent to get to the port side where you were Bill, to seek shelter behind the deck house. But, I discovered I could not move a muscle in my body! I could only stand there and watch him come on in -- until he blew up! After the explosion I clasped my hands together over my head and shook them real heartily, at the two loaders.

"The boy on that director -- shot that plane down. To the best of my knowledge, he was the only one firing at that instant. The twin 40's aft had lost power and were being manually operated, so they could not possibly have shot that plane down. In my opinion, he should be given a medal for his courage and skill."

"That boy" was nineteen year old L J Adams, from Pasadena, Texas. He recalls that event: "When our 5-inch guns opened up, even though it was out of our range, that bomber looked -- huge -- through my sight. After crossing our bow, Betty turned right and traveled down our starboard side, while our 5-inch guns continued to fire at him. All of a sudden -- up jumped the devil -- he made another right turn and flew right at me! I had his glass nose right in the middle of my sight, as I tracked him on in.

*This is an actual photograph of that exploding Betty, taken from the Ingersoll. Ingersoll had executed a right turn so the Betty ran down her port side. Wren is just out of the picture, to the left of the explosion! Thanks to LJ Adams -- we all survived!*

"I could hardly wait, as his glass nose kept getting -- bigger and bigger! My range finder, sitting next to me, kept shouting the range: '7,000 yards, 6,000 yards, 5,000 yards, then 4,000 yards.' I opened fire."

Quartermaster Third Class Ken Kutchin, loader on that mount, recalls his experience with Betty: "I was feeding clips into our gun as fast as it would take them. We had a line of ammunition passers delivering the clips on a hand off basis and we had practiced many hours, perfecting our rhythm, for those few minutes. Our gun crew clicked, as if we were a machine.

Ken continues: "I watched the nose of that Betty from the corner of my eye, as he continually broke through the smoke. The entire war came down to this minute. I thought he tried to get me, personally! When those 20's opened up I wondered -- will we all die?"

L J Adams, picks up the action as Betty came on in at the *Wren*: "All the way in that Betty seemed to disappear in the black smoke, so we kept thinking we hit her. Each time, just as we slacked off our fire, her glass nose poked through -- again and again!

"I was pouring my fire right into her nose and my range finder kept yelling, -- 'You're on him, you're on him.' When that 5-inch round exploded in the water ahead of the aircraft, it looked as if the concussion lifted his wing causing him to climb. I stayed right on him as his underside filled my sight. It was like watching the dangerous spectacle in slow motion. All of a sudden -- he exploded! The tremendous concussion seemed to rock our entire ship! For a brief moment I didn't know who got who."

Lowell Clark, bridge: "All three ships had been cruising in a column prior to being attacked by Betty. As she moved closer to *Wren*, *Cowell* in the lead and *Ingersoll* behind executed starboard turns, partially encircling the approaching aircraft. I had been giving a lot of thought to our column formation, but this partial triangle seemed to make more sense. But now he came right at me! I thought he had us! He was so close I could see the pilot's entire face!"

Our 20mm gun was loaded and ready to fire, so as clip handler I moved a few feet aft and watched the action from between the amidships deck houses. I could clearly see both engines and the glass nose which identified Betty. We called her the "Flying Cigar." It looked like he had us! I returned to my gun station. I did not see the explosion, but I heard it, along with the loud cheers and hand-clapping of *Wren's* crew.

John Powell, fire control officer, recalls: "I believe that Betty was within one hundred yards from *Wren* when he exploded."

LT Howard Cook, bridge OD says: "That Betty -- nearly landed on our deck. He was well under 100 yards, when he exploded."

Wouldn't you think *Wren* had enough for one picket cruise? No way! Admiral Ohnishi, had more for us. At 0920 another aircraft popped on *Wren's* radar and we went to flank speed again. This suicider, identified as a "Tony," passed down our entire port side, as we fired at him. He dove for the *Ingersoll* and narrowly missed her bridge. The Kamikaze crashed about fifteen yards off her starboard beam.

About 0950 still another suicide plane started his run on *Wren*, but about 4000 yards off our port bow our CAP shot him down.

*A "Tony," circled in the picture, exploded directly over Cowell's deck. Wren is in the foreground and Cowell in front. Cowell was covered with gasoline and aircraft parts!*

At the same time all three ships opened up on still another determined Tony, who exploded in midair directly over the *Cowell*. Shell fragments, gasoline, and his cockpit door landed on *Cowell's* deck, causing small fires. During the confusion, *Wren* scored a 5-inch hit on *Cowell's* anchor, cradled over her starboard bow.

Less than forty-eight hours on our first picket assignment, the destroyers USS *Robert H. Smith*, DD735, and USS *Shannon*, DD737 relieved *Wren* and *Cowell*. We spent the rest of the afternoon and the night of May 25, screening Hagushi Anchorage.

*Wren* cruised slowly back and forth like a mother hen guarding her chicks. As we patrolled the outer harbor, our responsibility seemed awesome. As far as we could see there were ships. This was the prize the Japanese suiciders were after. If the picket destroyers and CAP succeeded, the inner defense was not needed. Despite all the dying, the relentless Kamikazes still got through.

We remained at GQ most of the time while at Hagushi. The suicide planes approached directly over the water, got shot at, then circled looking for an unprotected way into the fat transports. One had to spend little time on deck at night to see aircraft falling in flames, like in slow motion. But occasionally we watched big explosions on the surface that marked the grave of another score by our enemy. If there's a hell on earth -- this was it. *Wren*, low on fuel and ammunition, went to Kerama Retto, the safe place.

### USS BUTLER, DD636, MAY 25, 1945:

While we fought for our own lives on RP 16, time ran out for the *Butler* at Hagushi. She had been converted to a high-speed minesweeper and reclassified DMS29. Bombs from a suicide plane exploded under her keel. The tremendous explosion instantly flooded *Butler's* forward fireroom and caused her to lose all steam and electrical power. Nine of her men died a violent death. Some survivors, in the after part of the ship, had their legs broken from the impact. The battleship USS *West Virginia*, BB48, remained at *Butler's* side. While aiding her they shot down two additional suicide planes. Next day she entered Kerama Retto for temporary repairs, then returned to the U.S. and sold for scrap.

### USS PC1603, MAY 24, 1945 and USS LSM135, MAY 25,1945:

The Patrol craft PC1603 was crashed into at Hagushi -- and devastated. The landing craft LSMR135 was sunk in the same action with *Bates*.

### USS BATES, DE68, MAY 25, 1945:

At 1115, while patrolling two miles south of Ie Shima, life ended for the *Bates*. Attacked by three suicide planes, the first dropped its bomb, then crashed into the starboard side of her fantail. The near-miss ruptured her hull. Plane number two crashed into her pilot house and inflicted heavy damage. Plane number three scored a near-miss with his bomb, but ruptured the port side hull. Thirty minutes later her crew was ordered to abandon ship. At 1923 May 25, still burning, *Bates* capsized and sank. Twenty-one of her crewmen died with her.

### USS BARRY, DD248, MAY 25, 1945:

At 1300 hours, *Wren* was relieved on picket station 16 and ordered to relieve *Butler*, put out of action at Hagushi, and the *Barry* took hits by two suicide planes! Patrolling in the same area we were in, *Barry* shot down the first, but the second Kamikaze got through heavy flack and crashed into her bridge. The explosion ruptured and ignited *Barry's* fuel tanks and threatened to blow up the forward magazine. Forty minutes later her crew abandoned ship. At 1500 hours the water had risen sufficiently to squelch the danger of explosion, so they went back aboard and extinguished fires.

The following day, they towed *Barry* to Kerama Retto, then determined her to be unsalvageable. Stripped of all useable gear, they decided to use the destroyer as a decoy for Japanese suicide planes. June 21, LSM59, towed her out to be anchored in the path of attacking aircraft. While under tow, she was attacked again and sank -- along with her towing vessel.

## USS ANTHONY, DD515, MAY 26, 1945:

*Anthony,* slightly damaged on this day and again June 7, had a long and hectic life at Okinawa. Her sister ship the USS *Braine,* was badly hit on May 27, and *Anthony* picked all survivors from the sea. Many great ships not hit by Kamikazes are not in our book and some, like Anthony, that were slightly damaged seem to be short changed. We will do all we can, in future printings of this book, to rectify this situation. Anthony received seven battle stars for WWll and the Navy Unit Commendation for her service at Okinawa. She was one of the great ones -- and her crew stands tall!

## USS O'NEIL, DE188, MAY 26, 1945:

The DE, crashed into and put out of service, went to San Pedro, California for repairs. Two men were killed and 17 wounded.

## USS REDNOUR, APD102, MAY 26,1945:

While operating with USS *Loy, Rednour* had a 10 foot hole blown in her deck, 3 men were killed and 13 wounded. June 14, she sailed to California -- her war ended there.

## USS STORMES, DD780, MAY 27, 1945:

At 0905, the same day *Wren* and *Cowell* returned to Hagushi, *Stormes* got hit and heavily damaged. She arrived at Okinawa two days earlier, immediately after shake-down. Not a good place to break in a new crew! *Stormes* encountered her first Kamikazes while patrolling the outer transport area. The Kamikaze passed between two U.S. Navy aircraft, then dove at the USS *Ammen,* DD527, directly ahead of *Stormes.* The suicider turned abruptly and crashed *Stormes* at her after torpedo mount. The bomb exploded in her 5-inch mount 3 magazine! Fires raged and the sea poured into the new 2200 ton Sumner class destroyer. They managed to shore up the holes, extinguish fires and save their ship. With 21 killed and 16 wounded, she slowly went to drydock at Kerama Retto. After temporary repairs *Stormes* started her slow voyage home to San Francisco. Her war ended almost before it began.

## USS ROPER, DD147, MAY 27, 1945:

The veteran Wicks class destroyer, reclassified APD-20, arrived at Hagushi three days earlier. *Roper's* life also ended abruptly. A Kamikaze crashed into her at the same time and place as *Stormes. Roper* returned to Mare Island, just to be scrapped.

## USS BRAINE, DD630, MAY 27, 1945:

The destroyer, hit in quick succession by two suicide planes, had her bridge demolished by the first, the second blew her number two stack overboard and smashed her amidships superstructure. *Braine* lost 150 men killed and 78 wounded. *Braine,* like her sister ship *Anthony* was a great ship and her crewmen -- stand tall. After temporary repair at Kerama Retto, she sailed to Boston for repairs. *Braine's* war -- ended.

## USS SANDOVAL, APA194, MAY 28, 1945:

At Hagushi anchorage on May 28, the transport and SS *Joseph Snelling* were crashed into and put out of service, with heavy loss of life.

## USS LOY, DE160, MAY 27, 1945:

*Loy* came under attack by three suicide aircraft. She succeeded in shooting down two, but the third crashed so close to her hull that she sustained severe damage and 18 casualties. En route to Hagushi for help and temporary repairs, she shot down still another Kamikaze. *Loy* had taken survivors aboard from the destroyer *Barry*, hit just two days earlier.

## USS DULTON, PSC1396, MAY 27, 1945:

The PSC, also took a hit on the bridge. Many of these smaller ships sustained damage at Okinawa, but their stories are too numerous to cover in one book.

May 26, the same day *Butler* and *Barry* entered Kerama Retto, *Wren* went there for fuel and ammunition. We replaced -- 766 rounds of 5-inch, 368 rounds of 40mm, and 360 rounds of 20mm ammunition. Having spent all of that in less than 48 hours, *Wren* and her crew survived an incredible challenge to their very existence. Captain MacDonald, himself, came down from the bridge and proclaimed, "I've got the best damn gunners in the United States Navy." Our crew felt proud, but also fear. Would we survive this ordeal?

The Keramas are a small group of islands located a few miles southwest of Hagushi Anchorage, near the southern end of Okinawa. They were taken from the Japanese March 27, a few days prior to the invasion of Okinawa. U.S. invading forces captured and destroyed 300 Japanese suicide boats during this short conflict. Kerama Retto was uniquely positioned to provide the best natural harbor for auxiliary and fleet repair ships. Ships of every conceivable type occupied the protected inner harbor; repair ships, tenders, oilers, ammunition ships, transports, and auxiliary craft were among those that this facility serviced.

The trip in, as we entered the outer islands, was the gateway to hell. A graveyard for fighting ships. We observed ships moving slowly and silently as the bodies of their dead were slipped over the sides in burial ceremonies. Battered and burnt hulks of ships were beached to prevent their sinking. Wrecks, including *Barry*, were under tow. Many of the ghostly hulks contained entrapped, decomposing bodies of crewmen.

Entering the main anchorage we ran into intermittent clouds of smoke laid down daily to shield our anchored ships from deadly suicide attacks. We observed ghostly hulks of battered fighting ships with twisted, mangled steel protruding in disconfiguration. They slipped slowly through the smoke in search of refuge. Ships with gaping holes where engine and firerooms once hummed with activity. Engineering spaces where all died a violent death from concussion, water, and clear superheated steam. Where fighting men were entombed in flooded compartments, sealed off to prevent their ships from sinking. Mangled bodies, entangled in wreckage were accessible only to the cutters torch.

In the inner harbor we observed abandoned remains of once proud destroyers, chained together and anchored in the harbor for spare parts. Other destroyers that should have been on the bottom, were still floating. Brave crewmen fought and worked to keep their ships afloat. Those were the grim results from a nation that chose and acted upon suicide as a national war policy. Kerama Retto, the sheltered place, the place of sanctuary -- the place of death.

While writing this book I have been hearing bits and pieces from various officers and crewmen about Howard Cook's "fishing trip". This is that story in his own words.

LT Howard Cook, OOD: "While in my bunk during the relative quiet and safety of Kerama Retto, I reflected on the past 48 hours, this had been war at its very worst. But, I was proud of the way our crew had matured under fire. I was beginning to feel less like the prey and more like the predator.

"My thoughts wandered back to the stormy tranquillity of Adak. What did our crew think of my fishing trip? Would they have any doubts about my ability to help lead our ship through what we now faced?

"I was approached by Chief Steward's Mate Orsolino with the proposal that we investigate a nearby stream on the east side of Adak where some good trout fishing was reputed to be. It seemed like a good idea, (anything was a good idea in that climatically inhospitable and lonely area of the globe).

*Return of the proud fishermen. L to R Chief Commissary Steward Orsolino, Captain Mac, and LT Howard Cook.*

"I replied to Orsolino that his proposal was excellent, and it would be in order to arrange for a ship's boat, provisions, crew, etc. Not much to my surprise, Orsolino stated that he had already arranged for provisions and crew, the latter a venturesome young sailor named Melvin "Frenchie" Mouton, from the New Orleans area, I believe. The resourcefulness of the enlisted branch never ceased to amaze me!

"The situation was ideal, beautiful calm weather, good companions, and an appetizing lunch provided by Orsolino.

"Orsolino, by the way, was the best fisherman I'd ever seen in action. His forebears were island fishermen in the Philippines, and he knew more fishermen's tricks than a dog has fleas.

"Frenchie Mouton, from the *Wren's* engineering division, was a perky lad with an unusually likable and pleasant personality.

"As mentioned, our destination was a trout stream on the east side of Adak. The approach was via a narrow channel, Kagalaska Strait, which separates Adak Island and Kagalaska Island to the east. It was our first foray into that area as we got underway from Kuluk Bay and headed east, proceeding along the headlands of Adak toward the channel separating that island from Kagalaska. Arriving at the channel we proceeded into it on a southerly course and were doing quite nicely when unhappily -- we came to a sudden jarring stop. We had stranded on a submerged rock -- my

*Coxswain Melvin "Frenchie" Mouton*

fault, I was steering. Passages between the islands were usually 200 to 300 feet deep, we managed to find an exception. Not good; we were in a remote channel between two small islands and out of sight of the fleet anchorage. The channel was not very wide at that point; perhaps 200 yards and about 75 yards from the Adak shore.

"After about 30 minutes trying to dislodge the boat, backing, rocking, full ahead, full astern, etc. we were faced with the unhappy prospect of having no other apparent recourse.

"I did not confide my apprehension to my two shipmates, but I was anxiously concerned about getting out of the predicament as soon as possible. Not the least of my concerns was the probability of sudden and overwhelming weather change, for which the area is notorious. This weather phenomenon known as a 'Williwa' is characterized by sudden and violent winds; no place for a small open boat.

"I decided that the best course of action was to send a swimmer to the Adak shore, cross the island and signal the ship for assistance. Thus, placing my fortunes with the great God of the sea, I swam, fully clothed, to the nearby shore. I have never been so cold; the water temperature was about 39 degrees Fahrenheit. When I reached shore, I was so drained of energy that I sprawled half in, half out of the water for a couple of minutes until I had the strength to crawl out. The next task was to cross the island by traversing the low peaked mountain range between me and the fleet anchorage.

"My equipment was rather meager, my sailor's sheath knife, a battle lamp that I borrowed from the whaleboat as my signaling light, slung around my neck, and the soaked clothing that I was wearing. I left the stranded whaleboat about 1600, crossed the island and reached a bluff overlooking the fleet anchorage, in the dark, about midnight.

"From my position on the bluff I commenced signaling, using the battle lamp (not exactly what it was designed for). It must have worked; I was later informed that every ship in the anchorage had her guns trained on me and my signal light.

"After a little time went by, out of the darkness a ship's boat from the *Wren* appeared. To my amazement, or surprise, who was aboard her, but Captain MacDonald -- in person. "I figured that he was going to hang me. My trepidation as to my status was quickly relieved when the Captain hailed from his boat, 'Where are the fish,' and I realized that 'my Captain' was more concerned about my welfare than he was about anything else -- I'll never forget him.

"So, back to the *Wren*, feeling some embarrassment for having precipitated such a circus. As a final note, the whaleboat with Frenchie and Orsolino had lifted off with the tide and had already returned to the ship, safe and well.

"The transit across the island was not too difficult, though I am not sure I would especially desire it today. On the descent, at one point I slipped and took a free fall of about twenty feet in the dark, including a complete head over heels somersault. Luckily, I landed on a clump of the spongy muskeg that covered the island. It broke my fall and no apparent injury was suffered as I continued down the face of the cliff."

Howard told me this story has been an embarrassment for him all of these years. Even though it spread throughout *Wren's* crew at the time, no one seriously criticized him. After all, he was just -- "goin fishin!"

LT jg. Lowell Clark: "While lying in my bunk in Kerama Retto, I pondered the problem we had keeping our guns unmasked. During the fury and excitement of suicide attacks, we had enough to deal with without worrying about shooting at our own ships. I started sketching different formations that might simplify the problem. Eventually, I came up with an idea that might solve everything. Three to four destroyers in a long, diamond shaped formation.

"This would allow each ship firing room outboard of our perimeter, and still keep us unmasked from frontal or after assault. If all ships executed either a port or starboard turn simultaneously, we would still have more firing clearance.

"The idea seemed good to me so I presented the sketches to Captain Mac, who agreed with the concept. The following morning, the Captain and I went over to Captain Moosbrugger's command ship to run the idea by him. He was very gracious and considered our proposal, then ultimately agreed to try it. From that time on, all picket destroyers traveled in the diamond shaped formation."

This idea of Lowell's probably saved many lives. It allowed all ships to shoot at a single target with greater flexibility and respond to multiple attacks. U.S. destroyers needed all the firepower they had to stay alive. The pallbearers stayed several thousand yards behind our destroyer.

*Typical tandem running formation, before Lowell Clark submitted his diamond shaped formation.*

May 27, *Wren* returned to Hagushi where we patrolled the outer perimeter of the transport area during the day and early evening. *Wren* was at general quarters most of the time. We would secure for a few minutes, then be called back. At 1755 we went to GQ with a plane and sub contact at the same time, but they slipped away without conflict. At 2005 we had another aircraft contact, many were in the area during this time. *Wren* laid down a smoke screen just before dark and continued screening duty until 2137, then anchored on the outer perimeter. Four destroyers were moored together with the USS *Drexler*, just outboard on *Wren's* port side.

During the short time *Wren* was off the picket line, ships had been blowing up all around us, in the -- safe area. But, by no means had things quieted down on the -- picket lines.

### USS FORREST, DD461, MAY 29, 1945:

*Forrest* was the next destroyer to fall victim to Japanese suicide planes. After several years in the Atlantic, they arrived at Ulithi March 9, 1945. She, too, had been converted to a fast minesweeper and reclassified DMS24. *Forrest* started sweeping mines at Okinawa on March 19, twelve days before the invasion. The efforts of these ships cannot be praised enough. Their job was hazardous, they were there first, at times all by themselves and they faced a suicidal enemy. *Forrest's* crewmen should be proud!

*Forrest*, attacked by three Kamikazes shot down two, but the third persevered and crashed her starboard side at the water line. Heavily damaged with five dead and 13 wounded, DMS24 headed for Kerama Retto to join the rapidly mounting numbers of ghost ships. The war ended for this gallant ship as it had for her sister ship, *Butler*, two days earlier. *Forrest* arrived home and was decommissioned -- and later sold for scrap.

*Wren lays down smoke before anchoring under its protection, for the night.*

# TWENTY -- ONE
# SINKING OF THE DREXLER AND
# WILLIAM D PORTER

After settling in for the night at Hagushi, under the protection of our smoke screen, a movie was called in the mess hall. We were happy, feeling the need of mental diversion. We just got into the plot when, "Ping .... ping .... ping .... all hands man your battle stations," GQ sounded. *Wren* was getting under way for, Picket Station 15, the hot spot. Before we cast off our lines the order came down: "Secure from GQ, the *Drexler*, is going out in our place." The movie continued, much to our delight.

We should have used the time to sleep, because *Wren* stayed at GQ from 0140 until 0405, then back at 0510. This time a Japanese "Pete" closed on the transport area. Ships on the northwest perimeter opened fire. *Wren* opened fire just before he splashed, about eight hundred yards off our port beam.

Once again we secured from GQ at 0515, but had no rest. At 0715 GQ sounded again. While running to man our stations word came over the PA, "The *Drexler* has been sunk!" *Wren* and *Watts* left together to replace *Drexler* and search for survivors. The seas were like glass and the winds calm, as *Wren* steamed at flank speed towards our rendezvous with disaster -- the USS *Drexler*, DD741.

In a very short time we arrived on the scene where the 2200-ton *Drexler* had disappeared beneath the sea. Her grave was marked with floating debris -- barrels, boxes, cans of every size, mattresses, life jackets, helmets and garbage -- mingled with fuel covered, shattered aircraft parts. Every available man on the *Wren* stood quiet vigil at our life line. *Wren* eased right through the middle of *Drexler's* remains, as we searched, in daylight, for any sign of life overlooked by *Lowry* and the LCSs.

Not having slept for days, we continued to examine the floating remains. It seemed like *Drexler* might somehow reappear. It felt like a -- nightmare! With our minds further blurred by the strain of not knowing from one minute to the next whether we would live or die, *Wren* continued slowly through the floating remains of this valiant fighting ship.

Words alone can never describe the remorse we felt. *Drexler*, oh *Drexler*, where are you? Where is your crew? One hundred fifty-eight now slept beneath us -- with their ship! Every crewman who observed that scene -- will take that nightmare to his grave!

During the morning hours of May 28, *Drexler* and USS *Lowry,* DD770, had been patrolling picket station 15. Skipper of *Drexler,* Commander Ronald Lee Wilson, himself among the fifty-two wounded, describes the action: *"We had been at general quarters all-night. As senior officer of our two ships, I had just ordered evasive action for another incoming enemy aircraft. We changed course to enable us to bring all guns to bear on the target and increased our speed. However, this plane was shot down by our Combat Air Patrol."*

Gunner's Mate Second Class Buford Mills, recalls: *"I was gun captain on the port side quad 40mm when about 0630 word came over our headset that marine fighters had made contact with six 'Frances II' twin engine bombers. Corsairs from our CAP shot down two, but the others continued to close on our position."*

Captain Wilson describes the action: *"At 0702 -- they were on us. Bomber number one was shot down by our TAF before he could attack. As aircraft number two appeared on our bow, we changed course to port to bring all guns to bear, and opened fire. He started his dive on Lowry, some eight hundred yards away from our position, in a hail of flack and smoke from our combined fire. The pilot appeared to be heading for a crash in the water as he nearly hit the Lowry. He managed to recover, momentarily, as his course took him -- directly at us. He approached our starboard side at the water level and crashed in a -- tremendous explosion. The bomber hit the after fireroom, also damaging the forward, as well as the after engine rooms. Huge gasoline fires were quickly extinguished through the superb efforts of LT Eugene C. Hicks, who was killed by aircraft number three. Thirty seconds after the first aircraft hit us, the second bomber was shot down by Drexler. We had no power, dead in the water, our decks ablaze and our crew in shock -- still, we fought back.*

*"While being riddled by the hot pursuit of two Corsairs and receiving many hits from our gunfire, bomber number three continued to close on our position. It appeared he was about to crash in the sea as the Corsairs broke off their engagement. He nearly hit our stacks as he zoomed over our heads, fighting to keep his aircraft under control. Regaining control, the determined suicide pilot flew a tight circle and came back. The two Corsairs quickly resumed the chase as our gunners continued to fire at him. While continually being riddled full of holes, this twin engine bomber also crashed into our ship at the base of number two stack. The second tremendous explosion was just too much for Drexler as she rolled over on her starboard side and sank, stern first, in forty-nine seconds after the last explosion!"*

Captain Wilson praised the courage and conduct of all his crew during the brief ninety seconds of their bitter battle for survival. He further stated: *"Many acts of heroism will never be known, as there were no survivors from the forward diesel generator room, plot room, lower handling rooms and magazines."*

Robert L. Anteau, fire controlman third class recalls: *""My GQ station was with the forward repair party, headed by Ensign Pappas. On station in the chow hall when* the first plane hit, we started the forward generator and water pump to extinguish fires started back aft. I grabbed the end of a hose and started down the starboard side of the main deck toward the fire. Looking up as I ran I saw the second plane being chased by two Corsairs, coming in directly at our starboard side. I immediately headed for the shelter of the port side, running between five-inch mount one and two. I was knocked down by concussion as mount two let go with a salvo right over my head.

"By the time I picked myself up and got to the port side, the twin engine bomber, a Francis II, was heading -- directly at me again. He had missed us on the first pass and was coming back for a second try. Reaching the passageway behind the wardroom I tried to return to the starboard side. However, this sheltered passageway was full of people with the same idea. No sooner had I squeezed inside when the second plane hit us with a tremendous explosion. Drexler immediately started to list to starboard as I helped cut a life raft loose. With our ship now listing about forty-five degrees, I slid down the port side of the hull into the water. As I swam away from our ship I looked back to see her bow sticking straight up in the air -- as she silently slipped away.

"With the oil on the sea now on fire, I swam into the wind to avoid it, heading toward a call for help. Getting to the spot, I found one shipmate with a working life belt helping another, with none. I gladly shared my working life belt with the second man as the other swam off to help still another shipmate in trouble. Shortly afterward we were picked up by a boat dispatched from one of the LCS's."

Torpedoman Third Class George Ream, recalls: "I was standing watch on the after bridge as lookout and operator of our torpedo computers. After the first plane missed the Lowry and headed for us, we were in each others' line of fire so all firing stopped. I saw the Japanese plane turn upside down and his props started splashing the water, as he came in. Just prior to hitting us he regained control and crashed at the waterline. The impact sounded like a -- huge thud -- shaking our entire ship.

"After missing us on the first pass, the second plane pulled a tight 180 degree turn and crashed into our number two torpedo mount with a terrific explosion. I was on the ladder to the 40mm gun deck when I was hit on the head with a flying piece of wood. Dropping to the gun deck I found myself entangled in the signal line. I called for help, but got none, so finally cut myself loose with a hunting knife I was carrying. As I recovered my footing, 40mm shells stored in a rack about five feet away started going off like firecrackers.

"I went up the starboard side of the bridge and started through the pilot house as the ship was listing about forty-five degrees to starboard. A radioman helped me get through to the port side. By the time I got there, our radar screen, on the top of the mast, was only about three feet from the water. The water was at our feet on the after bridge as the ship continued to sink, stern first, with the bow almost straight up in the air. Our torpedo officer, McQuilken, hit the water first, followed by the radioman. Bringing up the rear I could well have been the last man off of -- Drexler.

"Attempting to activate my life belt I found it leaked, so I started to swim, frantically. Thinking, if I don't make it, my mother will collect ten thousand dollars insurance money and if I do, I'll get a thirty-day leave. Totally relaxed -- I felt my body floating. Looking up I could see daylight, which I swam for with everything I had. Realizing my clothes were water soaked and pulling me down, I yelled for help. I heard someone yell, 'Hang on' and there was McQuilken swimming toward me with a floating net. We picked up Bruton, but didn't see the radioman."

Morris E. Carlton, water tender second class recalls: "I was in number one fireroom when we took the first hit. The lights went out and the emergency lanterns came on. With no communication we didn't know what was going on. After the second hit we lost all steam pressure, so we decided to go topside. Some men tried the port side ladder leading to the passageway, but it was on fire. Richard Cameron came back to the fireroom and told Roy Coleman and myself to go up the starboard ladder leading to a hatch that opened to the main deck. I was last of three to exit the ladder, reaching the hatch, the water was coming in on me. As I fought my way out onto the main deck, the life line was already under water, so I went over the side swimming away from the sinking ship. I looked back to see Drexler's bow protruding from the sea. It appeared to be about one hundred feet in the air as she -- slipped away."

Willard L. Jones, seaman first class, recalls: "I was on the main deck as the second plane hit above my head. I was knocked down twice and my hands were bleeding. Crawling through the midships passageway, the ship started going down, by the stern and rolled over on me. Jumping off from the ship I inflated my life belt which still worked, even though it had holes in it."

George (Duke) Payne, seaman first class, recalls: "I was a striker on mount 43, 40mm and as far as I know the only survivor from that gun. The second plane blew up our ammunition and I got blown off. I had pointer goggles on at the time, which got jarred to the dark position -- everything was black as I suddenly wound up in the ocean. With my face full of shrapnel, it seemed I was blind, until the water started seeping in my goggles."

In the aftermath of the sinking with one hundred forty men suddenly cast into the sea amidst the hazards of flaming oil soaked debris, many acts of heroism took place. Coxswain Geatano Caruso, saved several shipmates before perishing himself. LT Commander Robert Bidwell, saved a man's life by cutting him free of his tangled clothing which prevented him from swimming. LT jg. Nick Pappas, saved several others by aiding them in their desperate struggle to reach a life raft.

Knowing the weight limitations of the Japanese aircraft they originally thought it could not carry enough explosives to cause such damage. U.S. officials wondered -- could the Japanese have a new secret weapon?

In an effort to determine why *Drexler* sank in such a short time, the Navy Bureau of Ships conducted an investigation. (October 2, 1945 the results were published in a secret memorandum and they ultimately calculated it to be possible.) The first hit opened the after fireroom and the forward, and after engine rooms to the sea. Although there were no survivors in the area of the second hit, it is believed that the bomb exploded in the after engine room. This caused the after bulkhead to give way and flood the after crew's quarters. Weight of the flooding caused *Drexler* to sink stern first -- so fast.

Gunner's Mate Third Class Gene Brick, recalls: *"I was transferred from five-inch mount three to mount two a short time before May 28. This strange twist of fate has haunted me for a lifetime, as there were no survivors from mount three."* Gene's shipmates are also happy, as he organized a reunion.

Think, if *Drexler* had not replaced *Wren* on RP15 that fateful night, LJ Adams, might not have lived to be a preacher, Jim Hutzel, might not be spending winters in Florida, Joe Reinders, might not be running his boat out of Anacortes, Washington and there probably would be no book. We -- would all be dead! So would everyone else amidships, on the main and catwalk decks.

*Wren* continued to search the area for survivors, while USS *Watts*, DD567, joined *Lowry*, DD770, and the LCS's to take survivors on board for transport to various harbor facilities. At 1112 *Lowry* rejoined *Wren* to continue patrolling RP15, along with the four "Pallbearers."

The seas started to kick up during the afternoon and we learned typhoon number three would soon provide our own -- Divine Wind. Who would think *Wren's* crew would ever be happy facing a storm, after the Aleutians?

### USS SHUBRICK, DD639, MAY 29, 1945:

While patrolling RP16, where *Wren* had just survived her combined suicide attacks, *Shubrick*, took a severe crash from a Kamikaze. RP15, where *Wren* patrolled at the time, was only a few miles away. Those on the bridge witnessed the tremendous explosion!

Lowell Clark, bridge: *"Wren* was lead ship in a column with USS LCS's, 55, 56, 66, 114 and *Lowry* at the rear. While at GQ with many Kamikazes in the immediate vicinity, ships on RP16 opened fire. Captain MacDonald had ordered speed reduced to 10 knots, and we could almost hear a pin drop on the bridge. It was 10 minutes after midnight when we saw a flash and explosion very near our position. One aircraft came down in flames. At almost the same time a second huge explosion occurred on the surface. We knew one of our ships was hit! We all shared that sick feeling of apprehension on the bridge that night, but did not know which ship they hit.."

An unknown seaman's diary, given to this author by Bob Johns, also a survivor from *Shubrick*, recalls the details leading up to her destruction: *"We arrived at Okinawa*

*May 5, at 1800, and drew our first picket assignment, May 11. At 0500, on the 12th, we left our station to join the Drexler and other fleet units for an assault on Tori Shima. This tiny island was located a short distance from RP 16, about 60 miles west of Hagushi Anchorage. Drexler bombarded the island, but it appeared to be deserted, so Shubrick left for Okinawa at 1930 the same day, with other fleet units. Drexler remained behind to continue patrolling the area.*

*"Shortly after leaving, while running through the hot spot, we were attacked by four suicide planes. My ship gave a good account of herself, shooting down two of the attackers, one crashed near our stern. We survived our first challenge -- triumphantly."*

**The typhoon we had just gone through seemed anticlimactic to the ships of Squadron 57. This picture of mounts 4 and 5, taken aboard Wren's sister ship the USS Smalley, DD565, off northern Japan, is a typical fueling situation in calm waters. This operation could never be attempted in a storm.**

On May 25, midday, *Wren* and *Cowell* had been relieved at RP16, by the USS *Robert H. Smith* and *Shannon*, DM25. *Shannon*, a destroyer minesweeper, later relieved by the USS *Van Valkenburgh*, DD656, returned to sweeping duty. At ten minutes after midnight, on the 29th, *Shubrick* was nearing RP16, to relieve one of the two destroyers, when she came under attack by two aircraft. One Kamikaze crashed into the starboard side, setting off a depth charge, and blew a 30 foot hole at her waterline. With dead and wounded everywhere, without power and sinking -- *Shubrick's* situation seemed grim.

Onboard *Van Valkenburgh* the flash and explosion was also observed, so they gallantly sped to aid their sister ship. By 0113, she was alongside *Shubrick*, removing the badly wounded, as they transferred vital documents from the sinking ship. Eventually, flooding and fires came under control, and the tug, USS ATR9, arrived to take the badly damaged ship under tow, to Kerama Retto.

*Shubrick* lost 35 men killed and 25 wounded; however, after temporary repairs she managed to get one engine going for her long trip home to Puget Sound Navy Yard. After arriving, August 10, the Navy decided to -- scrap that SACRIFICIAL LAMB.

Both RP16 and our station RP15, had been patrolled by only two destroyers for the past few days; however, at 0500, *Wren* and *Lowry* were joined by the USS *Walke*, DD723. Bad weather increased, but *Wren* patrolled at GQ, with many enemy aircraft near our position, for most of the five days.

USS *Cogswell*, DD651 relieved the *Wren* at 0951, June 1, and we proceeded to Kerama Retto for fuel and ammunition. Once again -- *Wren* had been very lucky. The life of a destroyer at Okinawa had been calculated at ten days. We had already surpassed that by two, with seven days on the hot spot. How long could our luck hold out? This thought -- haunted everyone!

June 2, we patrolled Hagushi Anchorage until the 5th, when we left for RP5, relocated from the northeast side of the island to directly off Hagushi. We hoped this would be a gravy train; however, a surprising number of single and occasionally two aircraft were picked up on radar. *Wren* joined *Rowe* and *Lowry* at 1850 and formed Lowell Clark's "diamond formation." This was the first time we operated in that formation. As *Wren* left the transport area the battle between U.S. ships and the Kamikazes continued.

## USS LOUISVILLE, CL28, JUNE 5, 1945:

The cruiser had just returned to combat from Mare Island, where she had completed repairs caused by two Kamikazes, on January 6. While providing fire support for ground troops, she was crashed into for the second time. *Louisville* stayed out of action until June 9, then resumed her support duty until ordered back to Pearl Harbor on the 15th, for repairs. The cruiser did not return to the war.

## USS MISSISSIPPI, BB41, JUNE 5, 1945:

The battleship had just arrived from Pearl Harbor, where she had undergone repairs from the crashes of two suicide planes, on January 6. After leveling Shuri Castle, which had stalled the entire ground effort, *Mississippi* fell victim for the second time, but they stayed on the firing line until June 16, then went for repairs. The battleship entered port at Sagami Wan, Honshu, Japan, August 27, back on peacetime duty.

## USS J. WILLIAM DITTER, DM31, JUNE 6,1945:

While on picket station in the area of the old RP14, with USS *Harry F Bauer* and USS *Ellyson*, DMS19, the 2200 ton destroyer minesweeper was nearly severed by two Kamikazes. Attacked by a large group of aircraft, they shot down five with combined fire, but the sixth and seventh struck home. The first hit *J. William Ditter's* after stack. The second crashed her port side, near the main deck.

Dead in the water, with many casualties, her damage control parties kept the ship afloat until the tug, USS *Ute*, could tow her to Kerama Retto. *J. William Ditter* returned to New York -- and sold as scrap.

## USS HARRY F. BAUER, DM 26, JUNE 6, 1945:

Another 2200 ton destroyer minesweeper, damaged by a near miss that flooded two compartments, stayed with her stricken companion. *Harry F. Bauer* assisted *J. William Ditter* and escorted her into Kerama Retto. *Harry F. Bauer* was then repaired and an unexploded bomb removed. She returned to service.

USS *Van Valkenburgh* and *Wickes,* DD578, took over their old patrol station RP14, on a triangle with RP15 and 16. This station, supposed to have been eliminated with the reduction to five stations -- 5, 7, 9, 15 and 16, -- was closest to Japan. Captain Moosebrugger must have reactivated the RP station, out of necessity.

## USS LCS15, JUNE 6, 1945:

Immediately in the same action, the landing craft was sunk by a flaming Kamikaze. *Van Valkenburgh* went to her rescue. She plucked many badly burned survivors from the sea -- and her medical staff worked on them until the wee hours of the morning.

This was not a new experience for *Van Valkenburgh.* For the fourth time, this ship's decks were covered with wounded from other ships, and her wardroom became Doctor Smale's operating room. *Van Valkenburgh* received the Navy Unit Commendation for their outstanding duty.

## USS NATOMA BAY, CVE62, JUNE 7, 1945:

After riding out the typhoon, CVE62, provided air cover for ground troops. During this operation, a Kamikaze crashed into her. The "Zeke" came in on the port beam and the carrier changed course putting him on the stern. As the pilot came over the flight deck, he fired incendiary ammunition at her bridge. Reaching the island structure he nosed over, crashed into the flight deck and tore a 12 by 20 foot hole. The fo'c'sle and anchor windlass were damaged beyond repair. Fortunately, only four men were killed. June 20, *Natoma Bay* returned to San Diego by way of Guam, but her war ended.

Back onboard the *Wren*, with RP5 out of sight from Hagushi, we seemed to be all alone, except for our pallbearers, 3,000 yards behind. The sea was smooth as glass. This could have been a luxury cruise until GQ brought us back to reality. By the end of the second day, we were lulled into a state of relative tranquillity, when GQ sounded again.

As I rushed out of the electric shop, up the ladder and out the starboard hatch to the main deck, the shrill sound of mount 4 firing signal broke the silence. I looked up to the left and about had a heart attack. The gun muzzle was right over my head! I dropped to my knees and attempted to cover my ears. I did not make it! The mount 4 ready watch let go with their first salvo -- right over the water. Picking myself up off the deck -- I saw the Kamikaze headed right for *Wren*. As I got to my feet I felt dizzy. My head screamed from the inside. I ran up the starboard side towards my gun station -- and the Val exploded! Our ready watch shot him down, just in time. He could have had the *Wren* before I reached my GQ station!

Two minutes later a second Val followed his buddy in. *Wren*, now combat ready, traveled at flank speed. All guns opened fire and we blew another, would-be, Kamikaze out of the sky.

When studying the action reports from *Wren* and other ships, one can easily see how the Japanese got through to successfully crash U.S. ships. *Wren* had effective CAP overhead, but the aircraft flew right off the smooth sea, undetectable by air search radar. In his action report, Captain MacDonald said: "We detected the aircraft 7,000 yards away, the first shots were fired 20 seconds later and continued for one minute. The Kamikaze exploded, less than 1500 yards from *Wren*!" Our guns had to be manned at all times because things happened -- so fast. Those first shots had to count. A delay of two or three seconds could put a Kamikaze on our decks. *Wren's* gunners -- served her well.

At 1850, June 8, the USS *Fullam*, DD474, and USS *Dyson*, DD572, relieved the *Rowe* and *Lowry*, as we continued to patrol RP5. At 1740, June 9, the USS *Knapp*, DD653, joined the formation. At 0052, June 10, *Wren* left for Kerama Retto. At 1640 *Wren* got underway for Hagushi, where we anchored and patrolled for three days.

*Wren* served with *William D Porter* for a short time in the Aleutians, then she went south, before us.

### USS WILLIAM D. PORTER, DD579, JUNE 10, 1945:

While *Wren* anchored at Hagushi, *Porter* patrolled RP15, along with the four pallbearers. At 0815, a Val dive bomber dove from cloud cover -- straight at the destroyer. Quick evasive action by Captain, Commander C.M. Keyes, caused the Val to miss, but the aircraft hit the water alongside and wound up under the keel.

Like a mine, the bomb exploded near the after engine room.  The explosion lifted the entire after section out of the sea, then dropped her back with a thud -- like a rock. Sixty-one men had legs and feet broken or bruised, and many others were injured from the violent eruption.

*The William D. Porter settles in, as her crew scramble to get off.*
*Wren's sister ship, the USS Smalley, DD565, also took crewmen aboard and stood by, as Porter sank.*

USS *Smalley* DD565, had been relieved on RP15 by the *William D Porter*.  In a few minutes they received an emergency call to relieve *William D. Porter* again.  She was sinking, fast!  Second Class Fire Controlman Luther L. Farrar recalls:  *"That could, and probably should have been us.  We had just gone in for fuel and ammunition when the call came.  I'll never forget the sight and my feelings while watching her sink."*

Aboard the USS *Relief*, AH1, where the injured were taken, their stories were recorded by James J. Gillan, seaman second class, enlisted Navy Correspondent.  Thanks to Bill Glover, himself among the wounded, we have those stories.

Seaman First Class H. E. Farnham: *"I was washing down amidships, port side when I heard three short bursts.  I thought they were depth charges.  I looked up and saw a Jap plane coming in close to the water, straight at us. It was a Jap Val. Suddenly it hit us and I was bouncing around on the deck like a ball. Machinist Mate Anderson and Doctor Bernard helped me into a passageway and I picked myself up. The doctor asked if I was okay, then I ran off to my GQ station -- a five-inch gun, forward. They called it Gun One. My ankle started to swell badly and some of the crew helped me into a LCM standing by."*

Shipfitter Third Class S. R. Yurchey: *"After getting off watch, I was sleeping in my rack in the after crews quarters, just above where the plane hit. The explosion wakened me and I hit the deck, looking around for anyone who might be trapped. I checked the vents, then went topside to assist with carrying hoses and starting pumps. We shored up the bulkhead between the after engine and firerooms, then checked the compartments to see if any of our men were trapped below."*

Machinist's Mate Second Class D.L. Anderson: *"I was in sickbay, amidships, when I heard a shell explode. With only one shoe on, GQ sounded, so I hit the deck. While running down the starboard side I heard the terrific explosion, and flames and a water spout shot high in the sky. Suddenly -- I didn't know where I was. Later, I wound up on the port side, picking up shipmates. One was Farnham who I helped into the midships passageway, then I went aft.*

*"I tried to get into the after crews quarters, thinking some shipmates might be in trouble. The quarters were a mess, "sacks" (beds) were all over, bulkheads (walls) were buckled and I saw flames from an electrical connection box. I ran forward and the Executive Officer, Lt W. B. D. Stroud, asked me if I would get in the whaleboat to get submersible pumps and "handy billys" from other ships. Going over to another ship, I felt a depth charge explode. That destroyer was almost hit by a torpedo, while our men were dumping everything over the side. We made three trips to other ships, but when we saw we couldn't save our ship, we started rounding up the life rafts, which had been cut loose* and *were floating around the ship."*

Machinist's Mate Second Class N. J. Verteramo: *"On watch in the after engine room, I heard the alarm -- it only got out about four rings. I was knocked down, bounced around and ended about halfway down in the bilges. I was afraid of steam lines. A friend loosened a foot I got caught and I could see water swirling in the bilges by that time, so, I decided to try and get out. The steam was bad and getting worse. I finally got to the deck and then tried to go back, but the water in the room was deep by then. The engine room was about three-fourths flooded and there was no need to go back then. The man on the lower level from me was also knocked down, but he also got up, topside. The man in charge of the watch, Machinist's Mate W. M. Byrne, got free also, as did Machinist's Mate Third Class V. E. Phillion and Fireman First Class H. R. Bringle, who was on the lower level."*

Seaman First Class C.A. Williams: *"I was in the forward handling room. It all happened so fast I didn't know what had happened. I heard the general alarm ringing and a few rounds fired from a 40mm gun. I heard a big explosion, which lifted the ship out of the water, throwing me across the compartment. I got to my GQ station, a 20mm gun and waited. The First LT gave me his watch and told me to take a ship's draft every 15 minutes. The fantail, was then level with the water. The crew started throwing ammunition, depth charges, torpedoes, anchors and all loose gear overboard. We wanted to unload everything possible to save our ship. We were carrying hoses and wading in oil up to our knees. The ship was laying way over to the starboard side. We kept trying to pump out compartments for nearly three hours. But -- our ship was sinking. The LCMs came alongside and we went aboard. Those guys were wonderful, giving us coffee, cigarettes and treated us for shock."*

*William D. Porter laid over on her side and sank rapidly.*

Seaman Second Class A. E. Hingle: *"I was in my 'rack' in the after crew's quarters, when the explosion caved the bulkheads in. The oil pipes busted. I grabbed my pants but couldn't get to my shoes, so went up the after ladder to the fantail. When I got out of the daze, I went to my GQ station -- the only gun left in working condition, and started looking for another "Bogey." They took me off because of the pain in my heels -- you see, I hit the deck as it was coming up from the explosion. My heels -- took it hard."*

Seaman First Class Richard J. Stevens: *"I -- saw the plane coming in. I was standing on the fantail, when I heard a small shell burst, and saw the Bogey coming in fast and low. It hit and I was knocked to the deck and bounced around. I went to my 40mm gun station and stood by in case there were more planes, then helped unload the ship and assisted others who were boarding the LCMs."*

James Gillan states in his writing: One man who had a bad time was Radarman Third Class W. S. Clover: *"There I was in the after washroom, just aft of where the plane hit. I was -- blown into the number four handling room. I tried to run through the wash-room but the steam was so bad I had to go to the other side. Running forward to see what I could do, I stopped to help throw depth charges overboard."*

The Chief Yeoman said: *"I tried to help establish communications with others in the tactical unit. We got out the records, and checked the casualties off when transferred over to the LCMs. I tried to get a quick check of all personnel. We could account for every man."*

(Bill Clover provided me with these terrific stories -- told at the time.) -- "Thanks Bill!"

*William D Porter*, settled into the sea, then rolled over on her starboard side, as she started down. Stern first, with her bow straight up in the air, she expelled her last gasps of air -- then settled into her final resting place.

Navy Correspondent James J. Gillan quotes one man as saying: *"That's my home."*

Another said, *"Guess my home is gone."*

During *Wren's* three days at Hagushi, we spent much of our time at anchor, in the outer harbor. Fierce ground fighting took place above our heads in the southern hills, and as we moved on the open decks, the Japanese shot down at our white hats. This is the problem the blue dye, we lost during our big Aleutian storm, was supposed to prevent.

Danny Wann, one of the seamen who had guard duty on the bow stated, "We shot at everything that floated." The Japanese swam out, using floating boxes and bottles as snorkels, then snuck aboard U.S. ships and threw explosives in engineering and other vital areas. Everything had to be fired at, all night long.

One night while Danny, carried out this duty on the bow, he felt paranoid. He expected a Jap to pop out from everything that floated. Howard Cook, OD, walked out on the wing of the bridge and Danny yelled up to him, "I'm scared!"

Howard remembers that night well and recalls his answer, "So am I, stay there, it'll be OK."

The ground war was very close to where *Wren* anchored during those three days. The battleship *Missouri,* a short distance away, lobbed shells slowly but continuously at the Japanese. They had a spotter directing fire in close support. Each time one of her 2,000 pound rounds left its barrel it traveled as in slow motion, to its designated target.

*Wren* was host to at least one amphibious duck, full of hungry soldiers, who came alongside seeking handouts. We fed them well and sent them back to battle with additional food for their buddies.

June 13, *Wren* and *Cowell* left for RP16A, located between RP15 and 16 -- the reactivated HOT SPOT. We joined *Van Valkenburgh*, already on station, at 1425. *Wren* continued her cat and mouse game of 'gotcha' with the Japanese suicide pilots for four more days. We were at GQ around the clock with little to no sleep for the entire time. We were like -- walking zombies. I spent my rest time trying to cat-nap on the 20mm ready box, about the size of a coffin. Finally, at 0845, June 16, *Wren* had finished her last picket duty. We went to Kerama Retto for fuel and ammunition, then back to the southwest fire support area, arriving about 1700. *Wren* anchored for the night.

The war continued in the hills and several warships bombarded in support of the final stages. At 2030 -- a tremendous explosion occurred near where *Wren* was anchored.

Lowell Clark recalls seeing it: "I was relaxing in the wardroom a few hours after returning from Kerama Retto, when I saw a huge flash light up the darkening sky. The explosion had such force it seemed to rock our entire ship. This was just downright scary and too close for comfort. We had the word we would be leaving for the Philippines in the morning, and that was not soon enough for me. We knew one of our ships caught it --but didn't know just which one. We now know the ship was the USS *Twiggs*!"

## USS PUTNAM, DD537, AND USS TWIGGS, DD591, JUNE 16, 1945:

The destroyers had been operating together around the western fire support area. *Putnam,* on nearby picket duty, came under attack by a Kamikaze. Seconds before the attacker would have crashed the destroyer's decks, an unidentified U.S. CAP aircraft did a totally unprecedented thing in this crazy war. He deliberately crashed his fighter aircraft into the Kamikaze! How many of *Putnam's* crew lived long and full lives -- because of that one man's sacrifice? What words can adequately -- sing his praise? Who was he? His family should be told of this heroism! If anyone knows who he was -- let us know.

*Putnam* continued picket patrol for the fire support ships until 2030, when Captain Glen R. Hartwig, the squadron commander aboard *Putnam*, quickly went to aid the stricken *Twiggs*.

*Twiggs*, with *Putnam*, operated as picket for the Western Fire Support Group when a single torpedo plane attacked. His torpedo crashed into *Twiggs'* port side. Then the Kamikaze circled -- and crashed onto her decks! Another Kamikaze pilot completed his suicide pact with the Emperor. His torpedo exploded *Twiggs'* number two magazine, and engulfed the entire ship in flames. In less than one hour -- *Twiggs* sank. Among the 152 dead and missing was her Captain, Commander George Phillip. *Putnam* rescued 114 of *Twiggs'* 188 survivors.

## OKINAWA EPILOGUE

In retrospect, we have attempted to point out the total degree of devastation inflicted on U.S. Naval ships and personnel by the Japanese Kamikaze madness. Rather than relying on lists and information already available, I read the history of every ship commissioned in the U.S. Navy, myself, gathering my own information.

Ninety-seven destroyers, not including DMs and DMSs (destroyers minesweepers and destroyer minelayers) and APDs (destroyer transports) were at Okinawa. Most of those classes of destroyers took part on outlying picket stations, as Sacrificial Lambs, who fought like lions. In addition, 51 destroyer escorts served, generally in close screening duty around the islands.

A total of -- 97 destroyers crashed into by Kamikazes at Okinawa, included 11-DMSs, 4-APDs and 1-DM. Counted among the 97 Destroyers hit, 36 of all four classes, were either -- sunk outright, later by U.S. gunfire, beached or scrapped. Most of the remaining 61 stayed out of service for the remainder of the war.

Of the 51 destroyer escorts -- 22 were crashed by suicide planes, among those 7 were sunk or scrapped.

**SUMMARY OF ALL DESTROYER TYPES HIT BY KAMIKAZES AT OKINAWA: 148 TOOK PART, 119 WERE CRASHED INTO BY KAMIKAZES, AMONG THOSE 43 WERE SUNK OR SCRAPPED.**

It would be much easier to count the destroyers not hit! Judging from the information we have, it appears that about 80% fell victim. The traumatic effect of experiencing those events -- is apparent at ships reunions, nearly 50 years later.

In addition many other ships of the line fell victim to the -- Japanese suicidal madness. There were -- 8 fleet carriers, 3 escort carriers, 9 battleships, 5 cruisers and 55 auxiliary ships -- crashed into at Okinawa. We will probably never know the exact number of suicide aircraft the Japanese lost at Okinawa; however estimates range from 2,400 to 5,000, or more.

The Okinawa phase of the war ended officially on June 21, 1945. Our last two chapters will point out the considerable damage and loss of life inflicted by the continued desperation of a nation dedicated to the use of suicide -- as a weapon of war.

The U.S. Army, Navy and Marines paid a terrible price for that victory -- over 17,000 in all. General Buckner's Tenth Army suffered the lion share of the 12,000 killed on the ground, but the General also paid the supreme sacrifice -- he was killed during the last days of battle.

On June 21, General Ushijima, the Japanese 32nd Army Commander and his Chief of Staff, Lieutenant General Isamu Cho -- committed hara-kiri, rather than surrender. In this final gesture, they joined about 100,000 other dead Japanese soldiers.

U.S. Naval losses of over 5,000 killed and a like number wounded -- stands alone in Naval history. Such losses have never before been sustained in a single battle, or like period of time. Yet the 50th anniversary came and left -- without a whisper. U.S. Destroyermen and the **SACRIFICIAL LAMBS**, sailed into battle and stood tall and proud!

What is a hero? To the Japanese -- Kamikaze Pilots are all heroes. They now have a heavily visited memorial which glorifies them. Before leaving, the pilots often visited home and said good-bye to family and friends. The Japanese suicide pilot was strapped into his cockpit with only enough gas for a one way trip. Given a generous amount of saki, he left as a hero. We take nothing from him -- he was a hero!

In contrast, most Americans who had to face the Kamikazes were gone from home for so long -- we forgot what our mothers, fathers, wives and sweethearts looked like. We didn't want to be heroes. We just wanted to win that war and go home. Gun crews, people in magazines and handling rooms, engineering spaces or the bridge -- had no place to hide! Our gun crews -- "Looked them in the eye, to stand and die!" Thousands faced unwanted but certain death -- just as surly as Kamikaze pilots. But undauntedly, all stood their ground. Are they any less heroes than Kamikaze Pilots? In the United States the term hero is, now, handed down freely. When will America wake up? Our heroism continues to be unnoticed. Our country has never even officially said -- "Well Done."

How can liberal revisionist, who were not out there, ever pass judgment about the amount of force the United States applied against Japan? Thank God for giving the United States the bomb, first! LET THIS BOOK STAND AS THE U.S. CONSCIENCE!

### Wrote Commodore Moosbrugger:

*THE PERFORMANCE OF THE PERSONNEL OF THE SCREENING AND RADAR PICKET SHIPS, BOTH INDIVIDUALLY AND COLLECTIVELY, WAS SUPERB THROUGHOUT THE OKINAWA CAMPAIGN. ACTS OF HEROISM AND UNSELFISHNESS, FIGHTING SPIRIT, COOLNESS UNDER FIRE, UNSWERVING DETERMINATION, ENDURANCE, AND QUALITIES OF LEADERSHIP AND LOYALTY EXCEEDED ALL PREVIOUS CONCEPTIONS OF STANDARDS SET FOR THE U. S. NAVY. THE RADAR PICKET STATION GROUPS TOOK EVERY BLOW THAT THE JAPS COULD INFLICT AND ABSORBED TERRIFIC PUNISHMENT IN PERSONNEL CASUALTIES AND MATERIAL DAMAGE, BUT THE MISSION WAS SUCCESSFULLY...COMPLETED.*

# TWENTY -- TWO
# THE BEGINNING OF THE END

On June 17, at 1327, *Wren* with Squadron 57, joined Destroyer Division 113, along with the USS *Mississippi* and USS *Portland*, en route to Leyte Gulf. Steaming out of Hagushi for the last time, saddened no one. Three hours later on a zigzag course of 186 degrees at fifteen knots, *Wren* screened the larger ships. We were out of sight of all islands. The memory of *Twiggs* exploding while close alongside our ship last night, was a grim reminder our war did not end. But this definitely signaled a change from our last twenty-seven days as **SACRIFICIAL LAMBS.** *Wren* -- survived!

On the 19th, we conducted anticlimactic AA practice before entering San Pedro Bay, Philippine Islands on June 20, at 1642. Admirals Halsey, McCain, Radford, and Commodore Higgins, along with the flagships USS *Missouri*, USS *Yorktown*, USS *Shangri-La*, and USS *Flint* were already there. This was the location of the largest gathering of combat ships ever assembled in one place -- the mighty Third Fleet.

**USS LSM59; USS HALLORAN, DE305; USS CURTIS, AV4; USS KENNETH WHITING; USS ASM213; AND USS LST534, JUNE 21 AND 22, 1945:**
Despite the fact that the Japanese had lost the land war on Okinawa, their suicidal efforts against the remaining U.S. Fleet continued. The LSM59, was sunk and thirty-eight survivors were picked up by the USS *Steady*, AM118. The *Halloran* received severe damage with a near miss, killing three men. The *Curtis* was badly damaged, with 35 killed and 21 wounded. *Kenneth Whiting* had five men wounded when an Oscar crashed into her. The following day ASM213, and LST534, fell victim to continuing suicidal attacks.

June 25, *Wren* moved alongside the destroyer tender USS *Markab* for five days availability. During this time all three divisions were given liberty at a small section of barbed wire beach on Leyte. We enjoyed steak sandwiches and cold beer. It was the first time most of us had left the ship since Pearl Harbor. We all welcomed the R and R.

Leaving the tenders, we moved out in Leyte Gulf where I created my own recreation, the adventuresome kind I liked best. As the ship's only rescue swimmer, the quarter-deck OOD and accompanying watch seemed to turn their heads when hearing a splash alongside of the ship. They watched me climb the mast to the high searchlight platform, directly over their heads, in my swimming trunks and dive out clearing the whaleboat. They seemed to know I was off on another excursion. I swam under the ship and came up on the opposite side to avoid pushing my luck. Later, I asked the enlisted men standing quarter-deck watch under the OOD, "How did he react to my swimming excursions?" 'He just grinned and walked away.' they said.

Small islands in the middle of the gulf were of interest this time, so I took off on the mile or so swim to the nearest one. Arriving at the island, access to the heavily vegetated top was by means of scaling a cliff of some thirty or forty feet. I looked up, pondered the situation, and saw a monkey in a tree branch that hung out over the edge. Ah-ha, a mascot I thought.

I promptly swam back to the ship to get a shirt to be used as a capture device and returned to scale the cliff and retrieve a mascot. As I reached the top, the thick brush between the few trees made walking barefoot uncomfortable. I heard rustling brush so stayed with the sound, but it remained just out of sight until I reached the other side of the island. There I discovered what I had been chasing. I grabbed a hold of a tree and leaned out over the edge of the cliff to try to see the monkey, which seemed to be in the brush. I was startled when a very large lizard jumped over the edge and held on to the vertical wall. His large head appeared to be about twelve inches above the ground, and he hissed and spat out his tongue -- in a very unfriendly manner. In my quick retreat across the island, to where I came up, the brush seemed alive with similar noises. The -- monkey stayed there.

July 1, at 0609, the nine destroyers of Squadron 57 got underway again. This time we had company -- lots of it. As far as we could see in any direction, warships dotted the horizon. Battleships, cruisers, destroyers, carriers, and hundreds of supply vessels formed the many task groups of the mighty Third Fleet, underway to carry the war to Japan's doorstep. To -- end it! We now felt -- invincible. Squadron 57, part of Task Group 38.4; formed a circle screen around the carrier USS *Shangri-La*.

After the fleet organized, from 1355 to 1630, we practiced firing at towed sleeves. *Wren* fired 42 rounds of 5-inch, 855 rounds of 40 and 1800 rounds of 20mm. (July 4, the fleet celebrated in a like manner -- creating our own fireworks.) *Wren* continued her daily routine of AA practice, while we guarded the large fleet carriers. Like a who's, who of the U.S. Navy, they were all there. As we neared Japan, *Wren* went into her routine duty as part of the encircling screen of destroyers that guarded each fast carrier. At times when on distant picket duty by ourselves, it felt like basking in the sun -- after Okinawa.

July 5 and 6, the carriers started to launch routine flight operations. July 7, at 1006, we fished out LT jg C. W. Fox, our first of many pilots. He crashed while taking off from the *Shangri-La*. Carriers are able to make gi-dunks (ice cream), destroyers are not. So our bridge negotiated with the carriers to determine how many gallons each pilot was worth. *Wren* held him for ransom, then we transferred LT Fox back to his ship.

By throwing or firing a messenger-line they installed larger lines to support the chair, then rigged a boatswain's chair between *Wren* and *Shangri-La*. Pulled in either direction, the chair swung from the main line on wheels and traveled from ship to ship.

This often proved to be a very precarious procedure and slack occasionally allowed the chair to dip, often into the water. Even at best it was a very steep ride from the low deck of *Wren*, to the high hangar deck of *Shangri-La*. Naturally, we expected the ransom to be paid on the first trip.

At 1356, LT C. K. Hughes also crashed on take-off from the USS *Yorktown*. *Wren* repeated the process.

As rescue swimmer, I was always on the fo'c'sle in my swimming trunks, during those operations. I carried a shark knife to cut parachutes off if necessary, as they could pull the pilot under if his May West ( inflatable life jacket ) didn't work. I responded to deck officer, First LT Frank Olson, by doing what ever had to be done to get the pilots aboard. Some were injured, requiring more help then others.

*Bill Sholin brings a pilot aboard, as other crewmen come down to help.*

July 7, at 1810, *Wren* left the formation to become plane guard for the carrier, USS *Bon Homme Richard*, and we took a position 1000 yards off the carrier's starboard quarter. At 2045, we left to rescue crewmen from a crashed TBF. Arriving at the scene of the crash we found they had drifted off in the darkness, so we lowered our whaleboat to search for them. I was aboard that boat. We ran in a large circle, stopping occasionally to yell for survivors. In a short time, we were in voice contact with all three airmen. After taking the first two aboard, we headed toward the third; however he could not be found. We lost voice contact in the darkness and his fellow crewmen were panic stricken. While searching the ocean using hand lanterns, I saw the green marker dye given off by the airman's equipment. Even though I knew he was gone -- I said nothing.

Captain MacDonald ordered *Wren* to circle with the whaleboat, shouting and listening for a response. In sheer desperation and determination our Captain took the ultimate gamble. He turned our large searchlights on which drew a quick response from the Admiral, on his carrier safely off in the distance. Finally, with considerable reluctance, they called off the search. At 2110, the pilot Ivan H. Whitt Jr. and Airman Third Class Donald J. Majesky were taken on board and *Wren* returned to the fleet.

Lowell Clark, bridge: "As we took up our plane guard position on *Bon Homme Richard*, a dramatic discussion took place. The pilot pleaded, *'Please--Captain MacDonald don't give up the search.'* His airman, jumped into the discussion. *'Captain, we were in close voice contact with our man, and we know he is out there -- please go back.'* 'My hands are tied, we've been ordered back to our station,' our Captain argued.

Then other officers joined me in an effort to convince Captain Mac -- but our words fell on deaf ears. Our Captain was all Navy and the Admiral had given an order.

"Thirty minutes later we were back on plane guard with the fleet, but the desperate pleading continued. Finally, Captain Mac gave in to our combined pressure and called the Admiral for permission to go back and search. We left thirty minutes later, but found no one."

During our voice contact with the missing airman, he said nothing about being injured. If his May West did not open and he could not get his parachute off -- I knew he would be pulled under. Sharks were another factor we failed to consider at the time. I now know they consumed hundreds of men, after reading the history of so many stricken ships.

In spite of sympathy for our two surviving airmen -- we held them for ransom. Why should those floating hotels have all the goodies?

On July 10, at 0330, our task group bombed Tokyo with vengeance. The raids lasted throughout the day, into the next night, then we traveled north at 25 knots. July 12, we bombed Hokkaido. Those raids continued for several days. Then on the 16th, we went back to Tokyo. In this relentless way the Third Fleet kept pressure on the enemy. This was the beginning of the end for Japan. Our bombers were destroying their ability to continue.

During *Wren's* daily routine, ships we interacted with constantly changed. That day we were with the cruisers USS *Stockholm*, *Boston*, *Saint Paul*, many fleet carriers, and dozens of destroyers. Ships were mixed, they traveled back and forth in an effort to maintain balance and kept the Japanese guessing.

July 22, at 0855, a special secret order received from the Third Fleet Commander, directed Squadron 57 on an anti-shipping and bombarding mission. We were to proceed to Ogasswara Gunto, in the Bonin Islands, and destroy any ships we found, then bombard the town of Omura, Chichi Jima. The squadron got underway at 0916 on a heading of 240 degrees at 20 knots.

LT jg Lowell Clark, bridge: "Squadron 57 arrived on location at 1834 the same day, and *Wren* started sweeping down the west side of Ogasawara Gunto. We were in a column with the other ships on a 180 degree heading, at 20 knots, taking us about twelve miles west of Muko Jima. We continued to search with both surface and air radar, until 2353, then came to a 140 degree heading. We swept the south end of Haha Jima, at 29 knots until 0300, then came to a heading of 000 degrees true, at 25 knots and swept the east end of Haha Jima. With a few minor adjustments, this course took us to the bombarding location, at 0325. Omura was off our port side at 11,850 yards. The commence firing order came down. Three minutes later, after firing 102 rounds of 5-inch, we got the cease fire order. We left our 'calling card!' *Wren* departed at 30 knots on a heading of 045 degrees.

"It had been reported that the Japanese smuggled their troops off the island, on hospital ships. If we located any we were to board and search them. If we discovered any other ships, we would sink them. The Japanese radar had been tracking us all morning, so we knocked it out first. Chichi Jima had been by-passed by U.S. forces and we had little information about what the Japanese were doing.

"We secured from GQ at 0355 and continued our course of 000 at 23 knots until 0535. We then came to a heading of 290 degrees and rejoined Task Group 38.4 at 1144," Lowell concluded.

July 24, our group bombed the inland sea area around Kure and Koirse until 2100 the following day, then we left at 23 knots. At 0800 the 25th, after replacing fuel and ammunition, we rejoined Task Group 30.8. The USS *Wasp* joined our group of charges. Squadron 57 joined Task Group 38.3 on the 29th and guarded the carrier USS *Randolph*, while they bombed Tokyo and Nagoya, again.

### USS MARATHON, APA200, JULY 22:

As the Third Fleet knocked on Japan's door, their revenge for the loss of Okinawa continued. *Marathon*, anchored in Buckner Bay, was shaken by a violent underwater explosion. A Kaiten (manned suicide sub) launched from the Japanese submarine I-53, found its mark. Heavily damaged, a real effort was required to save the ship. The USS *Cowell*, sent rescue and firefighting parties to assist the stricken transport.

### USS UNDERHILL, DE682, JULY 24:

The Sacrificial Lambs were still paying a heavy price at Okinawa. Having left Okinawa for Leyte, Underhill escorted transports loaded with battle weary soldiers of the 96th division, when the DE was hit by

*Chief Callahan, shows a Kaiten Suicide Sub.*

a Kaiten suicide sub. *Underhill* was blown in two and quickly sank. USS PC's, 803, and 804, came to her rescue, but picked up only 25 survivors. Her captain LT Commander Robert M. Newcomb was numbered among her 133 dead.

### USS CALLAGHAN, DD792, JULY 28, 1945:

*Callaghan*, *Prichett*, DD561 and *Cassin Young*, DD793, were on picket duty together off Okinawa. *Callaghan* fired on an old Japanese biplane and drove him away, but he returned, low on the water and crashed into the destroyer's starboard side. One bomb penetrated the after engine room and opened it to the sea, while the aircraft and its second bomb hit the superstructure. Raging fires set off the ship's ammunition and prevented other ships from helping. At 0235 -- *Callaghan* sank. Forty-seven men were lost.

## USS PRICHETT, DD561, JULY 28, 1945:

*Prichett* stood by to help *Callaghan,* when a second Kamikaze was picked up at 5,000 yards. Under heavy fire, he closed DD561 and crashed in the water, six feet off her port side. Despite heavy damage to her hull and superstructure, the destroyer remained with *Callaghan*, and picked up survivors.

For the second time *Prichett* sustained damage from a Kamikaze, the first happened April 3. August 13 the destroyer started her long voyage home to Puget Sound -- her war was over. *Prichett* received a Navy Unit Commendation for heroic action.

## USS CASSIN YOUNG, DD793, JULY 29, 1945:

*Cassin Young* returned to Okinawa May 31, after being repaired from her first encounter with suicidal madness on April 12. After spending the night assisting her sister ships, DD793 became a victim, herself. A low flying suicide plane crashed into her starboard side. The tremendous explosion caused extensive damage. With 22 men killed, 45 wounded, and fires raging, the destroyer was in serious trouble. After extinguishing fires, she limped back to Kerama Retto. August 8, the destroyer went home to San Pedro, California--her war was over. *Cassin Young* also received the Navy Unit Commendation. This ship is now a museum in Boston harbor.

August 1, we rejoined the main group, Task Force 38, which included Task Groups -- 38.1, 38.3, 38.4 and Task Force 37 -- (Royal Navy). At 1826, *Wren* departed on another secret dispatch to Iwo Jima. We were alone, traveling at 18 knots and reached our destination at 0747 the next morning. This trip turned out to be taxi service, as we picked up fifteen officers to be delivered to Task Group 38.4. At 0525 August 3, we delivered our passengers and rejoined the fleet.

*Wren* had been underway over a month, the natives were getting restless and our job was becoming a drag. We just wanted to get the war over and go home. But, we wondered what that would entail.

Hap Rogers and his forward fireroom gang broke their boredom by plotting another batch of raisin jack! He recalls: "We knew we had to be innovative this time. We didn't want to get caught again. With all of those -- big boys -- to protect us we shouldn't need our life rafts, so what better place to hide our stash. Each raft had a large wooden container (several gallons) of fresh water. There was no way we would ever need that now, so I replaced the water in all rafts with our raisin jack. Well, as it started to ferment in the hot afternoon sun -- guess what -- it started to expand. Even though we thought we left plenty of room for this process, it started to drip...drip...drip... Naturally, someone told the Captain. He called me up on the deck. 'Rogers,' he said, 'What's that?'

"I don't know, Sir." I responded.

"By this time a sizable puddle had accumulated. 'Dip your finger in and taste it, Rogers.'

"Going through the motions -- I knew my goose was cooked. "Well, Sir, it tastes like some kind of wine, but that couldn't be, could it...?"

"He stood there staring me down. Captain Mac had that smug look. He distorted his face like he was -- really pissed. 'Rogers, I want you to empty all of those containers, take them down to the fireroom and steam them, then bring them all up to the bridge so I can smell them before they are refilled with fresh water.'

"Aye, aye, Sir, -- I cheerfully responded and carried out his order."

At 1030 August 5, while operating off Tokyo, *Wren* was dispatched to retrieve another downed pilot. He had to ditch between Japan and his carrier, the USS *Independence*. Three hours later we transferred LT jg Edwin Free back to his ship. After the transfer of several gallons of gi-dunks -- of course.

Each day about dusk, *Wren's* morning orders were posted in the scullery. After getting off watch, I decided to mosey up that way. The usual card game was in progress at the scullery, with my friend Jack Jarc,(now clean shaven) at the head of the table. With a few dollars on the table and blood in their eyes, this seemed a very serious poker game. It took a lot to disturb it, so I just said, 'Hi, Jack'.

The cork bulletin board happened to be in a dark place, so I usually removed the orders and took it in the light to read. While deeply engrossed in its very serious content, someone grabbed them out of my hands. Spinning around, I saw a very large first class machinists mate, considered the tough -guy of our crew, reading it. I quickly grabbed the paper from his hands, turned around and continued reading.

The next thing I knew he had jumped me from behind. As he towered over me continuing to rabbit punch the back of my neck, I ducked. He had taken me by complete surprise. But, the next few seconds revealed he made a serious mistake, so he broke off the conflict and stormed up the ladder.

After combing my hair I continued to read the morning orders. He returned with the OD and demanded, "I want this man put on report for hitting me." It so happened the OD was Frank Olson, the officer I worked with rescuing downed pilots, and the boys in the card game quickly came to my defense.

LT Olson grinned as he stood there and said: "You fellows shake hands now and forget this fighting. We can't have this on our ship."

The machinist's mate said, "Now, Bill, you do mean this, you're not going to catch me off the ship, are you?" I assured him I would forget the incident. Scratch -- one bully! For the most part, in spite of cramped quarters, heat and stress, everyone got along surprisingly well.

The content of those morning orders, dated August 5, 1945, revealed the picnic was over. Squadron 57 would enter Tokyo Bay and attack! At 2400, *Wren* would go in close to shore off Yokohama, without firing. Battleships and cruisers would steam miles off shore. While they bombarded specific targets for one hour, *Wren* was to operate as a spotter and could not fire on the enemy. That looked like a -- suicide mission! *Wren* would withdraw to join the other ships until 0200, then return to bombard Yokohama, at close range. This was a virtual -- death warrant -- for our ship! Our crew became very quiet, until they announced over the PA system, "All morning orders have been canceled, *Wren* is going to sea." We traveled east at 050 degrees the entire night.

August 6, the following morning, they announced, "Our forces have dropped an -- Atomic Bomb -- on the city of Hiroshima, Japan. We wondered, "What the hell is an Atomic Bomb?" We had never heard of such an animal. This dominated our conversation for the next several days.

We've never felt cheated by not going on that mission. Everyone knew we would have been blown out of the water. The resourceful Japanese had lined the hills that encircled Tokyo Bay with heavy guns, some removed from warships sunk in the harbor. It was a -- death trap!

August 8, Russia finally declared war against Japan. August 9, the second Atomic Bomb was dropped on Nagasaki! As Commander in Chief of all U.S. Military forces, should President Harry S. Truman have ordered those bombs dropped?

Every civilized man deplores the killing of innocent men, women, and children -- but as Commander in Chief, did our President have a choice? If you had been onboard any of the hundreds of ships we've written about, that were crashed by Kamikazes -- what would you think? What do U.S. Pearl Harbor survivors think? What would crewmen on any ships forced to invade Japan think? How about the soldiers and marines? The United States would have lost hundreds of thousands of men!

If *Wren* had gone into Tokyo Bay August 6 -- the fleet would have been swarmed by 5,000 Kamikaze aircraft -- held back for that event. *Wren* could not have survived! Why!? Finally, how would the Japanese have used the bomb if the situation had been reversed? Who -- started the war?

August 8, the fleet was back at northern Japan off Hokkaido, as air strikes continued in the area of North Honshu, and that island. At 1610, the following day, GQ sounded as a Kamikaze got through to the fleet. This was unusual, because the U.S. now had so many CAP aircraft to protect us. The Japanese had sent many Kamikazes, but few got through. They spotted the "Grace" diving from high altitude at the carrier *Wasp*, all ships opened fire. He soon burst into flames and crashed about 400 yards off the *Wasp*.

### USS BORIE, DD704, AUGUST 9, 1945:

The Clemson class destroyer joined Task Force 38; thirty days later she was hit by a suicide plane. The Kamikaze hit *Borie's* superstructure between the mast and her 5-inch gun director, killing 48 men and wounding 66. DD704 returned to Hunter's Point, California for repairs. *Borie's* war ended.

### USS HANK, DD702, AUGUST 9, 1945:

*Hank* and *Borie* operated together, when they found themselves in the midst of five Kamikazes. Three were shot down by combined fire of the destroyers. But the fourth Kamikaze hit *Borie* and the last nearly hit *Hank*. *Hank* had one man killed and five wounded from her second near miss. This one hit so close he sprayed the ship and crew with gasoline. *Hank's* last near miss killed three men on April 11. Even though we felt safe in numbers -- complacency had no place so close to Japan.

August 10, at 0758, they dispatched *Wren* toward Japan to rescue another pilot. Sub LT Inge Storheill of the Royal Naval Air Force, from HMS *Formidable*, was taken on board. We set an easterly course and arrived back with the fleet at 0600 the following morning. *Wren* transferred Lt Storheill to the battleship *Missouri*. One of the last pilots we rescued was badly burned. I believe it was the Sub LT. Getting him out of the sea and on board took a special effort.

*LT Frank Olson and Bill Sholin standing over a -- badly burned pilot. His clothing is being cut off by people kneeling in the background. Dr. Romig's hat is in the foreground*

At 1335 the same day, they dispatched *Wren* to rescue still another downed pilot. This time we took ENS Warner L. Salmin on board and transferred him to the USS *Schroeder*, at 1527. After completing logistics, the fleet headed southwest for additional air attacks against Tokyo.

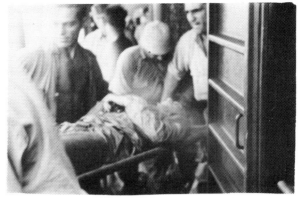

*A badly burned pilot goes into the wardroom for treatment, Dr. Romig backs in. One of the two burned pilots did not make it!*

August 12, at 0415, the air strikes began. *Wren, Watts, Stoddard* and the *USS Frank Knox* departed the formation and took up station "Watchdog" forty miles from the fleet. As air strikes continued against Tokyo, our four destroyers were targeted by many suicide aircraft. *Frank Knox* did a good job controlling our CAP and they shot down four Kamikazes. At 1900 we closed the fleet to 16 miles. The Third Fleet remained in the Tokyo area until the end of the war. We bombed everyday, around the clock, keeping pressure on the Japanese.

August 14, 1945, Japan offered to surrender; on her terms. However, air strikes continued against Tokyo throughout the day and night, until 0815 on the 15th. The Japanese finally accepted the mandated United States surrender terms. All U.S. attacks stopped! The Kamikaze attacks should also have stopped -- but no way. Our ships were kept busy warding off suicide attacks. It seemed every fanatic wanted to die for the Emperor. To die -- while he still had a chance. When Admiral Halsey was asked, *"What do we do about suicide planes approaching the fleet?"* He gave one of his last combat orders: *"Shoot them down -- but do it in a friendly manner."*

The Admiral also gave another, very unusual, order for the U.S. Navy: *"All hands spice the mainbrace."* This was the only time I know of when they served alcohol on U.S. Naval ships. *Wren* became a disaster area! I now understand the order was intended only for the British Navy. But an order from the Admiral -- is an order!

From August 15 to the 29th, the Third Fleet carried out reconnaissance of Japan. Air flights were conducted daily to ensure preparations were moving forward to an official surrender date. However, the Kamikazes continued their attacks.

Boatswain's mates are key deck people on destroyers. They performed many duties, like keeping the quarters shipshape, in charge of all deck hands and they are Master-at-Arms. They are also in charge of docking, mooring, fueling, and boatswain's chair transfers. At this time we lost First Class Boatswain's Mate Dick Easter, one of our best. He left *Wren,* by boatswain's chair, for transfer home. Dick had a long and distinguished wartime career. His first division replacement, Boatswain's Mate First Class Bill Ferguson, supervised the transfer.

During Dick's precarious ride from the low deck of *Wren* to the larger ship, the lines became slack giving Dick a shocking and unexpected bath. To this day, Dick jokingly blames his replacement, Bill Ferguson, for his embarrassing departure from the *Wren*.

August 30 and 31, *Wren* rendezvoused with a number of submarines to escort them into Tokyo Bay. This was it! At last the long war would end. Two long months at sea, in hostile territory, would end. During this time *Wren* had been kept very busy, sinking floating mines, rescuing downed pilots, on plane guard, and watchdog duty.

*Wren* also went to rescue an American PBM Mariner, a long-range flying boat, that ran out of gas and had to land on the sea. We dispatched our whaleboat to remove her crew. As they came alongside, the whaleboat crew used grappling hooks to the loud angry shouts from her pilot. *"You're wrecking my new airplane, get those things off"* he yelled. After removal of the passengers and crew, *Wren* immediately sank the PBM, with gunfire. This was a necessary -- not a facetious act. But, it devastated the crewmen.

*Wren's* crew looked forward to stepping back on dry land. We had only set foot on land once since leaving Pearl Harbor, many months ago.

*Top left Wren escorts subs into Tokyo Bay.          Top Right-Fleet carriers, always a familiar sight*
*Bottom left--shipmates relaxing on deck.  Bottom right-a depth charge begins to erupt, a frequent event*

# TWENTY -- THREE
## SURRENDER, OCCUPATION - AND HOME

At 1308, August 30, *Wren* rendezvoused with the submarines USS *Pilotfish* and *Hake* for the purpose of escorting them into Tokyo Bay. The following day we added the USS *Archerfish*, SS311; *Tigrone*, SS419; *Seacat*, SS399; *Muskallunge*, SS262; and *Haddo*, SS212; to our group. Some of those subs are now on the bottom at Bikini, destroyed in the U.S. atomic bomb tests.

LT jg Lowell Clark, bridge; "One of the submarine officers outranked Captain MacDonald, so he demanded to take over the point and lead us all into Tokyo Bay. Our Captain reluctantly gave in to his superior officer. Proceeding toward the harbor it became clear to me, as navigator, we were being led into an unswept minefield. I sounded the alarm to Captain Mac who immediately became assertive to his superior and took back his command. He shouted! 'You're leading us into a minefield!' Only a small opening had been cleared up to that time and my charts clearly showed the way. We entered the harbor out in front of our charges -- where we belonged."

When we got to the outer islands, the scene was tranquil and beautiful. It was difficult to imagine this as enemy territory. *Wren*, 3,000 yards ahead of our charges, slipped slowly through the calm outer harbor, into Tokyo Bay. We wondered, "Is the war really over? Or are we cruising into some sort of new sinister Japanese plot?" Entering the inner harbor, reality of the war that had just concluded, was everywhere. Partially sunk, beached, or burned out hulks of Japanese warships and freighters, cluttered the harbor.

August 31, at 1132, *Wren* anchored at buoy F-27 Tokyo Bay. At 1300 *Wren* piped her beloved Captain over the side for the last time. Captain MacDonald was going home. Many tearful eyes watched as he waved one last time before saluting the OD and the colors then walked down the gangplank into the gig. Captain MacDonald had fulfilled a promise made to the crew at *Wren's* commissioning: "We will take this ship into Tokyo Bay!" And -- there we were! His replacement was LT Commander Clayton Ross, but we all knew Captain Mac's shoes were too big -- they could never be filled.

*Wren* went dockside at the Yokosuka Navy Yard. For the next two days the harbor filled with U.S. warships. Then *Wren* anchored close to the USS *Missouri* where the peace treaty was signed September 2, 1945. *Wren* received an invitation to attend the surrender ceremony. The global war ended with the signing of that treaty. It cost the world -- four trillion dollars, and 40 million lives.

*B29s fly over Tokyo Bay, as the peace treaty is signed on the USS Missouri. Pictures taken from Wren.*

United States losses of 293,000 men were far less than either Germany, Japan, or the USSR; however, some sources indicate the killed surpassed the total losses of both the Union and Confederate Armies -- in the Civil War.

The same day the treaty was signed, before our crew could leave the ship, *Wren* got underway again. Dispatched to Iwo Jima to pick up passengers, freight and mail, *Wren* returned September 6. After completion of our deliveries to the -- USS *New Mexico, Idaho, Monterey, Indiana, Mount Olympic,* and USS LST648 -- *Wren* anchored in berth E-84.

***Wren tied up to the USS Piedmont***

The following day *Wren* moved to the Yokosuka Naval Base where we tied up to the tender USS *Piedmont,* for two days availability. This is where we got our first look at the face of our former enemy.

Given limited liberty, we were told to only go to the former Japanese Naval Base. But at least we could set foot on dry land. Bud Brennan, Bird Evans, several others, and I stayed together while we explored the deserted, high-walled, naval base. The Japanese had just walked off and left that large complex. There were empty furnished and equipped office buildings, partially filled warehouses, barracks with cots and an armory filled with guns -- for the taking. Most of our crew picked up a few souvenirs, like guns, swords, bayonets, helmets, and so forth, then set out to discover new territory.

We discovered the Japanese had unfinished caves throughout the many surrounding hills, where complete machine shops had gone underground. They also, had removed big naval guns from ships sunk in the harbor and installed them in the hills surrounding Tokyo Bay. (*Wren* would have gone into a deadly trap if we had carried out our mission to go into Tokyo Bay, as spotter.) Midget suicide submarines and suicide boats were also in plentiful supply.

The three of us climbed to the top of the wall and looked down onto the streets of Yokosuka. We were the first Americans the Japanese had seen. When we jumped off the wall, the street emptied quickly.

*Suicide submarines lined up, ready to go, Yokosuka Navy Yard in the background.*

*Two Japanese men take off with their cart, leaving a deserted street.*

Two little kids remained behind and looked up at us with big grins, so we gave them candy. Soon older people came from their homes and gathered around. We communicated with sign language and broad smiles. This first meeting seemed warm and friendly.

We found the Japanese, especially women and children, eager and curious at our first face to face contact. They bore many signs of malnutrition, with open sores on their

*"Bird" Evans wheeling and dealing with our former enemy.  He was a big hit!*

legs, arms, and hands, but seemed surprised and pleased with our friendly contact.  Up to this time men, women and children had committed suicide by the thousands.  At the very thought of American occupation -- they jumped off from cliffs.

*Bird Evans, on left and Bill Sholin posing with our former enemy.*

Given a short time for liberty, we returned to our ship.  It soon looked like a swap-meet, guns and war souvenirs of all kinds were piled on the fantail.  Everyone had stories to tell.

Dan Wann remembers the Yokosuka Navy Yard liberty: "Another guy was trying to fire up a steam engine with a couple of cars attached and I decided to help him.  We finally got it going, but couldn't stop it!  We both jumped off!  The last time I saw it the engine was going through a big door into a warehouse.  We didn't wait around to see the results -- just let her go and got out of there fast.

"Another guy took a suicide boat and started running it around the bay -- between U.S. ships. Others launched suicide subs into the bay, but they sank as fast as they hit the water. Some of our shipmates filled the LCVP with all kinds of guns from an old boxcar, then headed for the ship with them. Captain Ross saw them coming and told them to take the load out into the bay and dump it. Another bunch took an old whaleboat and rowed it around the bay. The tide was so swift they drifted out to sea and someone had to retrieve them."

Two days later, *Wren* moored out in the harbor at buoy 8, next to the destroyer, USS *Blue*. September 11, we changed mooring to berth F94, Tokyo Bay.

On September 15, at 1233 the Third Fleet got underway again. This time we provided a show of force to insure the release of prisoners of war, and to confirm the continued disarming of Japan. *Wren* guarded Rear Admiral T. L. Sprague's Carrier, USS *Bennington*. We carried out daily air reconnaissance until September 21, then the Third Fleet sailed to Eniwetok. We arrived on September 26, at 0810.

Those islands, merely sandy oases, barely projecting from the sea, were out there somewhere, but we couldn't see them from our anchorage. *Wren's* off duty section was given liberty, so once again I had duty as the lone shore patrolman for our ship. This meant I could go ashore with many friends in the opposite section, who I had not been able to go on liberty with before. It took about an hour to get to the tiny island designated for fleet R and R. A small building and single palm tree rose from the white sandy island. The surrounding water was blue, clear and beautiful.

This gala affair provided each man with a couple cans of beer and the familiar steak sandwiches. As usual, *Wren's* resourceful crew managed to improvise. They obtained extra rations of beer. I don't know for sure where it came from, but some of my friends had their own, in case quantity. Each ship had its own semiprivate section of beach, and our crew broke off in small groups. Machinists and electricians usually stayed together.

I had good intentions of mingling with our entire crew, socializing while showing a presence of authority with my SP band and billy club. (I knew this was totally unnecessary, someone had simply provided me with an opportunity for liberty with the opposite section.) After an hour or so it was obvious my services as shore patrol would not be needed as crews from the ships were adequately separated and each group kept pretty well together.

By this time I started to feel left out. Everyone offered me a beer, and I had many offers to join different groups. Finally I thought: "Oh what the hell, no one is going to get out of line on this island anyway. I might as well enjoy the outing." I had a beer with Cal Pfeifer, Dickey McCabe, Jerry O'Neil and several other friends I seldom got to drink with. Did I say -- a beer?

After a couple of hours of continual socializing, I decided to join others for a swim. No one had bathing suits -- but who cared -- we were thousands of miles from any women. We decided, since I was the only shore patrol, I should remain on duty -- so I left the SP band and club on. After a period of fun in the sun, a distant swim seemed like a good idea. So I swam alone, out to a small landing craft anchored some distance from shore. A sailor basked in the sun with the loading ramp down. I still don't know what purpose he served, perhaps they posted him as shark watch. I crawled out of the water onto the ramp and laid there to rest and sun myself, while shooting the bull with the sailor. Suddenly the PA system on shore echoed out over the water, "The last liberty boat for the *Wren* is now loading." Surprise, surprise! -- I started swimming back, but it was too far to catch them, so I angled in the direction the liberty boat would have to travel, in an effort to intercept the large launch. Well, it passed by in front of me. What now, I pondered!

The fleet was over the horizon, but I could see the motor launch, and the direction it was headed. So, what else -- I swam back to the ship, arriving among the fleet many hours later. Where the hell is the *Wren* I wondered? It was like looking for a single tree in the forest. While swimming undauntedly among the Third Fleet ships -- I hoped I would not get the Admiral's attention.

Eventually, I grabbed a hold of *Wren's* propeller guard ending my solo Pacific swim. My buddies said "We brought your clothes, we knew damn well you would swim back." Their confidence was -- reassuring. I quickly removed the SP band and club.

This had been the last mass movement of the Third Fleet. The ships spun off going to various ports of call, many went home to the good old USA. *Wren* was not quite so lucky, we returned to Tokyo Bay for the occupation.

Arriving back in Tokyo Bay we learned the occupation had become more of a routine procedure; liberties were granted freely in Tokyo, Yokohama and Yokosuka. From where *Wren* moored, Tokyo was a much longer ride by landing craft then Yokohama. Yokosuka, just a short distance, remained our primary liberty town.

Returning to Yokosuka after our absence, it had changed considerably. People now back out on the streets en masse, seemed friendly and unafraid of us. For the first time we could roam freely in the main downtown area, but outlying residential areas were off limits -- for enlisted personnel. It truly amazed us how selective our bombers had been with their targets. Residential areas remained virtually untouched, while the industrial and commercial parts of town were devastated. There were no shops, restaurants or grocery stores, just 2x12 boards connecting two apple boxes, where stores and shops once flourished.

The people seemed happy and relieved that the war was over. They sold what they had, mostly handmade items like art, clothing and kimonos. Their silk handcrafted items, such as kimonos, were beautiful.

The rate of exchange was established at fifteen yen to a dollar. The U.S. did not want dollars in Japanese hands, so they insisted we convert our money before going ashore, leaving our American money behind. This presented no problem for *Wren's* crew, as we soon learned to deal in hard goods. Candy and cigarettes were cheap and plentiful at our ships store. I did not smoke, but we could buy a carton of American cigarettes for fifty cents, and sell them to anyone of a hundred or so Japanese buyers waiting outside of the gate, for forty yen a pack. With a carton of cigarettes -- we were rich.

The powers that be, soon got wise to our new found wealth and allowed only two packs to be taken ashore. We were searched by Marine guards before leaving the Naval base, but any sailor could still hide a carton of cigarettes from them. Likely hiding places were either the many hidden pockets sewn into our uniforms, under our hats, or inside our socks.

The U.S. Military Government established a GI beer garden for all enlisted personnel in downtown Yokosuka. They dealt exclusively in Japanese money at that time, but sold only to American military personnel. This operation was in a large courtyard-like setting, and we could buy three cans of beer for ten yen and drink all we wanted.

In addition, the military government established the biggest brothel ever attempted in one place. There seemed to be many dozens of Japanese women, cycling Army, Navy and Marines through that brothel -- like a fire sale. The four deep line to get in -- extended for blocks. The cost of a ticket, good for one girl only, was ten yen. Many sailors stayed in the building using one ticket after another. It looked like a sideshow. It had rows of little narrow rooms with straw mattresses on the floor, accessed by long narrow hallways. The selection area was a large open courtyard with bench-seats around the outside, and ladies coming and going continually. You picked your girl from the dozens available at any given time, gave her your ticket and followed her to the individual room. Through the paper like partitions, shouting, cursing, and laughing echoed throughout the building. It sounded like a -- circus.

Danny Wann remembers that place well: "I saw a line of sailors about three or four blocks long -- thinking something good must be happening, I got in line. Well, I didn't know what was going on so I finally jumped over the fence to check it out and saw all of those Geisha Girls. Sailors picked out the one they wanted and went to the back of the building with them. I got out of there. Going over the fence again, I got caught by one of those Marine guards. Even though I hadn't done anything he made me take a 'Pro.' Curiosity finally got the best of me. I went back over the fence, for the third time -- then I lost my virginity."

You probably recall from earlier in the book, Danny lied about his age to join the Navy at 'sweet sixteen,' coming aboard *Wren* at seventeen. But, I'm sure he wasn't the only member of our young crew -- to lose his innocence at that Geisha House.

This is the way it was immediately after the war; however, the Americans treated the Japanese ladies outside the brothel, like their own back home, with courtesy and respect. Maybe the officials knew what they were doing, when they legalized the Geisha House. What would a pack of cigarettes, that cost sailors five cents, buy at that time? We could sell it for 40 yen. That forty yen would buy nine cans of beer, and get us laid. Things definitely looked up, but we still just wanted to go home.

For sailors as well as the civilian population, transportation was the major problem. The Tokyo train started running between Yokosuka and Tokyo, but getting around town was impossible. There were only a very few beat up old trucks, busses and no cabs. Those vehicles all ran on coal, and had a small burner pot with the top sealed to trap the gas, in the back. They had limited power, but ran quite well. If we were going someplace specific we commandeered those vehicles. We returned them to the Japanese when we arrived. During the time of *Wren's* occupation, bicycles and rickshaw became the primary transportation. But, we could see little change in the cities. Few shops and no restaurants were open, and no entertainment or outside lighting could be seen. A far cry from modern day Tokyo.

Most seamen on *Wren*, including Danny Wann, Al Copson and Barney Pullen slept up forward, all the way in the bow and hung out around the small boatswain's locker. This was by far the roughest riding place to live and work. The officers food storage locker was nearby.

While preoccupied carrying food from the locker, one of the steward's mates inadvertently left the key in the lock. Big mistake! Someone in that deck crew retrieved it. I doubt anyone in the crew realized the officers had to buy that special food themselves -- but I also doubt if it would have made any difference. The officers had enough perks to make them -- fair game. Sardines and canned boned turkey were among our boys favorites.

One of the empty sardine cans showed up in First Class Boatswain's Mate Bill Ferguson's bunk. It took Bill forty-five years to catch up with the culprit. Al Copson, confessed at a ships reunion, in Baton Rouge, LA. Even though electricians had little contact with the seamen, somehow I wound up with a can of that turkey.

Charley (Feet) Fullen, George Cantrell, Dickey McCabe and I went on liberty in Tokyo, so I took the turkey along for trading stock. We walked down the street and tried to pick up girls, using the only Japanese slang words we knew -- "skivi, skivi, ten yen." When a beautiful young woman responded in perfect English, the four of us stood there, red faced, totally startled and embarrassed.

"What is it you wish,?" she asked. After six months at sea, I landed on my feet, and struck up a conversation.

"Where did you learn to speak such perfect English," I inquired.

"I was raised and schooled in Los Angeles, California and was visiting in Japan when the war broke out." she responded. After introducing myself and my friends to her she said, "My name is Madori Nakadushi, I'm very pleased to meet you boys."

Dickey asked, "Where are you going?"

"To work at Mitsubishi Dinki, would you like to come along?" We unanimously agreed and joined her.

The Maranuchi building, one of the few buildings in Tokyo to survive the bombings, remained relatively intact. Even though the windows were all blown out, commerce returned, and the Mitsubishi Aircraft Gasoline Company occupied one floor of that building.

We entered one very large room full of small desks neatly arranged and occupied, mostly by women. A few men, usually foremen, mingled among the desks. As we entered -- all work stopped. People gathered around us as Madori interpreted. We gave out all of the candy and cigarettes we had, much to the delight of the women; however, to the chagrin of the men. In Japanese society, at that time, women were very suppressed, and the men resented our American custom of treating women like ladies.

Madori showed us a typewriter that looked right out of the dark ages to us. It had a large flat platform containing the entire Japanese alphabet, with a two-way carriage. To use it, the carriage had to be located over the desired letters and the lever pressed, this left a single symbol on the paper.

After our visit at her place of work, Madori accompanied us on a shopping trip in the building. With her help, I selected a hanging piece of needlework for my mother, which turned out to be a good choice.

Returning Madori to her job, we seemed to have worn out our welcome from the men. They gave us unfriendly scowls. We had wanted to find a regular Japanese Geisha House, so Madori wrote the directions to one on a slip of paper, in Japanese. She told us to give it to the conductor on the Tokyo-Yokosuka train.

After saying our good-bye's, she gave me her home address; however I did not get back to see her. Before leaving, I gave her the can of turkey I had been carrying. You would have thought I had given her a fortune.

"I can't accept this. You have no idea of its value," she said. "I don't care what it is worth I just want you to have it," I answered.

While looking for the train at Tokyo station, we were joined by Bob Havey, electrician and Al Ceccato. We found our way aboard the train, but it was packed full of Japanese, still they continued to stop about every block, jamming more in. George

Cantrell, the designated Shore Patrol for that day, wore his club and arm band, the only authority the Japanese knew. He got pissed off about being squeezed by so many people and ordered the conductor to stop the train -- and kicked everyone off. He gave the conductor the note. We went to the Geisha House -- all by ourselves.

The conductor dropped us off in a small residential area. Between the buildings they had walkways about six to eight feet wide, with no streets. The walkways were crammed with people clotting along in their wooden thongs, in a sort of shuffle step, making a very strange noise. We knew this place was out of bounds for enlisted men; however it did look interesting so we moved on, in search of the Geisha House. We towered above the heads of the crowd and could see two regular military SP's approaching. Quickly, we removed our white hats and tucked in the white stripes on our uniforms. Slouching over -- we picked up on the shuffle step with the rest of the crowd. In the dusk we slipped by them, unnoticed.

We found the Geisha House, took off our shoes and entered. A nice looking, young, Japanese lady greeted us and showed us to one of several rooms off a long hallway. We suddenly heard a loud commotion and shouting. It soon became obvious -- the place was being raided by U.S. Military Police. They yelled, "American skivi, you got American skivi," as they obviously knocked the Japanese around. We knew the SP's were looking for us. In a few minutes the lady came back in the room with our shoes. As the noise and threats continued, she snuck us down a back stairs. We later learned we had accidentally entered a special brothel for Chief Petty Officers.

Back out on the walkway we were approached by a Japanese man selling whiskey. The label read, Scotch type whiskey bottled in Tokyo. We had been warned to be careful of Japanese liquors, some had been poisoned, so we made him drink from each bottle before buying it. After drinking our whiskey, we commandeered another truck, and returned to the liberty boats.

As we approached the dock I looked to my left out over the bay, when a sailor stepped out of a crowd and plastered me in the face with a punch from left field. I didn't even see it coming. He mingled with his buddies as I started after him, in hot pursuit, but Cantrell and (Feet) Fullen on either side, picked me off the ground and carried me away from the conflict. I was pissed! That meant fight to me and I yelled at my buddies, calling them yellow so and so's. Even though they felt we were hopelessly outnumbered by those -- battleship sailors, I was still mad on our long ride back to our ship. Since when do *Wren* sailors shirk a fight with battleship sailors -- just because we're outnumbered?

Lowell Clark, recalls: "When our men raided that food locker, our new skipper, Captain Ross, would not let it go. It was Captain Queeg time on the *Wren*. He wanted me to conduct a full scale investigation. 'I want you to find out who those culprits are and court martial them,' he said. Not being something that any of us wanted to do, he became furious and ranted and raved, very similar to the original Captain Queeg, but we simply refused to act on his order."

The novelty of Japanese liberties soon wore thin for *Wren's* crew, morale was low and most of us hardly ever went ashore. We just wanted to go home. By December 1, we got our wish, as *Wren* was homeward-bound, by way of Midway, Pearl Harbor, San Diego, Balboa, Panama, Colone, and Philadelphia.

With news of our going home, we could now start piping the heavy songs to our crew -- Charle Spevac's, It's Been a Long Long Time, I'll Be Seeing You, by Tommy Dorsey, It All Comes Back to Me Now, by Hal Kemp and Glen Miller's, It Had To Be You -- were among the favorites and our moods were extremely upbeat!

Some of our crew decided to celebrate with a party of their own. Leonard Lamoreaux and the after engine room boys, started the party by hijacking several cases of beer from the hole below the after crew's quarters. The party in the after engine room soon spilled over into the after fireroom. Captain Ross got wind of it! Most involved were leaving the Navy and going home, so they weren't too worried about the consequences.

Hap Rogers, now fireman first class, in charge of both firerooms, recalls: "For once in my Navy career, I actually knew nothing about that party. Facing Captain Ross was a new kind of experience for me. He was after blood. He busted me back to fireman second class, and hit me where it really hurt. I was restricted and not allowed to go home when we got to San Diego, even though I lived nearby."

Four years after the war started -- *Wren* sailed triumphantly back into San Diego Harbor. We moored dockside at the destroyer base, to the music of a Naval Band and greetings from the Red Cross. They served coffee and doughnuts. *Wren* was -- home from the war.

On December 8, 1945, the following article, in the "San Diego Union" announced Squadron 57's arrival back home.

### 1568 RETURNEES ARRIVE HERE ON DESTROYERS

*A destroyer division that probably saw more diverse and continued action in the Pacific than any other fleet unit. Destroyer Squadron 57 arrived in San Diego yesterday with returning Pacific veterans.*

*A total of 1568 passengers came in on the destroyers Rowe, Smalley, Stoddard, Watts, Wren, John Hood, Bearss and Jarvis of the squadron, LST 766 LSM 134, destroyer tender Dobbin and the destroyer Black.*

*With the arrival of 2130 Navy, Marine and Coast Guard veterans on 20 ships today, the weekly figure of returning servicemen disembarked here will come to 18,521. The destroyer squadron, delayed in arriving here until late afternoon because of low-cast fog in the outer bay, saw duty at the Aleutians, bombarding the Kuriles from there in the spring of 1944. Departing from the fog and winds there, they steamed for a hotter climate and action in the central Pacific, where they participated in the Okinawa campaign on the picket line, intercepting Jap suicide planes.*

*Returning from occupational duty at Honshu, and other northern islands in Japan, the ships arrived for their first visit in the U. S. since early in 1944. Squadron commander is Capt. E. N. Dodson jr., U. S. N., of Plymouth, Mass.*

While still assigned to the *Wren*, we got our first stateside liberty -- we had planned every move for months. Dickie McCabe, and I went ashore together; we started out with a big steak dinner at the Golden Lion Inn, near Persian Square, then had our picture taken together. This experience, like coming back to life, felt as if we were from another planet. The bright lights, taxicabs, cars honking, neon signs, and good old American civilians out and about, overwhelmed us. I had a lot of difficulty talking to American girls! I felt like a total outsider and I had always been outgoing. Shortly after that liberty, I packed my sea bag -- and left my ship for home.

*Wren* left again, continuing her trip to the Philadelphia Navy Yard by way of the Panama Canal. Upon reaching Colone at the entrance to the Atlantic Ocean the "Squad Dog" decided to race to the Delaware River. He wanted to take one last shot at the *Wren,* to see if he could beat her.

Jack Clemens, chief engineer: "When Captain Ross called for a full head of steaming capability, I was unable to provide it as we had key components torn down, being worked on. Captain Ross was furious -- he threatened me with everything, including court martial. We put the machinery back together in record time. As the others steamed off, we thought we had seen the last of them, but much to our surprise and delight, *Wren* overtook and passed them all -- winning! Needless to say -- this vindicated me with Captain Ross."

*Wren* steamed into her final resting place with the remainder of her wartime crew. Squadron 57 was greeted once again by Philadelphia Record, on December 24, 1945.

### FIVE DESTROYERS REACH NAVY YARD FROM TOKYO BAY
*Home for Christmas from Tokyo Bay came approximately 1000 officers and men aboard five destroyers that docked at the Philadelphia Navy Yard yesterday.*

*The five ships are the 2100-ton Watts, Rowe, Stoddard, Wren and Smalley. They saw action in the waters adjoining the Kurile Islands, the Aleutians and as part of Task Force 38 they withstood the attack of the Jap kamikaze planes off Okinawa.*

***Left Tokyo December 1*** *After the surrender of Japan, their squadron moved into Tokyo Bay as part of the naval occupation forces. They left Tokyo December 1, stopped to refuel at San Diego and came through the Panama Canal. The vessels looked as though they had been through plenty of war when they docked yesterday. They will be* *thoroughly overhauled here during the next two months, after which they will join the Atlantic Fleet.*

Commander John Powell was one of the first to board Wren, many months ago, and now he was one of the last to leave. John and his wife, Peggy, are still our friends.

### WREN'S FIRE CONTROLMEN -- THE BEST IN THE BUSINESS

*L to R back row John Powell, Joseph Luckman, Red McCluge, Paul Chery, Joe Churney, Wallace Cregg and Bill Harris*

*Donald Sturm, Hank Caveneas, Frank Harting, Lester Tohl, Bill Harrison, Paul Lund, Art Maloney, Robert Doesr, Don Hanline, Robert Stolf*

*Without Bill, Wren's crew might never have reorganized. After 45 years he put forth the maximum effort necessary to locate everyone--in honor of his father.*

*Bill was given an honorary membership at Wren's first reunion, in Baton Rouge, Louisiana, in 1989.*

*Bill Ferguson Jr. -- honorary member of Wren's crew*

The first words of a book written long ago about two cities would seem a proper end for ours; "They were the worst of times -- the best of times." **THE END**

# POST SCRIPT

No Bomb = 1,000,000 American lives what-could have-would have-Happened? The truth must now, at last, be told.

At Okinawa the U.S. suffered 49,159 casualties including 9,760 Navy men from Kamikazes. In the first 30-days at Normandy Americans suffered 39,000 casualties, terrible--but should Okinawa be forgotten?

## THE SHOCKING RECENTLY DECLASSIFIED, TOP SECRET, PLANS FOR THE INVASION AND DEFENSE OF THE JAPANESE HOME ISLANDS (FROM THE USS LST ASSOCIATION NEWS BULLETIN)

By mid-morning of the first day of the invasion, most of the American land based aircraft would be forced to return to their bases, leaving the defense against the suicide planes to the carrier pilots and the shipboard gunners. Initially, these pilots and gunners would have met with considerable success, but after the third, fourth and fifth waves of Japanese aircraft, a significant number of kamikazes most certainly would have broken through.

Carrier pilots crippled by fatigue would have to land time and time again to re-arm and refuel. Navy fighters would break down from lack of needed maintenance. Guns would malfunction on both aircraft and combat vessels from the heat of continuous firing, and ammunition expended in such abundance would become scarce. Gun crews would be exhausted by nightfall, but still the waves of kamikazes would continue. With our fleet hovering off the beaches, all remaining Japanese aircraft would be committed to nonstop mass suicide attacks, which the Japanese hoped could be sustained for 10 days.

The Japanese planned to coordinate their kamikaze and conventional air strikes with attacks from the 40 remaining conventional submarines from the Japanese Imperial Navy, beginning when the invasion fleet was within 180 miles off Kyushu. As our invasion armada grew nearer, the rate of submarine attacks would increase. In addition to attacks by the remaining fleet submarines, some of which were to be armed with "long lance" torpedoes with a range of 20 miles, the Japanese had more frightening plans for death from the sea.

By the end of the war, the Imperial Japanese Navy still had 23 destroyers and two cruisers which were operational. These ships were to be used to counterattack the American invasion and a number of the destroyers were to be beached along the invasion beaches at the last minute to be used as anti-invasion platforms.

As early as 1944, Japan had established a special naval attack unit, which was the counterpart of the special attack units of the air, to be used in the defense of the homeland. These units were to be saved for the invasion and would make widespread use of midget submarines, human torpedoes and exploding motorboats against the Americans.

Once offshore, the invasion fleet would be forced to defend not only against the suicide attacks from the air, but would also be confronted with suicide attacks from the sea.

Attempting to sink our troop-carrying transports would be almost 300 Kairyu suicide submarines. These two-man subs carried a 1,320 pound bomb in their nose and were to be used in close-in ramming attacks. By the end of the war, the Japanese had 215 Kairyu available with 207 more under construction.

With a crew of five, the Japanese Koryu suicide submarines, carrying an even larger explosive charge, was also to be used against the American vessels. By August, the Japanese had 115 Koryu completed, with 496 under construction.

Especially feared by our Navy were the Kaitens, which were difficult to detect, and which were to be used against our invasion fleet just off the beaches. These Kaitens were human torpedoes more than 60 feet long, each carried a warhead of more than 3,500 pounds and each was capable of sinking the largest of American Naval vessels. The Japanese had 120 shore-based Kaitens, 78 of which were in the Kyushu area as early as August.

Finally, the Japanese had almost 4,000 Navy Shinyo and Army Liaison motor boats, which were also armed with high explosive warheads, and which were to be used in nighttime attacks against our troop carrying ships.

The principal goal of the special attack units of the air and of the sea was to shatter the invasion before the landing. By killing the combat troops aboard ships and sinking the attack transports and cargo vessels, the Japanese were convinced the Americans would back off or become so demoralized that they would then accept a less than unconditional surrender and a more honorable and face-saving end for the Japanese.

In addition to destroying as many of the larger American ships as possible, "Ketsu-Go" also called for the annihilation of the smaller offshore landing craft carrying our G.I.s to the invasion beaches.

The Japanese, had devised a network of beach defenses consisting of electronically detonated mines farthest offshore three lines of suicide divers, followed by magnetic mines and still other mines planted all over the beaches themselves.

A fanatical part of the last line of maritime defense was the Japanese suicide frogmen, called Fukuryu. These "crouching dragons" were divers armed with lunge mines, each capable of sinking a landing craft up to 950 tons. These divers, numbering in the thousands, could stay submerged for up to 10 hours, and were to thrust their explosive charges into the bottom of landing craft and, in effect serve as human mines.

As horrible as the defense of Japan would be off the beaches, it would be on Japanese soil that the American armed forces would face the most rugged and fanatical defense that had ever been encountered in any of the theaters during the entire war.

Throughout the island-hopping Pacific campaign, our troops had always outnumbered the Japanese by two and sometimes three to one. In Japan it would be different. By virtue of a combination of cunning, guess-work and brilliant military reasoning, a number of Japan's top military leaders were able to astutely deduce, not only when, but where, the United States would land their first invasion forces. The Japanese positioned their troops accordingly.

Facing the 14 American divisions landing at Kyushu would be 14 Japanese divisions, seven independent mixed brigades, three tank brigades and thousands of specially trained Naval Landing Forces. On Kyushu the odds would be three to two in favor of the Japanese, with 790,000 enemy defenders against 550,000 Americans. This time the bulk of the Japanese defenders would not be the poorly trained and ill-equipped labor battalions that the Americans had faced in the earlier campaigns. The Japanese defenders would be the hardware of the Japanese Home Army. These troops were well fed and well equipped, and were linked together all over Kyushu by instantaneous communications. They were familiar with the terrain, had stockpiles of arms and ammunition, and had developed an effective system of transportation and resupply almost invisible from the air. Many of these Japanese troops were the elite of the Japanese army, and they were swollen with a fanatical fighting spirit that convinced them that they could defeat these American invaders that had come to defile their homeland.

Coming ashore, the American Eastern amphibious assault forces at Miyazaki would face the Japanese 154th Division, which straddled the city, the Japanese 212th Division on the coast immediately to the north, and the 156th Division on the coast immediately to the south. Also in place and prepared to launch a counter-attack against our Eastern force were the Japanese 25th and 77th Divisions.

Awaiting the southeastern attack force at Ariake Bay was the entire Japanese 86th Division, and at least one independent mixed infantry brigade.

On the western shores of Kyushu, the Marines would face the most brutal opposition. Along the invasion beaches would be the 146th, 206th, and 303rd Japanese Divisions, along with the 6th Tank Brigade, the 125th Mixed Infantry Brigade and the 4th Artillery Command. Additionally, components of the 25th and 77th Divisions would also be poised to launch counterattacks.

If not needed to reinforce the primary landing beaches, the American Reserve Force would be landed at the base of Kagoshima Bay on November 4, where they would be immediately confronted by two mixed infantry brigades, parts of two infantry divisions and thousands of the naval landing forces who had undergone combat training to support ground troops in defense.

All along the invasion beaches, our troops would face coastal batteries, anti-landing obstacles and an elaborate network of heavily fortified pillboxes, bunkers, strong points and underground fortresses.

As our soldiers waded ashore, they would do so through intense artillery and mortar fire from pre-registered batteries as they worked their way through tetrahedral and barbed wire entanglements so arranged to funnel them into muzzles of these Japanese guns.

On the beaches and beyond would be hundreds of Japanese machine gun positions, beach mines, booby traps, trip-wire mines and sniper units. Suicide units concealed in spider holes would meet the troops as they passed nearby. Just past the beaches and the sea walls would be hundreds of barricades, trail blocks and concealed strong points.

In the heat of battle, Japanese special infiltration units would be sent to reap havoc in the American lines by cutting phone and communication lines, and by indiscriminately firing at our troops attempting to establish a beachhead. Some of the troops would be in

American uniform to confuse our troops and English speaking Japanese officers were assigned to break in on American radio traffic to call off American artillery fire, to order retreats and to further confuse our troops,

Suicide troops with explosive charges strapped on their chests or backs would attempt to blow up American tanks, artillery pieces and ammunition stores as they were unloaded ashore.

Beyond the beaches were large artillery pieces situated at key points to bring down a devastating curtain of fire on the avenues of approach along the beach. Some of these large guns were mounted on railroad tracks running in and out of caves where they were protected by concrete and steel.

The battle of Japan, itself, would be won by what General Simon Bolivar Buckner had called on Okinawa "Prairie Dog Warfare." This type of fighting was almost unknown to the ground troops in Europe and the Mediterranean. It was peculiar only to the American soldiers and marines whose responsibility it had been to fight and destroy the Japanese on islands all over the south and central Pacific. "Prairie Dog Warfare" had been the story of

Tarawa, of Saipan, of Iwo Jima and Okinawa. "Prairie Dog Warfare" was a battle for yards, feet and sometimes even inches. It was a brutal, deadly and dangerous form of combat aimed at an underground, heavily fortified, non-retreating enemy. "Prairie Dog Warfare" would be what the invasion of Japan was all about.

In the mountains behind the beaches were elaborate underground networks of caves, bunkers, command posts and hospitals connected by miles of tunnels with dozens of separate entrances and exits. Some of these complexes could hole up to 1,000 enemy troops.

A number of these caves were equipped with large steel doors that slid open to allow artillery fire and then would snap shut again.

The paths leading up to these underground fortresses were honeycombed with defensive positions, and all but a few of the trails would be booby-trapped. Along these manned defensive positions would be machine gun nests and aircraft and naval guns converted for anti-invasion fire.

In addition to the use of poison gas and bacteriological warfare (which the Japanese had experimented with) the most frightening of all was the prospect of meeting an entire civilian population that had been mobilized to meet our troops on the beaches.

Had "Olympic" come about, the Japanese civilian population inflamed by a national slogan, "One Hundred Million will die for the Emperor and Nation," was prepared to engage and fight the American invaders to the death.

Twenty-eight million Japanese had become a part of the "National Volunteer Combat Forces" and had undergone training in the techniques of beach defense and guerrilla warfare. These civilians were armed with ancient rifles, lunge mines, satchel charges, Molotov cocktails and one-shot black powder mortars. Still others were armed with swords, long bows, axes and bamboo spears.

These special civilian units were to be tactically employed in the nighttime attacks, hit and run maneuvers, delaying actions and massive suicide charges at the weaker American positions.

Even without the utilization of Japanese civilians in direct combat, the Japanese and American casualties during the campaign for Kyushu would have been staggering. At the early stage of the invasion, 1,000 Japanese and American soldiers would be dying every hour. The long and difficult task of conquering Kyushu would have made casualties on both sides enormous and one can only guess at how monumental the casualty figures would have been had the Americans had to repeat their invasion a second time when they landed at heavily fortified and defended Tokyo Plain the following March

The invasion of Japan never became a reality because on August 6, 1945, the entire nature of war changed when the first atomic bomb was exploded over Hiroshima. On August 9, 1945, a second bomb was dropped on Nagasaki, and within days the war with Japan was at a close.

Had these bombs not been dropped and had the invasion been launched as scheduled, it is hard not to speculate as the cost. Thousands of Japanese suicide sailors and airmen would have died in fiery deaths in the defense of their homeland. Thousands of American sailors and airmen defending against these attacks would also have been killed with many more wounded.

On the Japanese home islands, the combat casualties would have been at a minimum in the tens of thousands. Every foot of Japanese soil would have been paid for, twice over, by both Japanese and American lives.

One can only guess at how many civilians would have committed suicide in their homes or in futile mass military attacks.

In retrospect, the one million American men who were to be casualties on the invasion, were instead lucky enough to survive the war, safe and unharmed.

# The End